# ELECTION DAY

## An American Holiday, An American History

Kate Kelly

Facts On File

*New York • Oxford*

**Election Day : An American Holiday, An American History**

Copyright © 1991 by Kate Kelly

Facts On File, Inc.          Facts On File Limited
460 Park Avenue South   Collins Street
New York NY 10016       Oxford OX4 1XJ
USA                              United Kingdom

A British CIP catalogue record for this book is available from the British Library.

**Library of Congress Cataloging-in-Publication Data**
Kelly, Kate, 1950–
    Election day : an American holiday, an American history / Kate
Kelly.
        p.      cm.
    Includes bibliographical references (p.  ) and index.
    ISBN 0-8160-1871-5
    1. Elections—United States—History.   2. Election Day—History.
I. Title.
JK1978.K45   1991
324.973—dc20            90-3994

Facts On File books are available at special discounts when purchased in bulk quantities for
businesses, associations, institutions or sales promotions. Please call our Special Sales
Department in New York at 212/683-2244 (dial 800/322-8755 except in NY, AK or HI) or in
Oxford at 865/728399.

Composition by Facts On File, Inc.
Manufactured by the Maple-Vail Book Manufacturing Group
Printed in the United States of America

10 9 8 7 6 5 4 3 2 1

This book is printed on acid-free paper.

# Contents

*For my parents, Pat and Bret Kelly*

# Acknowledgments

This book could not have been written without the help of others. Coralee Paull offered invaluable aid in researching this book, as she tirelessly and enthusiastically devoted herself to locating the hard-to-find personal election stories. Her diligent efforts are revealed throughout every chapter in this book.

I also want to acknowledge the many historical society researchers who searched their files to find the kind of material I needed, many of whom then spent time on the telephone describing to me the nuances of local practices. Their states are the richer for having people like them to keep history alive.

I also owe a debt of thanks to the Larchmont Public Library. Everything from out-of-print books to unpublished doctoral dissertations and microfilm of 100-year-old newspapers were brought to Larchmont for me to use. Jacqueline Anderson deserves special mention for her willingness to track down anything and to beg for extra time when I needed it.

What's a book without an editor? I was lucky to have wonderful ones. Kate Kelly (no relationship!) brought the project to me and provided important guidance, and Neal Maillet's detailed questioning and persistent follow-up have made the book what it is. Carole Campbell added immeasurably to the book through skilled copy editing. My gratitude to each.

Finally, I could not have written this book without the love and support of my husband, George Schweitzer, who made a family commitment to this book so that it could be written in the presence of three very active and wonderful young daughters.

Kate Kelly

# Introduction

When we go into the voting booth to cast our ballots today we rarely think of the rich heritage of election day—but it has a history more complex than any other holiday, for it combines the history of our voting practices and suffrage laws with the very wonderful story of how our forebears celebrated election day.

In colonial times, election day was celebrated as a day of reunion. Colonists who had not seen friends and other townspeople for some time would make the effort to come in to vote and to catch up on the news. Eating and drinking were all part of the festivities (leading some to label the votes the "voice of grog").

By 1840, people still enjoyed the camaraderie of the day, but they were also relishing the politics of it. Everyone loved the "log cabin and hard cider" campaign excitement, and the activities, ranging from massive barbecues (where attendees were measured in acreage rather than numbers) to several-mile-long parades, were as much fun as today's tailgate parties before a big football game.

As the country grew older and election history progressed, there are funny tales like the election day bet that had to be paid off by rolling an apple across Brooklyn Bridge with one's nose; or the amazing reports of the Wide Awakes, robed in glazed black capes and caps parading by the thousands by torchlight to support the Lincoln campaign; and there are 20th-century stories of soldiers voting from the battlefield as well as accounts of the mobs who for years thronged Times Square on election night to hear the news. And most sobering, there is the dark history of Reconstruction when black voters were tricked, threatened, beaten and killed in an effort to deny them their right to vote.

Political shenanigans are as old as the practice of voting, and American ingenuity has meant that many have found ways to get around the system over the years. Sometimes the miscreants have been political parties handing out bogus tickets to illiterate voters or making outright purchases of votes; other times the voters themselves have taken advantage of primitive registration systems that permitted them to vote as often as they desired. (In the early 19th century, one New Jersey election boasted 14,000 votes in a county where 4,500 voters were expected.)

Only through this pushing and pulling of our voting practices have we obtained the electoral system we have today—one that is basically sound and can be said to be admired the world over. Our elected officials govern under the oldest Constitution in the world, and our voting rights have increased through the years—more Americans than ever are eligible to vote.

From the Jamestown settlement where the first votes were cast in this country to the voting experience today, *Election Day* presents a tapestry of campaign stories, voting incidents and political trickery (and resulting reforms) that show the quality and the strength of our political heritage.

# Election Days in
# Colonial America _____ 1

In 1619 British settlers in Jamestown, Virginia, participated in what must have been the New World's very first election day. Just as the colony was starting out, an elected body of colonial representatives was chosen to combine with a governor and council (appointed by the Virginia Company, the group of British business partners who founded the colony) to form a general assembly. This assembly, much like a miniature parliament, would make the laws for Virginia. The date of the election (actually probably different days in various parts of the settlement) is uncertain, but it would have taken place sometime between April 29, the date of the arrival of the new governor who called for the election, and the convening of the first assembly, which occurred in late July.

The French, Dutch and Spanish settlers in America were willing to accept rule from their homelands, but the British came with an intense desire for self-government, and they brought with them a sophisticated system of representative government. In England, local officials and church officers as well as members of Parliament's House of Commons were elected. Precedents were well established for everything from how voters should be notified of an election and who could participate, through to the methods for the casting of votes. Over the 170 years of colonial rule in North America, settlers would put these traditions to good use, and colonial legislatures and assemblies would become increasingly powerful. Needless to say, the elections to these bodies would also increase in importance. What was remarkable about the American colonists was their ability to adapt the British electoral methods to the requirements of a turbulent existence in a new land.

When 20th-century Americans think of the reasons colonists came to North America, they tend to think of the Pilgrims and other Puritans, who sought religious freedom. In fact, the colonies—even those that *were* settled for religious reasons—were largely business propositions. After England's long war with Spain and James I's ascension to the throne, Great Britain looked toward the colonization of America as a way to create new markets for its goods and to provide more natural resources than the small island country could possibly produce.

To settle the land, England offered land grants to individuals and joint-stock companies. These entities, in turn, offered enticements to prospective settlers who would be willing to set sail to try to carve out a life in the unknown. Land entitlement and various attractions varied from group to group, but one feature was constant. The charter companies and proprietors knew that the colonists would expect to participate in their colonial government. All joint-stock companies and colonies settled by proprietors or under royal charter had plans for setting up a representative government elected by the colonists themselves. While some governors were slow to implement the system, or called for the elections only infrequently, or even used the bodies only as advisory committees rather than legislatures, almost everywhere plans were soon in place for colonists to hold elections.

## Colonial Election Day

In the typical early American colony elections were held for local, church and militia officers; practices for each varied from community to community and from year to year. These elections were sometimes held independently of assembly type elections. Local elections were held at almost all times of the year, and elective offices ranged from North Carolina's sole elective office (public register of land) to a long list of what the colonists felt were important jobs—everything from clerks and constables to the surveyor of the highway, the collector of rates, fence viewers, chimney viewers and the packers of beef (Connecticut).[1]

Colonies with an established church held elections for church positions (in some places even the minister was elected), and these were generally held at separate times from other area elections—Maryland and the Carolinas tended to hold their church elections on Easter Monday.[2]

Election day for representatives to the colonial assembly, however, was usually treated as a major celebration. Since colonial settlements were usually some distance apart, it was a time for friends and neighbors to meet, catch up on news and generally have a good time. In Eastchester, New York, it was the custom for travelers coming by horseback and by foot to meet up with others traveling from the same direction to form a parade on the way into town. The event was capped with a feast held on the eve of election day.[3]

Even the stern Puritans who settled New England viewed the colony-wide election as a day of great import, and they celebrated it with as much pomp as their religion allowed. (For them, it was the most important colonial annual holiday.) Shops and schools were closed, and town inhabitants, dressed in their finery, gathered in the marketplace. Especially in port towns, the residents were usually joined by visitors who wanted to observe the celebration. In communities where nearby Indian tribes were friendly, sometimes an Indian chief, dressed in ceremonial garb, came to town to witness the holiday.

For most of the early colonial elections in New England the assembly meeting and colony-wide elections took place on the same day. The governor and past elected officials typically met in a designated location in order to march with other qualified voters, all of whom were accompanied by the militia and a band, to the place where the meeting (usually called the general court) would be held. In Newport, Rhode Island in the 1670s, meetings were held under a buttonwood tree near the center of town where the local mill provided filled grain bags on which participants could sit.[4] Elsewhere, homes, churches and meetinghouses were the typical places where people decided upon town business and voted.

At the opening of this general court, the first order of business was always the election day sermon. (These were unique to New England, but they were a lasting tradition. Sermons were given in Connecticut from 1674 to 1830, in New Hampshire from 1784 to 1831, and in Vermont from 1777 to 1834. In Massachusetts the tradition continued for 250 years–from 1634 until 1884.)[5] Each year a different minister was chosen to deliver the sermon, and the responsibility was always a great honor. Though only a small proportion of the population was usually able to attend the general court, the clergymen knew that their words would be spread by other ministers in attendance. (The May meeting of the General Court in Boston was also chosen as the time for the "Convention of Congregational Ministers," when area pastors came to town to talk and compare notes.)[6] From the late 1660s on, the sermons were also printed as pamphlets for wider distribution.

Kept to an hour or under because of all the other business to be covered during the day, the sermons were usually quite theatrical. In weaving an epic story for listeners, the minister covered many topics. Always thankful for the good of the past, the clergyman also found time to catalog what was wrong with New England, plead with the audience to do better and take a look at what might lie ahead. Voters were also reminded to elect good men and then leave them alone to govern. There was usually a message preached about the evils of change.[7]

Following the sermon, business issues of the colony were covered first, and, since these matters more directly affected the residents, the vote was usually larger on such matters. Later in the day—as attention turned more toward political concerns of the court—more and more of the townsmen were likely to drift off toward the tavern. For those who stayed at the meetinghouse, a snack of election day cake (a yeast cake with raisins and sweet spices) was often provided by the women of the community.

During the meetings, the women gathered in nearby houses to talk as the young people socialized and the children played in the village common.

After court ended, there was usually parading in the streets, and sometimes an ox (which had generally been led through town the night before) was roasted. In the evening, there would normally be entertainment for the general public with a select few expected to dine with the governor.

Outside New England, colonists did not usually attend a civic meeting on election day but the day was still an important time to catch up on local news. Voting typically took place on the village green or in a nearby building—eventually the courthouse—large enough to accommodate a crowd, and voters expected to be "treated" throughout the day. Though many colonies had laws forbidding the use of food or money in connection with elections, this law seemed to have been largely ignored and, typically, large quantities of rum punch, ginger cakes and barbecued beef or pork were used to persuade voters to cast their ballots for a particular candidate. Virginian Edmund Scarburgh was just one of many politicians who gained his seat in the legislature after wining and dining the voting public. In 1738, Scarburgh treated at a race and then at a muster (a formal military inspection) and made sure liquor was available near the courthouse door as the men went in to vote. Despite an investigation, Scarburgh retained his seat.[8] Even George Washington participated in this kind of ritual. Because of military commitments, the president-to-be could not be present for his election to the Virginia House of Burgesses in 1758, so he left instructions that 28 gallons of rum, 50 gallons of rum punch, 34 gallons of wine, 46 gallons of beer and two gallons of "cider royal" be purchased for the voters—both those who voted for and against him. If, in later elections, the will of the voter was sometimes dubbed the "voice of grog," it was often with good reason.

Colonial elections were generally held in the spring when travel was again possible after the usually difficult winters, but elections were also held throughout the year—midwinter to midsummer. The New England settlements (Massachusetts Bay, Connecticut, Plymouth and Rhode Island) had fixed dates for elections, generally in the spring. Elsewhere, colonies awaited the issuing of writs (orders from the governor, under the seal of the reigning British monarch). Generally, there were requirements as to how often assemblies were to be elected (annually, every three years, etc.), but these guidelines were not always followed.

Interestingly, an effort was usually made by nearby towns and counties to avoid holding elections on the same day. According to custom, landholders had the right to cast a vote anywhere they owned property, even if that meant voting in several locations. If elections were held concurrently, then an effort was made to extend the election for a week or more to allow voters to travel to the various election sites to vote. It was generally provided that an election continue for more than a day if necessary until all the votes were accounted for. Georgia's constitution specified that an election could not last for more than 20 days.[9]

Although elections in England were always held between 8:00 and 11:00 A.M., the colonies needed to adapt old traditions to their own situation. Some held morning elections, but more often morning and afternoon sessions were held in order to permit more voters to participate.

## Voting Procedures

Each colony had its own provisions for notifying voters of an election. The Hartford Constitution of 1638 provided that the constable of each town go from dwelling to dwelling to notify townspeople. Virginia, too, required the sheriff to go from house to house (or farm to farm) to notify voters. In 1662, this arrangement was found to be ineffective and in its place the sheriff was directed to provide each minister in the county with the appropriate writ concerning an upcoming election. In turn, the ministers would have to return copies of the writ confirming that they had announced the election to their flocks; they faced heavy fines if they failed to do so.

In Massachusetts, the sheriffs notified selectmen to assemble voters. New Jersey posted advertisements about the election in three of the most frequented areas of town. Pennsylvania and Delaware required that written notice be placed on a tree or a house on the most common paths leading into each township where an election was to be held.

In the Carolinas and Maryland, announcements were generally posted in churches, since Sunday religious services could be depended upon to bring colonists in from their farms.

Colonists inherited from England methods for the actual casting of votes. It was sometimes done by "ereccion of hands" (i.e., a show of hands) or by "declaring the choice upon the view"—voters stood on one side of the town green or another depending on how they felt on an issue. With these two methods, the sheriff, who was generally in charge of running elections, would look the groups over (being as precise—or imprecise—as he wished) and give his opinion as to the victor. It was not an exact science.

But it was *viva voce*, the practice of voting orally, that was most widely used. During the 18th century, at least half of the colonies used it at one time or another.

*Viva voce* was popular because colonists believed that elections would be more honest if men had to stand up and be vocal about their beliefs. This practice precluded many kinds of fraud. Though the voter beholden to a certain candidate might not have been able to be entirely true to his opinions because of the public nature of his vote, there were not too many ways to cheat the system. (Oral voting did encourage one kind of voting control—if friends of a candidate saw that the totals in a polled vote were going to the opposition, they would leave the site of the election and travel to neighboring farms to bring in voters who were likely to vote the desired way.) The public nature of almost all forms of the voting probably made each voter think very carefully about the negative results of voting a certain way.

Sometimes oral voting was as simple as voting by acclamation. The sheriff would ask the crowd to signify its vote by calling out "aye" or "nay" at the proper time. If an election was largely uncontested, then sometimes the entire slate of officers was read, the crowd cheered and the "voters" all adjourned to the tavern. In Pennsylvania as late as the 1680s, voters preferred this method because other voting methods took too long. Those who had made the effort to come in to vote were eager to socialize and then start for home as soon as possible.[10]

If a more precise count was needed, a more specific polling took place. The sheriff, the candidates and usually two clerks, one for each candidate, would take their places on the green or in front of the courthouse. The clerks were to record the name of the voter, his residence and for whom he was voting. All was done orally and in full view of the others who were at the poll. Generally, the sheriff arranged to hang a large piece of white cloth on which to keep a tally of the votes. As each voter declared his preference, his vote would be recorded by the clerks as well as on the white sheet and shouts of approval would come from one side and hoots from another. Betting on the election outcome was common, and, as the odds changed, new wagers would be laid. Historian Daniel Boorstin also notes that expression of thanks from the candidate was important. After each vote was cast, the favored candidate would rise, bow and express his gratitude to the voter. A typical thank you might run: "Mr. Buchanan, I shall treasure that vote in my memory. It will be regarded as a feather in my cap forever."[11] This traditional sign of gratitude was so important that when George Washington was called away to head up the militia in 1758, he asked a prestigious friend to sit in for him in order to thank each voter.

Some of the colonial states continued the practice of oral voting for quite some time. Electoral votes in Virginia were by ballot starting in 1800, but some other elections there continued as *viva voce* as late as 1870.[12] Just after the Revolution, Maryland was still electing state legislators, representatives to Congress and presidential electors orally while sheriffs were elected by ballot.

New England's voting methods were, as a rule, somewhat different from those described above. Interestingly, New Englanders were the ones who most objected to the public aspects of oral voting, and the corn and bean method was a voting system created and used there for reasons of secrecy. When freemen voted for the men who would hold the position as one of the governor's assistants—also known as magistrates—the methodology hardly varied. Each candidate would be announced orally, and votes in favor went into the hat as corn; votes against went in as beans. A similar method was used with bits of paper with and without writing. If a voter cast a paper with writing, it was considered in favor of the candidate; a blank was known to be a vote against.

In southern Delaware, the corn and bean method was also sometimes used for balloting, and, in the late 1600s, an ingenious device was invented that assured, the colonists felt, absolute secrecy in voting. A box was divided into two compartments, and in the lid of the box was a chimney-like structure large enough for a voter to thrust in his hand. Voters were told in advance which compartment was for each candidate; thus once a voter's hand was inside, a ballot could be cast for either candidate without onlookers knowing for whom the vote was cast.[13]

Given the New Englanders' preference for secrecy in voting, it is fitting that the first known use of the written ballot in America was in 1629 at the election of officers of the Salem Massachusetts church.[14] New England was ever after to be a leader in the use of voting "by papers."

South Carolina used a secret ballot starting in 1721 where oral as well as nonsecret balloting had been used. (Voters cast written votes, but they were signed or announced orally.) With this secret ballot, the voter wrote on a piece of paper the names of those whom he wished to have as his representatives, rolled up this ballot without signing it and dropped it into a box, glass or paper container. As a man voted, his name was "entered in a book or a roll, for that purpose provided . . ." to prevent any person's voting twice at the same election.[15] When the votes were tabulated, if two were found rolled together, neither was counted. In 1743, North Carolina adopted the method of voting on a scroll of paper rolled up and evidently unsigned but by 1760 had abandoned that method in favor of neighboring Virginia's system of oral voting.

Illiteracy was a fact of life; in Pennsylvania in places with written ballots, the sheriff was instructed to open the ballot and read aloud the names contained to let the illiterate voter verify that this was, indeed, the way he chose to vote.

Distance from the polls presented difficulties for colonists, and though many colonies provided that polls could be moved in order to make them more accessible to more voters, in actual practice, the location was rarely altered. Some colonists lived 60 miles and more from the nearest voting place, and for many that was often just too far to travel.

In England, the voter's presence was always required for legal voting, but New Englanders soon tried to circumvent this requirement because of the problem of distance. Sometimes, freemen wanted to remain home for fear of Indian attack or to try to tend their crops in a bad year. Because of these difficulties, the colonists began to develop methods of voting by proxy—the forerunners of our current system of absentee ballotry. (Since the colonies were still under royal domain in one way or another, official descriptions of voting by proxy were often deliberately obscure—to prevent royal representatives from learning of the practice.)

As early as the 1630s, Boston provided that certain towns should have "libertie to stay soe many of their freeman att home for the safety of their towne as they judge needful, and that the said freemen that are appoyncted by the towne to stay att home shall have liberty for this court to send their voices by pxy."[16] The law was made applicable throughout the colony in the following years because of the "great danger and damage that may accrue to the State by all the freemen[2] leaving their plantations to come to the place of elections."[17]

By 1760 Newport, too, felt that the voters' presence in town could be "very injurious to the interest and public weal of the colony."[18] Proxies could be submitted in writing on a specific day in the local area and carried to the general court by deputies elected by the local freeholders. To be accepted, each proxy had to be signed on the back by the voter.

During the 1640s, the Massachusetts government decided that voting by proxy was so effective that it tried to pass a law specifying that all votes should be cast in this manner, with only elected members of the general court coming to Boston to vote in person. But the colonists cared so deeply about their suffrage rights that the law was soon replaced with one allowing for voting in person or by proxy.

## The Right to Vote

Who actually voted? At that first election in Jamestown in 1619, it appears that all men who desired—servants as well as gentlemen—were able to vote. This was a very unusual practice for the time. Though movement for broadening the voting franchise was afoot in England during the 17th century, British law still required all voters to own property that produced income of 40 shillings or more per year. This requirement limited the franchise to freeholders (those who owned land), automatically excluding the poor, criminals and servants.

Nonetheless, when Virginia was first being established, an early law required "every man and manservant of above sixteen years of age"[19] to pay taxes, and each male was also to vote. Skilled craftsmen were needed in the community, and it is likely that early colonists were reluctant to disfranchise those whose efforts could make or break the success of the enterprise, whether or not they were wealthy. In 1646 the Jamestown assembly decided to fine colonists who failed to vote (the fine was 100 pounds of tobacco), but exempted servants from the fine. However, the "good life" didn't last much longer for the lower classes. In 1654, the Assembly took the vote away from servants and former servants. And though popular demand returned the vote to former servants, since they paid taxes, people in servitude were no longer given voting privileges. (In actual practice, leniency was common.)[20]

After this early period it was almost a given that voters would be male and over 21. Otherwise, suffrage requirements could be bent to solve problems of the moment. Minority groups (blacks, Indians, Jews, Catholics) were usually excluded from voting in the areas where their numbers were sizable enough to make a difference. If minorities in the area were insignificant in number or if they posed little threat to the ruling electorate, the legislature often didn't bother to formulate laws prohibiting them from voting. (Blacks and women for instance, were not excluded from voting in New Jersey until 1807.) Interestingly, when Maryland was led by Roman Catholic Lord Baltimore, Catholics were allowed to vote. But when Baltimore was ousted from power for a time, laws against voting by Catholics were passed. (Lord Baltimore ultimately had to convert to Protestantism in order to regain control of the colony, and exclusion of Catholics continued.)

In New England, the Puritans were very worried about losing their sense of religious community if too many people of other beliefs settled in the area. For that reason, the original settlers demanded that newcomers be accepted into the "freedom" of the town—through which one then gained political rights, the right to own land and voting privileges. Those who were accepted became known as "freemen." (This same term was used in the colonies outside New England to mean "free man," someone who was not a servant; it also was sometimes used synonymously with freeholder—someone who owned land.)

But for the most part, property ownership was what decided whether or not a colonist could vote; the requirement varied somewhat according to locale. In rural areas where land was plentiful, the freehold requirement of 50 acres was just right for letting the leading men of the community vote; in an urban setting, such a large property requirement would have prevented almost everyone from voting. Before the turn of the 17th century, a property requirement of some local measurement was standard in the British colonies.

The land ownership requirement was important to colonists because it solved what they viewed as a host of election day problems. Most settlements were sponsored by businessmen who had put up the money for the colonists to come to the New World, and these investors wanted to protect their investment. Since the companies controlled the ownership of the land, they also controlled who would or would not vote. Furthermore, "improper" voters, paupers, idiots, the insane and criminals (who would later be excluded from the vote) were rarely property owners, so they weren't a problem. By the 1700s Virginia restricted voting to men who owned either 25 acres with a house and plantation or 100 acres of uncultivated land. Most colonies had similar requirements, and records show that about one-third of all settlers had some landholdings. More lenient settlements based their requirements on the worth of real property— sometimes based on whether or not a person paid taxes.

In the end, rigid suffrage laws could be seen by colonists as the solid foundation for a colony's stability. In defense of an increasingly burdensome property requirement, a representative of the New Jersey proprietors noted: "If everybody were (though of Never so little worth) to be Lawmakers, those Persons of best Estate in the Countrie, and the Proprietors Interests, would be at the disposal of the tag, rag, and Rascallity."[21]

Different kinds of elections often required different qualifications. Sometimes the quantity of land required to qualify varied for local and colonial elections. To vote in church elections in New England, a colonist had to be a member of the church or had to pay taxes in support of the church (with the coming of a certain degree of religious tolerance, colonists who were members of other churches were not forced to support the established church financially). But broadest of all was the franchise for the militia. Because many colonies felt that all who could be required to serve in the militia should also participate in selection of officers, many places provided that all able men between the ages of 16 and 60 had the right to vote for military officers.

By the time of the Revolution, the colonies had begun to specify other requirements (race, color, sex, age, religion and residency), but by then every one of the 13 colonies had a property requirement. Only seven (New Hampshire, Rhode Island, New York, New Jersey, Virginia, North Carolina and Georgia), however, required that the property be in the form of real estate. The other six colonies offered alternatives to the property qualification in the form of the holding of personal property or the payment of taxes.[22]

But what is truly amazing about the colonial electorate was how very small it was. Even with compulsory voting, which was first stipulated as early as 1636 in Plymouth and was enforced in Virginia, Plymouth, Maryland and Delaware, the figures for eligible voters were still very small. For example, in Pennsylvania in the early 1700s, voters were required to own 50 acres or have property valued at £50 or more. Not many in the city had a net worth of that amount, and those in the country lived far from polling places. Historians have analyzed the data from the period, and they show that about 8% of the rural population in Pennsylvania qualified to vote, but that only about 2% in Philadelphia qualified. Virginia and Rhode Island had relatively high percentages qualifying with about 9% of the white population eligible to vote. Massachusetts and Connecticut show that about 16% of the population qualified, but that only about 2% of the overall colony actually voted. New York City and Virginia show a far larger proportion—8% of the population—as actual voters. Overall, the potential voters seemed to vary from about one-sixth to one-fiftieth of the population.[23]

While we consider 20th-century voter participation scandalously low, the colonial statistics show that the property qualification, poor methods of communication and difficulty traveling to the polls meant that amazingly few colonists were able to participate in the democratic process.

## The Right to Run for Office

The number of people eligible to run for office dropped lower still. Early on, colonists were overworked and stretched to capacity in settling the new land, but they considered government to be a bounden duty and civic diligence was expected of members of the gentry. (Since class distinctions were made on the basis of wealth, it was easier to achieve the status of gentry in the New World—most colonies offered land entitlement for no money down.) It was not unusual to have one person serve as justice of the peace, judge of the county court, a member of the legislature and hold an official position in the church.

Many colonies had increased requirements for those who desired to be elected officials. Members of South Carolina's state legislature were required to own 3,500 pounds currency; North Carolina's had to possess at least 100 acres of land. Georgia took these requirements to ridiculous extremes. In 1732, the trustees of Georgia intended that the settlement would build its riches from silk production. In order to encourage settlers to pursue this insect husbandry, the trustees took a somewhat innovative legislative action. In 1751, the trustees voted that no person could be a deputy (the equivalent to a colonial assembly representative) unless he had a "hundred mulberry trees [on which silkworms could live] planted and properly fenced upon every 50 acres he possessed." After 1753, a Georgia deputy was to be a person who had strictly conformed to the "limitation of the number of negro slaves in proportion to his white servants, and who had at least one female in his family instructed in the art of reeling silk, and who yearly produced fifteen pounds of silk upon 50 acres of land, and that quantity upon every fifty acres he possessed."[24] Because the trustees realized that few could meet these qualifications, they exempted members of the first assembly from these rules.

If a settler qualified for candidacy, even when the standards were so idiosyncratic, then the nomination and campaign were very humble affairs. In the New England colonies, candidates generally had to have their names placed in nomination (they could also nominate themselves) at one general court in order to run for any elected office to be voted on at the following court. A candidate would announce his intentions to run in advance of the election, generally by claiming that his neighbors and friends had prevailed upon him to take office. Colonial decorum prohibited candidates from implying that they thought highly of themselves and the supposed confidence of friends and neighbors was considered necessary to justify a candidacy. Little campaigning was done on the issues, and candidates were forbidden to solicit votes or even to vote for themselves. One New Yorker put it this way: "To ask a man for his Vote is a Confession in the Candidate that he is suspicious of his own merit. 'Tis proof of his Apprehensions that the sense of the Public is against him."[25]

*In a colonial Williamsburg reenactment, a colonist steps forward to vote orally (viva voce). Present at the table would have been the sheriff, the candidates and usually a clerk for each candidate to keep a tally of the votes. After each voter expressed his preference, the candidate for whom he had voted would rise and thank him. (Courtesy Colonial Williamsburg Foundation.)*

## Election Abuses

England was never known for its lack of election tampering, and colonists brought to the New World the potential for abuses as well as for democracy. Not surprisingly, some of the best-documented stories of election abuses in the colonies concern the office of the sheriff, who—outside of New England—was generally the manager of the election with power to schedule the time and place of elections, open and close the polls, decide on the qualification of voters and submit the returns. In some towns, he was appointed by the governor; in other locations, he was selected by the gentry from among themselves.

Sheriffs were sometimes accused of making improper returns, excluding qualified voters from the poll, neglecting to give due notice of the time and place of the election, appointing clerks illegally, intimidating voters and failing to administer oaths to challenge voters. Other documented abuses included the relocation of the poll by several miles without the consent of the candidates; keeping the poll open for two weeks and then suddenly adjourning it to the edge of the county without consent and keeping the poll open for several days until certain candidates were in the lead, at which time the election was declared closed.

In one 1743 case in Hunterdon County, New Jersey, charges against the sheriff had enough merit for an election to be declared void. In this instance, the sheriff had opened an election in Trenton at 3:00 P.M. on March 1, and the voting continued until after 8:00 P.M. closing only after the town crier had gone around the city three times announcing the upcoming closing of the polls. The next morning the poll reopened at 9:00, with the understanding that the poll would stay open until 1:00 P.M. or until at least one-half hour after the last vote had been received. Late in the morning, when voting had slowed, the sheriff sent the town crier out again and he "went into several of the Taverns and desired the people who had not voted to give in their Votes or the Poll would be closed." Shortly before noon, the sheriff announced his intention to close and ignored the pleas of colonists, who informed him that a group from nearby Maidenhead should arrive soon. When the 42 voters arrived shortly thereafter, the polls had already been shut. The excluded voters protested, and eventually the colonial Assembly declared the election void.[26]

In 1710 in Middlesex, New Jersey, a sheriff ran the election with great partiality. He permitted the advocates of one candidate to vote freely without taking the prescribed oaths, and he summarily turned away the advocates of the other candidate. As soon as his candidate had secured a slight majority, the sheriff "shut up the Pole so Suddenly and abruptly that the very Clarks at the Table knew not of it but lost their votes . . ." Forty-one petitioners protested, but the Assembly set their pleas aside.[27]

Abuses by the sheriff were just one kind of problem. For the rich, the property requirement for voting could be twisted into a source of support—all they needed to do was make their friends landholders. In an election in Virginia in the 1730s, one candidate brought scores of men from other counties and had small lots deeded to them to make them eligible to vote. To prevent this kind of abuse from occurring again, the House of Burgesses soon passed a law requiring a voter to own land with a structure on it. At the next election, one enterprising candidate sent his friend home with a shack from another property in order that the lot deeded to the friend would have the required "structure." At a meeting of the legislature shortly after, the size of structure was stipulated in order to prevent further abuse.

Other kinds of election irregularities occurred. Pennsylvania was an area where the Quakers, the Scotch–Irish and the proprietary governor were often at odds, and, in close elections, local politicians helped Germans get naturalized quickly in order that they might help the colonists' cause. These kinds of incidents recurred everywhere, with dishonesty on both sides. In New Jersey in the early 1700s, one Dr. John Johnston brought scores of men from Monmouth, Somerset and Hunterdon counties and had small lots of land in Perth Amboy deeded to them in order to make them eligible to vote there. But the governor must have gotten wind of the plan as he brought in his own schooner- load of "voters" to bring about Johnston's defeat.[28]

In New York, two rival families battled out many elections for local and national offices, and typical maneuvers included marching tenants to the polls and observing their votes as well as the stationing of bruisers at the polls to protect or intimidate.

On one occasion in New Jersey, a candidate was allowed to cart the unlocked ballot box from poll to poll in his horse-drawn sulky. Though no reason for this action is given and tampering couldn't be proved, it happened during a highly contested election in Hunterdon County, and residents later petitioned against the legality of election because of this as well as other questionable acts.[29]

## The Seeds of Revolution

Long before the revolutionary era, the politics of dissension had begun to establish itself. As early as the 1760s, a Massachusetts political "machine" existed. As the struggle between colonists and the Crown heightened in Massachusetts, colonists met in secret caucuses to designate candidates for public offices. Ballots with the appropriate people listed were prepared, and each member would leave with a supply to distribute among friends and acquaintances on the day of the election. As the Revolution neared, the clubs began to operate more openly. Gatherings generally would consist of people from the same neighborhood, or workers of the same profession, and these groups, in turn, would link up with similar caucuses or clubs in order to expand their reach.

Although, of course, no national political parties existed, there were most definitely factions—generally those in favor (and who were benefiting from) the leadership of the proprietor or governor and those who were not. Peppered throughout were local protests against the wishes of the British government or of the proprietors. While the Boston Tea Party is probably the best known incident of the colonists' disagreement with the Crown's representatives, the local people took issue with laws made in England on numerous occasions long before the Revolution. The colonists found that their assemblies could vote to withhold funds for gubernatorial salaries, which gave them some leverage to negotiate for their needs.

As the Revolutionary War neared, elections assumed a new importance in the British colonies, and as tensions heated up in the colonies, it was actually the cancellation of an election day that led indirectly to "the shot heard round the world." In the fall of 1774, colonists were still seething about Parliament's reaction to the Boston Tea Party (the other colonies had rallied to help Boston once the port was cut off). Massachusetts Governor Thomas Gage sent out the usual writs of election for the October General Court, but because of Boston's blockade, the governor called for the Court to be held in Salem, the new seat of government. This only heightened public outrage, and Gage was so angry at the reaction that he cancelled the election. Nonetheless, 90 members of the General Court arrived. When Gage failed to appear, those in attendance declared his behavior unconstitutional and adjourned to reassemble in Concord as a Provincial Congress. Convinced that Massachusetts was ultimately going to take up arms and that the solution was to quell the renegades while the trouble was still local, Gage obtained permission from Parliament to use troops against the colonial upstarts if necessary. When the Provincial Congress met the following April in Concord, Gage waited until adjournment and then sent his soldiers in to capture ammunition. The battles of Lexington and Concord followed.

Of course, what Gage had miscalculated was the reaction of the other colonies. Tensions were at an all-time high; this was the final affront. As far as the colonies were concerned, war had begun.

# The New Constitution and the Vote to Ratify      2

The Revolutionary War and the years following were politically tumultuous times in each of the colonies (now more properly known as states). By the time the War of Independence broke out, two factions were easily identifiable among the colonists—the revolutionaries, who were in favor of the Revolution, and the Tories or loyalists, who wanted to remain connected to Britain. (For the most part, the revolutionaries attracted laborers, farmers and the underprivileged, but they also pulled into their midst Virginia planters and some merchants from other colonies who were angry at the unfair tax and trade treatment they had received from Britain.) Within each state political battles occurred about whether radicals or conservatives would control the revolutionary government during this unsettled period. The radicals benefited from the committees of correspondence established throughout the states by Samuel Adams, which had been able to organize and to gain control almost everywhere. The Tories, caught by surprise by the Revolution, were isolated and unable to gain much power.

Shortly after the Revolution began, colonial legislatures drafted state constitutions; in most cases, the people did not have the opportunity to voice their approval or disapproval of the documents, but in general, the laws pertaining to suffrage did not differ greatly from the ones under which the colonial governments had been operating. (It was the other laws imposed by England to which the colonists objected.) Connecticut and Rhode Island, which already enjoyed popularly elected governors, added bills of rights (added by other states as well) to their previous documents and worked with the same government structure that they had under their royal charters. Other states were careful to rein in elected leaders and ensure that they did not attempt to capitalize on the power vacuum created by rebellion against the Crown. This was particularly true concerning the office of state governor. (Some even provided that their legislatures were supreme.) Every state but South Carolina opted for one-year terms for governors and assemblymen, believing that annual elections would prevent tyranny. Test oaths of allegiance, designed to exclude loyalists (and in some cases, Catholics) were common. In seven states every male taxpayer could vote; elsewhere there were moderate property qualifications. Many more changes were yet to come.

But, by 1787, the men who had led the American Revolution knew that the nominal national government was in serious trouble. Since 1781 the states had been guided by a document known as the Articles of Confederation, which kept the power within each state while loosely linking all 13 of them. In trying to avoid all the hazards of a strong central government, American leaders had created one with no power at all, and it was failing miserably.

That the states' first attempt at a national government was flawed is not surprising. When the Continental Congress appointed a committee to draft a wartime confederation to unify the independent states, the members of the committee had fresh in their minds all the tyranny and abuse of British rule. For that reason, only minimal centralized federal powers were granted the Articles of Confederation. Any power that had been abused by England was denied to the new government. As a result, the federal government could not levy taxes, enlist troops, punish lawbreakers or compel the states to observe treaties. No national executive existed; nor was a national court system established. The expenses of running a government were to be paid under a system of state land-value assessments, but Congress had no power to collect the money. The entire power of the government rested on whim—each state decided whether or not to cooperate on any given issue.

In 1785 an economic downturn quickly slid into a country-wide depression. The crisis made the problems of governing under the Articles of Confederation increasingly apparent. The government was hardly exempt from the crisis and became overwhelmed by the interest payments on its internal and external national debt (largely attributable to the expenses of the Revolution). Trade throughout the colonies came to a standstill. On farms, crops were being left to rot in the fields because no one could afford to buy them.

In addition to economic problems, other disputes arose. The new states were fighting over boundaries, some were entering into their own negotiations for trade with foreign countries and Indian affairs were being managed poorly. Conditions were bad enough that there was talk of war between the colonies.

In 1786, a revolt by a group of farmers in western Massachusetts signalled to Americans everywhere the extremity of their plight. In the fall of 1786, mobs of farmers prevented some Massachusetts courts from sitting because, were the courts to convene, judgments would be handed down against people in debt and farmers would be stripped of their holdings and put in jail. Led by a former Revolutionary War soldier, Daniel Shays, the farmers—pitchforks and staves in hand—attempted a raid on an arsenal and then planned to prevent the sitting of the state supreme court at Springfield.

Within a few days, the rebellion was put down, but the struggle had brought to light disturbing weaknesses in the country's government. Even though other Americans identified with the plight of Massachusetts, they were powerless to offer help. No federal governmental body, and certainly no individual, had the authority or the money to step in and deal with the situation. The rebellion made it clear that a government had to be created that would have the ability to take action when and where needed. The survival of the nation—and the freedom of the people—were at stake.

These problems were foremost in the minds of the political leaders in the fall of 1786, when only five states appeared at a convention in Annapolis to discuss United States trade. Alexander Hamilton of New York and James Madison of Virginia urged the small group to put out a call for a federal convention to address the weaknesses of the Confederation and to devise further provisions "to render the constitution of the federal government adequate to the exigencies of the Union."[1] The hope and goal were to provide for a strong central government for national purposes while still maintaining the independence of state governments and the authority of state governments over local concerns.

## The Federal Convention Meets

Fifty-five men representing 12 of the 13 American states (Rhode Island declined to attend) met in Philadelphia for four months during the summer of 1787 and drafted a completely new Constitution. They knew that merely strengthening the Articles of Confederation was not the answer, and they set out to create a strong, well-balanced central government, with dispersed authority among three independent branches of government—the legislative, the judicial and the executive—and to establish a system of checks and balances so that no branch of government could encroach on the other. They did so, and in the process they established a government that has worked as well for 50 states consisting of 240 million people as it did for the original 13 eastern seaboard states, populated then by about four million.

Unsalaried and paying their own way, most of the representatives who came to Philadelphia had extensive experience in government. Most famous were George Washington, 55, and Benjamin Franklin, then 81 years old. James Madison and Alexander Hamilton were also present, as were two college presidents, three professors and 28 men who had served as part of the Continental Congress. Conspicuous by their absence from the Convention were a few who were vital to the American Revolution: Thomas Jefferson, who was serving as minister to France, and Patrick Henry, who didn't want to be a delegate because he disagreed with plans for a strong central government.

It's not surprising that the resolution of many election-related questions was an integral component of the Convention's proceedings. In fact, Convention members argued most hotly about the electoral system of the new government. Together with the impetus to form a stronger federal government was a counterbalancing concern that the government truly be held responsible to the people. No matter how wonderfully designed the new government might be, it would not be worth much if it couldn't guarantee a fair choice of America's rulers.

Among the early questions dealt with were the requirements that would be necessary for Americans to vote. Some felt, Pennsylvania delegate Gouverneur Morris among them, that suffrage for national elections should be held only by landowners. John Dickinson of Delaware and James Madison argued also that the rights of public liberty were safe only in the hands of freeholders (a point on which Madison reversed himself many years later).

Connecticut's Judge Oliver Ellsworth countered that such restrictions were risky— that Americans would be quick to reject the new Constitution if they were to be disfranchised! Said Pierce Butler of South Carolina: "There is no right of which the people are more jealous than that of suffrage."[2]

Nathaniel Gorham of Massachusetts drew on practical personal experience noting that "he had never seen any inconveniency [sic] from allowing such as were not freeholders to vote." He pointed out that "the elections in Philadelphia, New York and Boston, where the merchants and mechanics vote, are at least as good as those made by freeholders only." He continued: "The people have long been accustomed to this right in various parts of America and will never allow it to be abridged."[3]

The delegates were unable to reach a consensus, and the suffrage issue was left to a Committee of Detail, an appointed group of the delegates who were assigned to wrap up such loose ends. Given the range of opinion, they concluded that suffrage requirements could not be enforced on a national basis; that it would be very unfair if someone were eligible to vote for representatives to the state legislature, but were excluded by the Constitution from a vote for the national legislature. For that reason they left such questions for the states to decide.

The Convention fared better deciding on the structure of Congressional selection. The selection of senators was decided upon early. In June, John Dickinson of Delaware first made a motion that senators should be chosen by state legislators. Though Pennsylvania's James Wilson proposed that a popular vote for senators would be the most democratic method, the delegates promptly voted Wilson down, and adopted Dickinson's motion officially, with Virginia and Pennsylvania dissenting. (This method was used until it was changed to a choice by popular election with the passage of the 17th Amendment in 1913.)

Although delegates intended to cement the Senate's identity as an august and powerful body, the identity of the House was more open to question. Each delegate seemed to have his own ideas for the election to and structure of this assembly. Accordingly deciding on how members of the House of Representatives would be chosen was much more difficult. Discussions were heated, and the problem blocked progress for several weeks. The large states wanted population-based representation, while the small states, which had enjoyed one-state/one-vote under the Articles of Confederation, feared that the large states would usurp all power. Slavery was a heated issue (some thought the Constitution should legislate against it), but the sheer numbers of slaves in the large states also figured prominently in this discussion. Though it had been discussed before, on July 16 Roger Sherman put forth what has been called the Connecticut Compromise. It specified that the Senate would feature equal representation (two senators from each state chosen by the respective state legislatures) and that the House of Representatives would be popularly elected and apportioned according to the number of free inhabitants; slave states could incorporate 3/5 of their slaves into their population figure.

The delegates found this proposal satisfactory. Other election details were to be left to the states.

## The Most Difficult Question

Although large states and small states, free states and slave states had many major disagreements during the summer, the one issue that most split the Convention was the method for electing the chief executive officer of the country, the president. Pennsylvania delegate James Wilson noted: "The subject has greatly divided this House . . . It is in truth the most difficult of all on which we have to decide."[4]

Meeting in secrecy, the Convention had not been underway for many days when a rumor soon surfaced among the people that the delegates were planning to crown George Washington king. As debate continued over the method of selecting the president—many of the delegates may have wished that the issue had been so simple.

The idea of a popular election, by which the citizens themselves would vote directly for president, was discussed very early in the proceedings, but it was soon rejected, primarily because the delegates knew that problems in communication among all 13 states would seriously hamper such a method. The nation had only 80 newspapers, and the postal service was slow and unreliable. Philadelphia and New York were two to three days away by stagecoach; and the trip between Boston and Philadelphia was made by both stagecoach and ferry in 10 days and entailed crossing seven rivers. The delegates found it difficult to imagine how one man could become well enough known throughout the 13 states to be elected by the majority of the people. One delegate, George Mason of Virginia, compared making the selection of president by popular vote to referring a "trial of colours to a blind man."[5]

Along with Mason, Elbridge Gerry of Massachusetts, Roger Sherman of Connecticut and Charles Pinckney of South Carolina were also vocal in their feelings that a popular election was unworkable. They also hoped, apart from questions of practicality that by avoiding a popular election, the government would also eliminate the possibility of "dangerous commotions" among citizens at election time. With the removal of the property requirement in several states, some foresaw a day when more and more people would be eligible to vote—and be likely to riot if their candidate didn't win.

But when the first formal plan set forth at the Convention called for the national legislature to choose the president, the representatives quickly rejected it; they argued that the chief executive should be independent of the legislature to be a true guardian of the people. The next plan called for the state assemblies to be given a proportional number of votes, to be cast directly or through electors. This method, too, was defeated because it was decided that it would be improper to make the president beholden to the state legislatures.

As the summer wore on and the issue continued to confound the representatives, the idea of the popular election was again discussed; the system had worked well in New York and Massachusetts in selecting their early governors.

In all discussions, two stumbling blocks arose. The first was the "favorite son" problem. Voters in each state would almost certainly vote for their own state's best candidate, and the representatives felt that it would be difficult for one candidate to ever win a majority of the votes; if one did, the system would certainly favor the larger states with more voters.

The second sticking point was the southern delegation's opposition to a popular election. Because blacks were not allowed to vote, the South, whose population included a large number of black slaves, would not be represented in the final tally according to its actual population. Southerners thus proposed a system of "electors," whereby each state would be assigned a fixed number of official voters based on the state's population. For southern representation in the House of Representatives, it had already been decided that 3/5 of all slaves would be counted toward determining representation for the South. Delegates suggested that the same formula could be used to determine the number of electors from each state as well.

On August 6, the Committee of Detail had been appointed to wrap up items on almost all of the rest of the Constitution, yet the issue of selecting the chief executive was still undecided. Late in August, the idea of a popular election was voted upon, as well as the suggestion of voting through electors, but both proposals were defeated. Finally, in desperation, the representatives, tired and eager to go home, appointed a Grand Committee consisting of a representative from each state still present, and on August 31 they began a series of meetings to work out a viable system for selecting the president of the United States.

After five days of deliberation, the Committee set forth a report recommending a four-year re-electable term for the president, and a rather complicated method for electing him: Each state would appoint a number of electors equal to the combined number of senators and members of the House of Representatives to which the state was entitled. The body of electors as a whole was called the electoral college. Electors would meet and vote by ballot for two persons, one of whom must not be a resident of their state. The results would then be sent to the president of the Senate. If one clear victor were apparent, he became president. If a majority had given an equal vote to two or three candidates, then the Senate was to choose from the top five. Congress was left the responsibility for devising the electoral timetable.

When this proposal was presented in early September, it was greeted with approval from the other delegates who objected only to the provision of a vote by the Senate in the case of a tie. The delegation as a whole decided that the House—as the legislative body most representative of all the people—be given the tie-breaking responsibility. With this change, the proposal passed and was made part of the new Constitution.

The committee had devised a plan that, at the time, satisfied everyone. The population-based apportionment of electors pleased the large states; the smaller states liked the fact that when the vote was thrown into the House for a final decision all states had only one vote, giving them all equal power in the ultimate decision-making. The southern states were pleased that the number of a state's electors would be appointed according to the number of their congressional delegation, which reflected the 3/5 of the slave population. The states' rights advocates appreciated the fact that the state legislature could select how electors were chosen; and the delegates who had favored the direct vote were able to see how the electoral system could represent the will of the people.

Left ambiguous was the manner in which the electors were to be selected. The Constitution states: "Each state shall appoint in such manner as the legislature thereof may direct, a number of electors . . ." Left to the interpretation of history is what the Founding Fathers really intended. Above all, they certainly meant to respect states' rights in the matter. Some contemporaries contended that the Committee really meant to suggest a popular vote for the electors but was reluctant to explicitly ordain it. In any case, the Federal Convention delegates surely envisioned the presidential electors as honorable men who would come together to choose a president who was wise and capable and above the influence of different factions. Had they foreseen that the office of the presidency was to become very much a part of the political party system, they almost certainly would have come up with a very different method.

The process had been arduous. No fewer than 60 ballots had been taken on the issue of selecting a president. Five times the Convention had voted in favor of having the president appointed by Congress; once they had voted against it, once for electors chosen by the state legislators, twice against that, and then voted again and again to reconsider the whole topic. At last, the issue had been resolved, and the delegates could think about adjournment.

But none of these debates would mean anything if the new document was not accepted, or ratified, by the American people. Here, the Convention had taken a huge gamble and had opted to submit the Constitution to popularly elected assemblies of the people for ratification. Though it would have been simpler to offer it to the state legislatures for approval, the delegates recognized the attendant risks. By seeking approval from the men who represented the old guard, the very men whose power might be lessened by a change, they risked defeat. Risky, too, of course, was the unknown of submitting the Constitution to the people. Both Massachusetts and New Hampshire had used this method for approval of their state constitutions, and, in both cases, numerous drafts and a great deal of time were necessary before the people were satisfied. But Rufus King of Massachusetts pointed out that a public referendum was the only way "of obviating all disputes and doubts concerning the legitimacy of the new constitution."[6] Even if the document did not guarantee popular elections in most cases, few wanted to foist this system on the American people without their final say-so. In this sense, the popular elections concerning the ratification of the Constitution may have been the most important election days the country has ever seen and were proof of the democratic bedrock of the American system of government.

The one concession that the delegates made in letting the people ratify the Constitution was in not requiring approval from all 13 states. Foreseeing that total agreement might be very difficult, the Federal Convention provided that only nine states need ratify the Constitution before the United States could begin operating under it; the other states would come under its jurisdiction as each of them ratified.

The Founding Fathers must have left Philadelphia feeling well satisfied, but they also knew that much work was still ahead of them.

When the Federal Convention ended, newspapers eagerly printed the Constitution in its entirety as soon as they could get copies of it. Then the public debates started, and much newsprint was occupied with opinions for and against this new form of government. The Convention had been a rehearsal for the questions, doubts and rejection or acceptance that would ultimately be voiced by the people.

The people were concerned about many things. Would a strong central government bring tyranny? Tax them excessively? Drag them into foreign wars? They feared loss of their own state's independence, and they didn't understand why there was a need for a vice president and viewed it as "dangerous." Massachusetts, where democracy was so strong, was terribly alarmed that there were no provisions for annual elections— six years for senators and even a four-year term for the president seemed like a very long time. And when people read of the provision for the Federal City—10 miles square—they were concerned. A Baptist preacher in North Carolina, candidate for his state's ratification convention, told a meeting of frontier parishioners that the Federal City would be "walled in or fortified. There an army of 50,000 or perhaps 100,000 men will be finally embodied and will sally forth and enslave the people, who will be gradually disarmed."[7] The thought of a national army was terrifying, but most alarming of all was that the government would have the power of taxation.

The fight over the Constitution was not a class, a sectional or an economic split. If it was anything, it was age *vs.* youth with the younger convinced that the immediate peril was dissolution and that without a strong federal government, the American experiment in government would fail. Supporters of the Constitution used pamphlets and newspaper articles to educate the people (most famous and effective were the articles that appeared in a New York newspaper written by Madison, Hamilton and John Jay over the common signature "Publius.") But probably the most persuasive argument for the Constitution was the knowledge that Franklin and Washington were in favor of it.

Many of those elected to attend the ratification conventions were prominent citizens who had been politically active throughout the period. Many of the delegates to Philadelphia were delegates to their state conventions as well; if they were not, as in the case of Elbridge Gerry of Massachusetts, they were usually invited to address the group anyway.

Perhaps foreshadowing some of the difficulties that would arise in choosing presidential electors, problems arose for the people in defining what kind of person they wanted to have attend the ratifying conventions. Should he be open-minded and make a decision based on the information presented at the convention, or should he be elected because he campaigned for or against ratification? In York County, Virginia, in the summer of 1788, a crowd of freeholders gathered to listen to convention contenders speak for and against the Constitution, until finally a freeholder stood up and suggested that all present candidates be rejected as being too opinionated. Instead, the freeholder suggested, the people might nominate two well-respected citizens who would approach the Constitution with an open mind. Though the men nominated weren't even in attendance, the crowd agreed with what the freeholder proposed and off they marched to Williamsburg, the home of one of the crowd's nominees. When Chancellor George Wythe was asked, "Will you serve?" the startled chancellor lost control of his emotions and could only respond, "Surely—How can I refuse?"[8]

In Massachusetts, farmers from the western part of the state represented both sides of the question. Amos Singletry, an elderly farmer from Worcester with no formal education who had sat in the state legislature, noted:

"Does not this . . . constitution take away all we have—all our property? Does it not lay all taxes, duties, imposts, and excises? And what more have we to give? . . . These lawyers and men of learning, and moneyed men that talk so fincly and gloss over matters so smoothly, to make us poor illiterate people swallow down the pill, expect to get into Congress themselves . . . and get all the power and all the money into their own hands."[9]

But a young farmer, Jonathan Smith from the Berkshire Hills, replied:

"I am a plain man, and get my living by the plow. I am not used to speak in public, but I get your leave to say a few words to my brother plow joggers in this house. I have lived in a part of the country where I have known the worth of good government by the want of it . . . Now, Mr. President, when I saw this Constitution, I found that it was a cure for these disorders. I got a copy of it, and read it over and over. I had been a member of the Convention to form our own state constitution, and had learnt something of the checks and balances of power, and I found them all there. I did not go to any lawyer to ask his opinion. We have no lawyer in our town, and we do well enough without. I formed my own opinion, and was pleased with this Constitution."[10]

Once called, many of the ratification conventions went on for several weeks. The people met and read carefully through the entire Constitution with debates, questions and persuasive speeches applicable to the various parts under discussion. Often the level of contention was very high. Whether or not a strong central government was the only way to save the nation was an uppermost question in everyone's mind.

Interestingly, despite all the problems surrounding the issue at the Federal Convention, the method by which the president was to be selected was very well received by the public. As the delegates spoke out, urging ratification, they tended to explain the electoral system based on their own leanings. Those who had favored direct vote explained that though the election would be by indirect vote, the vote for president would still be representative of the will of the people. Others emphasized the importance of the states' roles in selecting the electors.

While many of the delegates arrived to listen and to study, others had been mandated to vote only as their community instructed. In Massachusetts (where the vote for ratification was very close—187 to 168, and then only ratified with the provision that a bill of rights be added), lawyer William Symmes from Andover—after listening to the debates—felt it right to ratify, despite the contrary instructions of his constituents. He assumed they would understand, but they did not. The reaction of the neighbors was so unpleasant and violent that Symmes was forced to move to a new community.[11] Another delegate indicated that he wished there had been time to go home and present to his constituents the argument he heard on the Constitution. He voted against ratification.

Delaware, Pennsylvania and New Jersey ratified almost immediately, but such influential states as Massachusetts, New York and Virginia were slow to act. Ultimately, Massachusetts had the strong support of shipwrights, metalworkers and other mechanics reinforcing the lawyers, merchants and many of the farmers. In New York, Alexander Hamilton campaigned vigorously, and in Virginia, every bit of George Washington's influence was needed.

New Hampshire had the honor of casting the ninth vote, making the Constitution effective as of June 21, 1788. (Virginia, New York, North Carolina and Rhode Island had not yet ratified, and the latter two did not do so until after Congress adopted a Bill of Rights—thus, neither North Carolina nor Rhode Island participated in the first election.)

In most cases, though the harangues had been serious and the debates fevered, once settled, the people in favor of the new government were ready to celebrate, and those who had been against it were ready to admit that it was time to try something new. The ratifying states celebrated with bonfires, speeches and toasts.

Now it was time to test the machinery. The first opportunity to do so was in the Congressional election that could take place as early as November of 1788, only a few short months from the date of ratification.

# A New Nation Elects Its Government _____ 3

In the fall of 1788, the new nation looked toward electing a federal government, but confusion—coupled with hopefulness—reigned. Given that ratification was uncertain, no state legislature had prepared for federal elections, and politicians and statesmen were still puzzling over how the electoral college was to operate. The means of choosing electors still had to be decided in each state, and no one was certain whether to choose electors who could be trusted to judge for themselves who should be president, or whether electors were to directly represent the will of the voters in their state. Time for contemplation was scarce, and much work was to be done before the country would have its new government.

To add to the difficulties, there was an immediate delay in making the nation operable. The date the new government was to begin was to be determined by the Congress elected under the Articles of Confederation, and, though ratification of the new Constitution had occurred in late June, Congress didn't decide on the timetable for the government until September 13, 1788. (The reason for this two-and-one-half-month delay was the difficulty in deciding where to establish a temporary seat of government—finally New York was chosen.) The outgoing Congress also directed that electors of the president and vice president should be appointed or elected by the first Wednesday of January 1789, and that they should meet in their respective states and deliver their votes on the first Wednesday of February. The newly elected Congress was to meet in early March, and its first order of business would be the count of electoral votes.

But the very first popular national election in the new nation was a Congressional one. Legislators were summoned so that laws could be passed to nominate and elect candidates. Because of slow communications, distant state capitals did not even receive the news of Congress's new schedule for two weeks, leaving only a few weeks to accomplish much.

Though the new Congress was due to meet in New York in early March of 1789, organizational problems in various state elections for representatives resulted in election dates ranging from November 24, 1788 to June 22, 1789. New Hampshire and Massachusetts provided for popular elections, but when none of the candidates in New Hampshire and half the district representatives in Massachusetts failed to receive majorities, the elections had to be held again. Shortly thereafter, one of the three New Hampshire Federalist representatives resigned, so a special election was held the following June.

New Jersey's election lasted for more than a month—from February 11 until March 18, and, in the end, it was contested. New York did not vote for representatives until March 3–4, and results were not known until the end of the month—long after the representatives were due in Congress. Maryland spent a great deal of time drawing up its districts, and when it held elections on January 7–11, the district divisions made certain that a Federalist carried each district.[1]

Ultimately, seven of the states held some kind of a district election so that each representative had a specific constituency; four states elected their representatives at large. All of the men were elected by the middle of March 1789 except for one from Massachusetts and one from New Hampshire. All the state legislatures, except New York, had also successfully chosen their senators.

Though chaos abounded over the holding of a statewide election, the actual voting procedure posed no particular difficulty in this election year. As colonies, the states had been holding elections for a long time, so the changeover in government did not require specific changes in the actual conduct of election day. Some of the states had more liberal suffrage requirements, so in some places more people were eligible to vote. (The decade after the Revolutionary War began to see a further breakdown in the property requirement for voting, and two states had substituted a tax-paying requirement for that of property ownership.)[2]

Two very nominal political party-type groups dominated the electorate: Federalists, who strongly supported the Constitution, and Antifederalists, who sought to limit the centralized powers of the federal government. These campaigns addressed only a few national issues. The Federalists were greatly concerned that the election of too many Antifederalists would impede an effective beginning for the new country, so they continued their work for ratification by remaining involved and supporting candidates who would back the new Constitution.

The national financial crisis was another issue of concern to many; Maryland and Pennsylvania were particularly concerned about repayment of continental creditors. Some Massachusetts candidates won popularity by speaking in favor of the national assumption of state debts. But local issues and personalities and factions were largely crucial to election results.

Because the elections were spread out over time and news traveled slowly, it took a long time before the government leaders realized that the people were voting in favor of the Federalists. (Ultimately, only 10 of the 59 representatives and two of the 22 senators were Antifederalists.) Even the Antifederalists, tired of defeat after defeat, seemed willing to give the Constitution a try. Thomas Jefferson, a supporter of the Antifederalist cause, later looked back and explained the consensus of the election: "The inconveniences of an inefficient government, driving the people as is usual, into the opposite extreme, the elections to the first Congress run very much in favor of those who were known to favor a very strong government."[3]

Although George Washington was evidently quite satisfied with the ultimate roster of representatives, James Madison had another view: "I see on the list of Representatives a very scanty proportion who will share in the drudgery of business."[4]

The 66 men who served in the first House of Representatives came from diverse economic backgrounds ranging from being sons of large landowners to the son of a tradesman. The majority were lawyers, an occupation that generally implied office-holder, but there were doctors, merchants, farmers and planters as well.[5]

## *The States Choose Electors*

Despite the turbulence that would surround the various methods and schedules for the choice of electors in each state, one element that kept the fragile system from breaking apart was the unanimous certainty in all the states that the next president would be George Washington. As will be seen, because of the confusing way that votes were counted, the only real contest would surround the office of the vice president.

The state of Maryland was one of the few that was well enough organized to hold elections for both representatives and electors on the same day, and that state showed the most election activity on this first presidential election day. In a brief but frenzied campaign, featuring public meetings, the use of militia companies to get out the vote, parades, barbecues and strong ethnic appeals to those of German descent, the event gave indication of elections to come. To hardly anyone's surprise, candidates in favor of George Washington's presidency took the day.

If the other states seemed overwhelmed at only conducting Congressional elections, the prospect of choosing electors was that much more daunting. With barely four months to summon legislatures and decide how electors would be chosen, the states had very little time for any prolonged philosophical discussion about the selection of electors or to prepare for a popular election.

The Constitution's framers who had spoken out on the issue expected that electors would be chosen "by the people," but this was not a foregone conclusion by any means. For instance, a newspaper correspondent in Philadelphia, pointing to the time constraints of the election schedule, wrote on October 1, 1788:

> It is evident that Congress construe [from] the Constitution that the legislatures of the several States, not the people, are to choose the electors, as that body has ordered the choice of said electors to be on the first Wednesday of January, and their meeting for the choice of President four weeks later. For if the people, as hath been asserted, are to choose the electors, is it possible that in the large States

of Massachusetts, Virginia, etc., the returns can be made for the choice, notice given to the persons chosen, and the persons thus chosen have time to meet together in the short space of one month? No, it is impossible, and can only be remedied by the legislature, who, in fact, are "the States" making the choice.[6]

Many of the states, particularly those in the South, had no experience in running state-wide elections. Simply selecting the electors in the state legislature was far easier than devising a new system for statewide elections, which would raise such thorny questions as how to set up nominating procedures as well as logistical difficulties like districting.

And, in fact, in five of the 11 states (Connecticut, New Jersey, Delaware, South Carolina and Georgia) entitled to participate in the election (Rhode Island and North Carolina had not yet ratified), the governors did not summon the legislature in time to arrange for a popular election.

Pennsylvania's legislature was in session in early fall of 1788, so this state became the first to decide how its electors would be chosen; in this case in a statewide general election. Interestingly, Pennsylvania's main argument against choice by legislature was the expense of having to call a special legislative session for the purpose.[7]

The legislature of New Hampshire assembled on November 5 and passed an act for the election of representatives and electors on the third Monday in December. The people were to bring in their votes for five electors, the full number to which the state was entitled. The votes were to be returned to the legislature, which was to be in session in early January, and the persons having a majority were to be declared elected. As it happened, no elector received a majority, so the General Court appointed the full list. This resulted in great rancor. The Senate claimed equal power with the House in the appointment, and the House insisted upon a joint ballot. Heated discussion kept the legislature in session long into the night, and finally, just before midnight—so that George Washington wouldn't lose New Hampshire's votes—the House yielded (protesting that this was not a precedent) and concurred in the list of electors chosen by the Senate.

Equally venomous was the situation in the New York legislature, which was unable to resolve a dispute similar to New Hampshire's and ultimately lost its votes. New York's lack of enthusiasm for the Constitution doubtless contributed to its inability to resolve the issue.

The other states found that nothing in the process was simple. Massachusetts established a system whereby the people in each representative district were to vote for two persons who lived in the district. Of the two persons in each district having the highest number of votes the General Court chose one and also chose two independent electors at large. The law prescribed that the choice be by joint ballot.

In the states that provided for a popular election, voting was light. In Pennsylvania, the turnout for the presidential election was less than half that for the Congressional election and far below state elections. In Massachusetts and New Hampshire, more votes were cast for representatives than for electors. Lack of competition probably contributed to this seeming indifference. Parties (of sorts) consisted of those in favor of the Constitution and those against, and political sentiment seems to have been largely one way or the other in each community. For that reason, there was little contest in each area. Federalists dominated some localities; Antifederalists dominated others. About half the Federalists bothered to vote, the Antifederalists hardly appeared at the polls, often not even having candidates.

As in the Congressional election, in states where electors were chosen by popular vote, the Federalists were mounting campaigns to vote for men who had pledged their votes for Federalist candidates. Pennsylvania paved the way for politics to come. Delegates from 18 counties met on November 3 to agree on electoral ticket and Congressional nominees. Friendly newspapers publicized the slate.

Accounts of the actual voting are few. The Worcester, Massachusetts *Spy* made note that the electors had their ballots for Washington and Adams prepared before they came together. Having organized, they voted quickly and adjourned. "There was not a word spoken, except in the choice of a chairman."[8]

When the electors finally gathered in 1789, five states had appointed the electors in the state legislature. Massachusetts let the people select all but two of the electors, who were then appointed by the state; and four states gave the vote to the people. New York didn't participate.

The electors, as the Founding Fathers had intended, were free agents in the choice of president and vice president, but in this election, all electors found it fitting to name Washington as the first president.

## Choosing a Vice President

What drama there was in that first election revolved around the office of the vice presidency. When this position was established, it had no purpose other than to facilitate the selection of the president. It was feared that in years when the presidential choice wasn't as clear-cut as in 1789, that there would be a "favorite son" problem with the larger states easily overpowering small states simply by having more ballots to cast for their own candidates. The framers of the Constitution came up with a system of double balloting for the presidency, which was soon to become known as the "fatal defect." The instructions on double balloting were that the electors were to cast two undiscriminating votes for president. One vote could be for a resident of the elector's state; the other vote had to go to a nonresident. The hope was that this way some sort of consensus on a leading national candidate would be reached. The person with the second-highest number of votes would be the vice president. Those who did foresee a role for the office that John Adams, the first vice president, referred to as "His Redundancy," also pointed out that because both votes were equal it should mean that there really wasn't a subordinate officer. Theoretically, both candidates were equally qualified to be president.

Although the plan seemed like a good one at the time, it ran into problems from the beginning. Alexander Hamilton, who had not attended the Federal Convention, quickly saw the fatal flaw in the system. Writing to James Wilson, he noted: "Everybody sees that unanimity in Adams as vice president and a few votes insidiously withheld from Washington might substitute the former for the latter."[9]

Another scenario might run like this: if equal votes were cast for George Washington and John Adams, the latter of whom was wanted for vice president, then there would be no majority winner. As provided in the Constitution, that would throw the decision into the House of Representatives for a final vote. Washington didn't want any competition, and Hamilton feared he might not accept the presidency if any snags developed along the way. As a result, he counseled several states to withhold their votes from Adams—an act that certainly didn't endear him to the man who was eventually to become the second president. As it happened, several states cast their votes for "favorite sons" anyway, and George Washington emerged with 69 votes to John Adams's 34.

## Counting the Votes

When the new Congress convened in early March, there was no quorum (the minimum number of congressmen needed to conduct business). Only eight senators and eight representatives, out of 22 and 59 respectively, had managed to appear. This was a great disappointment and caused Washington great consternation. He had only reluctantly agreed to accept the presidency if elected, but he didn't want the government to fail. Throughout the month, express riders shuttled between New York and Mount Vernon with the latest news on the likelihood of achieving a quorum.

Finally on April 5, a month and a day late, the last Congressional laggard arrived, providing Congress with enough members to validate the electoral count.

On April 6, John Langdon, a senator from New Hampshire, was elected president of the assembly "for the sole purpose of opening and counting the votes for President of the United States." A message was sent to the House of Representatives saying that the Senate was ready to count the votes in the presence of the House. Both the House and Senate were to appoint one or more members to sit at the clerk's table to list the votes as declared, and the Senate appointed one to the House's two. The president of the Senate opened and counted the votes.

Out of 91 possible electoral votes, only 69 were included. Rhode Island and North Carolina, with three and seven votes respectively, had not yet adopted the Constitution, and the eight votes of New York were wasted by that state's bungling of its election. Two electors from Maryland and two from Virginia failed to appear in their states on February 4, the day of voting within the states. The ice in the rivers and bay prevented one of the absent Maryland electors from attending, and the other was home sick with gout.

Even if more votes had been cast, it is unlikely that the results would have changed. As it was, George Washington, the only president ever to win a unanimous vote from the electoral college, won the presidency with 69 electoral votes from the 69 electors who cast ballots.

## Washington and Adams Are Notified

Special messengers were sent to Washington and Adams to tell them the news. Because of proximity, Adams was notified first, and he set out from Braintree, Massachusetts, where he lived. Well-received all along the way, Adams was escorted by relays of horse troops as he traveled to Boston, and through Massachusetts and Connecticut to Westchester, New York, where he was met by a troop that accompanied him to New York City. Introduced to the Senate on April 21, Adams was later to tell his wife Abigail: "My country has in its wisdom contrived for me the most insignificant office that ever the invention of man contrived or his imagination conceived."[11]

At the time of the counting, George Washington was at Mount Vernon, Virginia, so messengers were sent with the official word of his election. While he had long known what was coming, he greeted the news with mixed emotions. At 56, he longed to stay at Mount Vernon and enjoy life as a country gentleman, and he worried about criticism of the new government from such prominent citizens as George Mason, Patrick Henry and Edmund Randolph. However, it was this very criticism that ultimately won him over. Caring deeply about the future of the country, Washington felt compelled to step forward to lead this great experiment in democracy.

But whatever Washington's feelings about taking office, he must certainly have been heartened by the reception he got on his trip to New York, the city chosen to be the first capital of the nation, for his inauguration. The mood was triumphal, and people all along the route came out to wave and cheer the man who had been empowered to lead this great new country. In Elizabethtown Point, New Jersey, officials feted Washington and put him aboard a specially built barge. Other decorated barges joined that vessel, and the flotilla went into New York to Murrays Wharf to the sounds of pealing bells, roaring cannons and hurrahs from all the spectators. Upon arrival, though carriages were waiting to take him, Washington chose to walk into town, tipping his hat to the ladies all along the way.

The morning of April 30, people assembled in churches throughout New York City and in the other states and prayed for the success of the new government and for the prosperity of the president. Washington was escorted from his house to Federal Hall at Nassau and Wall Streets where he was to take the oath of office. When no Bible could be found on which to swear the oath, there was some consternation, but Chancellor Robert P. Livingston had one fetched, and shortly thereafter, George Washington was sworn in as the first president of the United States—the end result of that first presidential election.

# The Country Copes With Political Expansion _____ 4

For most Americans election days in the 1790s were much the same as they had been in previous years. Whether it was a town meeting day in New England or a voting day elsewhere, people came walking, riding on horseback— sometimes two astride, being drawn in carts by oxen or in wagons by teams of horses, which were sometimes decorated with flags, ribbons and sleigh bells. They continued to look forward to the opportunity to get together to cast their votes.

Once at the voting place, the throng made for an assorted collection. As one historian describes the typical scene:

> Here an old German with a long black beard, dressed in red and blue striped homespun—not far from him, a stout, hale, rawboned, ruddy farmer, evidently of Scotch–Irish origin—in one corner, an old woman with a little table spread with cakes, and early apples, and a boy or two to replenish her table when required.[1]

This was also the day to take care of business. Land and slaves were auctioned; lawyers had their hearings before the justices; fights and duels were often scheduled. As the day wore on and liquor began to have its effect, rowdiness and unscheduled fights frequently broke out.

If the people noticed a change in the nature of election day, it was in the candidates whom they considered. No longer was the would-be politician the landowner from next door. With multicounty and statewide elections, the fellow was often a stranger. And because of this, elections were becoming even more fun, for electioneering in the form of "hustings speeches" (a tradition revived from the British homeland of giving formal campaign speeches from a raised platform) became a favorite entertainment and "treating" became more important than before.

At this level—the level of the politicians, both local and national—the stress and strain of the upheaval in the political system were manifested.

Locally, politicians could no longer think only of winning the votes of their neighbors—they were wrestling with how to campaign on a district or state level. They needed to develop methods for becoming known in a wider arena.

Nationally, politicians knew that the new Constitution meant that the political focus could no longer be on what was good for each state; the country as a whole needed to be taken into consideration. It was a time of turmoil, and the politicians were also painfully aware that the fate of the United States was still very much in doubt.

Several national issues had begun to affect the lives of the people. In the three years of Washington's administration, the people had gained Congressional approval of a Bill of Rights, but it was too early for that to have had local impact. Of more pressing concern was the monetary situation. Secretary of the Treasury Alexander Hamilton was setting up a strong financial structure for the federal government, and the government had begun levying taxes—something that directly affected people's pocketbooks. Especially concerned were the Scotch–Irish farmers who had settled in western Pennsylvania. In 1791, Hamilton had pushed through an excise tax that hit hard on whiskey—a commodity the farmers found easier to transport to the eastern seaboard to be marketed than the grain from which it was made. Several area legislatures protested the tax, and there was local unrest. (Washington did not send in troops until 1794.)

On the foreign front, tensions were mounting between France and England, and Americans still felt keenly their loyalties to one country or the other. France had won favor with many during the Revolution because of the instrumental part it played in helping the colonists win that war; yet Britain was the former mother country and the nation upon whom the U.S. was still heavily dependent for trade. If trouble erupted, American loyalties would be awkwardly split.

In any case the fate of the federal government was far from certain—the Articles of Confederation had lasted only a few years, so who was to say this government would do much better? The United States was still a young country, and the government had a long way to go before it would build up confidence in all of the people.

## Election-Related Issues of 1792

In its last session prior to the presidential election, Congress set up a new timetable for choosing electors. Leaving the choice of the exact election date to the states (if states chose electors by popular election), Congress stipulated that the choice had to be made within 34 days preceding the first Wednesday in December, the day on which the electors were to meet in their states and vote by ballot for two men. (They were to make no mark on their papers to disclose which of the two they preferred for president or vice president.) The electoral votes had to arrive before the first Wednesday in January, and the votes were to be counted in Congress on the second Wednesday in February.

This schedule meant that states could choose to hold elections any time between the first week in November and the first week in December, but in actual practice, most elections took place sometime during the first two weeks in November.

The lack of a uniform date for the elections presented an interesting situation, not unlike the modern day problem of election outcomes being known before polls close on the West Coast. Since the state electoral votes were not kept secret, the results of the presidential election might already have been determined and reported in newspapers or—as in 1800—the whole election might hinge on the vote of the final state. (One of the Constitution's framers, Charles Pinckney of South Carolina, noted in 1800 that it was intended that the electoral vote not be known until after the ballots were officially counted, but it immediately became the practice to make public the votes cast by electors.)[2] The 34-day period during which elections could be held prolonged excitement and provided time for more intrigue.

Within the government, factions were developing into full-scale political parties. Alexander Hamilton, as architect of a federal banking program that was well liked by the business community and the wealthy, became champion of the party that became known as the Federalists. Thomas Jefferson, who had a primarily agrarian philosophy, felt that every man could be a landowner and every landowner a voter, and his party called themselves the Democratic–Republicans (or the Republicans). Jefferson also favored stronger state governments, while Hamilton sided with bolstering federal power.

While Hamilton maneuvered comfortably with the security of the current administration behind him, Jefferson and James Madison, a fellow Virginian and a member of the first House of Representatives, realized the value of a North–South coalition in building any sort of opposition to the government-based party. Because national electioneering was thought unseemly, Madison and Jefferson made a summer trip to New York to form a coalition with Governor George Clinton and his political lieutenant, Aaron Burr, under the guise of observing the local flora. The Virginians also made contact with Madison's Princeton classmate, Philip Freneau, and invited him to come to Philadelphia (ostensibly to work as a government translator) to start an Antifederalist newspaper to challenge *The Gazette of the United States*, which was friendly to the Washington administration. The birth of the *National Gazette* under Freneau was the most visible sign of the beginning of a national two-party system. It was also the beginning of the practice of each party having a newspaper mouthpiece, a custom that spread throughout the states.

Some historians cite these national events as the beginning of the two-party system, but what happened nationally almost certainly could not have succeeded if grass roots activity weren't growing up to meet the party system that was developing in the highest echelons of Washington's cabinet. In the Chesapeake area in the 1780s, the states had drawn together behind a manifesto designed to help overcome the terrible debt crisis that the region was struggling with as a result of the Revolutionary War. This early interstate linkage and other multicounty linkings of local groups certainly contributed to the base on which the national parties could build.

The development of the two-party system laid the groundwork for the political battle that was to take place in 1792. But first, Washington had to be convinced that he should run again for president. Not even the opposition felt that the country was ready to proceed without him, partly because of lack of a logical successor. Thomas Jefferson was not popular in the North, and he personally preferred to go back to Monticello; diplomat John Jay had just lost an election in New York and had managed to alienate various groups; and John Adams, it was felt, was too monarchical.

Washington was no more eager for the presidency than he had been the first time. He was turning 60, had been quite ill in 1790–91 and longed to return to Mount Vernon. He had already consulted James Madison about the wording of his farewell address, but concern over the stability of the country and the impact of foreign influence kept him from making a final announcement.

Though Thomas Jefferson had political differences with the president, he urged Washington to seek a second term: "The confidence of the whole union is centered in you . . ."[3] Perhaps more convincingly, Attorney General Edmund Randolph pointed out that Washington would certainly be pressed into service if the United States were to be dragged into the Franco–English war. Randolph suggested that Washington might prefer to solve problems in office rather than in the midst of battle. Hamilton counseled the president that it would be better to leave office early than to refuse to run at such a crucial time. Ultimately, the counselors swayed the chief executive, and he did agree to run.

Like the election of 1789, the drama of this election was at the vice presidential level. To indicate dissent from Federalist doctrines, the Republicans wanted to mount opposition for the vice presidency. However, choosing a candidate proved to be quite difficult. Jefferson's personal reluctance to run for the office was buttressed by the fact that, as a Virginian against Virginian George Washington, he would automatically forfeit the electoral votes of that populous state because only one of the two votes cast by each elector could be for a native son. George Clinton had been a likely candidate, but his recent election for governor of New York had been tainted with fraud. Aaron Burr, a U.S. senator from New York, was also considered. Just a few weeks short of the early November elections, representatives from Virginia, New York, Pennsylvania and South Carolina met in Philadelphia (now the nation's capital) and decided upon Clinton, overlooking the problems he had encountered in the New York election. Excitement over marshalling an opposition candidate was palpable among party notables.

The excitement did not carry over to the people, however. In most states, newspaper reports were lackluster and the people did not feel involved. Even in Pennsylvania, where two partisan newspapers actively covered national politics, only about 4,000 votes were cast—in contrast to 35,000 votes cast a month earlier in the Congressional election.[4]

In 1792, 15 states participated in the presidential election (Rhode Island and North Carolina had ratified the Constitution, and Vermont and Kentucky had just been admitted to the Union). Electors were appointed by the legislature in nine states (Vermont, Rhode Island, Connecticut, New York, New Jersey, Delaware, South Carolina, Georgia and Kentucky); four states held popular elections (Pennsylvania,

Maryland, Virginia and North Carolina) and, in New Hampshire and Massachusetts, a combination method was used whereby some electors were chosen by the legislators while others were elected popularly.

The method used for counting the electoral votes set a pattern that was followed for a great many years. Both the Senate and the House assembled in the Senate chamber at noon on the second Wednesday in February. One teller from the Senate and two from the House were appointed to inspect and make a list of the votes as the president of the Senate (the nation's vice president) opened and read them. The victor was then announced by the president of the Senate.

The electoral voting was solid. Every elector had again given one vote to Washington, for a total of 132 electoral votes. For second place, Adams came in with all of New England, giving him a total of 77 electoral votes to Clinton's quite respectable 50. Though Adams was the obvious victor in the vice presidential race, the Republicans had garnered enough strength to give legs to a two-party Federalist–Republican system—an alignment that was to persist and broaden.

As long as Washington was available for the top seat, the first elections functioned more or less as tryouts for what was to come. The political leaders were learning the value of party alignment for building strength behind specific candidates, and they were seeing that pleasing various parts of the country was vital to winning. At this point, they were finished with auditions, and it was time for serious rehearsal to begin.

## 1796: The First Election Without Washington

Anxiety was high in 1796, the year of the next presidential election. Feelings had begun to mount against Britain in 1794. Great Britain was holding trading posts in the Northwest Territory in flagrant violation of the Treaty of 1783, it was encouraging Indian unrest, and royal ships were illegally seizing American ships bound for the French West Indies and "impressing" sailors—ostensibly searching and removing *British* subjects from the ships, although American sailors were almost always taken. To calm the cries for war with Britain, President Washington, knowing that such a war could be calamitous for the new nation, had sent diplomat and Chief Justice John Jay to Britain to work out a settlement. Though Jay gained a promise that the western posts would be given up within two years and obtained important commercial trading privileges, there was surprisingly violent reaction from many Americans who were angry at the concessions that Jay had to make (which included recognition of America's obligation to pay prewar debts to British merchants and a lack of concessions from Britain on other trading rights, impressment and incitement of the Indians). Jay was burned in effigy; and the wrath of the people, incited by the press, exploded onto the streets. The treaty was to become a central campaign issue of 1796.

There was also continued concern about the future of the country. Most felt that Washington would step down, but they worried about whether the country could continue without him. Could a mere "mortal" walk in his shoes?

Fearful of what an early farewell announcement would do to the country, George Washington waited until September 16, about six weeks before electors were to be chosen (using the same timetable as in 1792), before making official the fact that he would decline to seek office again.

Because of the delayed word from the president, few preparations had been made for the upcoming election. And since no precedent existed, confusion led the way. Many thought it logical for the vice president to succeed the president, so John Adams was the obvious Federalist candidate. Though he disliked the party system and would have preferred to have been automatically deemed the successor, Adams let party leaders know of his availability—he wanted the presidency very much.

Adams was a brilliant man, but his pomposity and aloofness even from those with whom he aligned himself made him difficult to like; his experience as vice president, "the first planet from the political sun," was vital to his candidacy. He also pointed out the benefits of his advancing age and indicated that because of it he, too, would step down after a brief time. (Though sorry to lose Washington's leadership, the Constitution's framers had been quite pleased with the precedent of two terms set by Washington. There was still the fear that a president might try to dominate the office for 15–20 years—too long a term, in the framers' estimation.)[5]

Because no official system for selecting candidates existed, it soon became custom for members of Congress from each party to meet informally with top party leaders to select the candidates. This practice was the precursor of the more formal "caucus" procedure soon to come. While these meetings were not entirely secret, they were not publicized and formal minutes were not kept. Criticism arose—pointing out that people did not intend their legislators to go to Philadelphia to partake in party business—but for a time, the system prevailed.

James Madison, a leading Antifederalist, had spoken to Jefferson about running, but Jefferson had indicated he wasn't interested. But when no other candidate surfaced, Madison saw no alternative and put forth Jefferson for president at the Republican caucus. As their second candidate, the group settled upon New York's Aaron Burr.

Continuing with the example set by Washington, the candidates did little campaigning for themselves. (The exception was Aaron Burr, the Republican candidate for vice president, who spent six weeks touring New England and speaking to potential electors.) The supporters were expected to drum up interest, and they did so by playing up the differences between the parties. The Republicans campaigned for free trade, low tariffs and money borrowable at low interest rates—items of benefit to an agricultural society. The Federalists sought ways to favor the merchants and traders—the constituency from whom they would draw their strength.

The campaign was venomous. Part of the uproar was started by Thomas Paine, whose widely distributed pamphlet, *Common Sense*, had been so crucial in rallying the American people to the cause of the Revolution. After imprisonment in France in the early 1790s because of his involvement in the French Revolution, Paine had finally been released after James Monroe interceded on Paine's behalf; but Paine felt abandoned by his friend, George Washington, whom he felt should personally have rescued him from his predicament. After writing a scathing private letter to Washington, Paine released the diatribe to the antiadministration Philadelphia newspaper, *Aurora*, which excerpted parts of Paine's *Letter to George Washington* during the summer of 1796. In it, he accused the president and Gouverneur Morris, who had been minister to France when Paine was imprisoned, of scheming against him. He denigrated Washington, personally and professionally, and launched a vigorous assault on John Adams as well. While there was an outcry at the time over his libeling of the two highest leaders of the land, neither man responded to the assault, and Paine ultimately did more harm to himself than to anyone. Even Adams's political rivals were uneasy about using the material Paine had written against Adams because of the hysterical nature of Paine's attack.

The electors theoretically were not pledged to any one candidate, thus much of the electioneering took place *after* the electors had been chosen in November. The partisan press participated, and handbills and pamphlets denigrating the other side were distributed. Federalists pointed out Jefferson's sympathy for the French Revolution, the possibility that he might become a "foreign tool" and his lack of belief in God as vital reasons to vote against him. The Republicans focused on Adams's high-toned style of government and his lack of belief in the people. The Federalists targeted their campaign and worked on votes they thought they could sway. The Jeffersonian Republicans wanted to address the ordinary citizen. Handbills were printed and nailed to doors of houses and gate posts, and townsmen were hired to ride through the state scattering Antifederalist broadsides. The prevailing messages were that Adams was a monarchist, and Jefferson was a friend of the rights of man and a champion of democratic principles. Though the Federalists were successful in the short run, the Republicans had hit upon a system for building grass-roots support for their candidates.

On the highest party level, Hamilton was again busy. Never a fan of Adams, he so badly wanted to see Adams defeated that he saw no harm if Thomas Pinckney ended up in the top spot. He counseled some states to throw away their vote for Adams, but when word of this leaked out, New England responded by crossing out Pinckney's name to protect Adams. This uncovered another pitfall in the double balloting system, and the result still seems astounding (though it was not viewed as particularly peculiar at the time). Adams became the Federalist president with Republican Jefferson taking the vice presidential spot. The final tally was Adams with 71 of the electoral votes; Jefferson, 68; Pinckney, 59; and Burr with only 30.

The perils of double balloting became very clear in this election. As the Federalists withheld votes from their own nominee, Pinckney, so that he wouldn't best Adams for president, it resulted in Adams becoming a Federalist president with Antifederalist (Republican) Jefferson as vice president.

With the addition of Tennessee to the Union, 16 states took part in this election. Ten of the states chose their electors by the legislature; the remaining six (New

Hampshire, Massachusetts, Pennsylvania, Maryland, Virginia and North Carolina) held popular elections.

The role of the elector was still very much in question. Although electors weren't supposed to pledge to a candidate prior to their election, they were backed and supported by the newly formed political parties. The Federalists put up local tickets of electors in several states, and the Republicans did the same, with the appropriate newspapers backing and publicizing each ticket. Though some contemporaries thought electors were to be independent men who were to consider the options and decide the vote for themselves, this was not the reality. When one Federalist-sponsored Pennsylvania elector decided to switch and cast his vote for Jefferson and Pinckney, he was viewed as a traitor: Wrote one citizen to the *United States Gazette*: "What! Do I chuse Samuel Miles to determine for me whether John Adams or Thomas Jefferson shall be President? No! I chuse him to *act*, not to *think*!"[6]

Despite much remaining uncertainty about the presidential election process itself, the country did accept the fact that John Adams had been elected president. "The sight of the sun setting full-orbed, and another rising (though less splendid) was a novelty,"[7] wrote Adams to wife Abigail about the peaceful changeover of the presidency. And a novelty it was. For the first time in modern history, there had been a peaceful surrender of a head of state as one stepped aside for his elected successor.

## Local Election Activity

On the local level, politicians were struggling to become known in larger voting districts. Up through the Revolution, campaigning was basically nonexistent because votes were generally sought only from neighbors. Voter and candidate generally knew, or knew of, each other because they shared a common community. Political preference was based on personality. Did a voter know and like the candidate? Was he influential in the voter's life? Would it be detrimental to vote against him? Who a candidate married, who his friends were and how much he had contributed to the community were also meaningful to voters. (Even before television, public image was important.)

Now candidates had to campaign beyond their hometown and among unfamiliar voters. Methods for campaigning consisted of campaign speeches ("hustings speeches"), personal letters, circulars, pamphlets and items in the press. More and more newspapers were springing up with partisan editors, and better postal service also helped spread the word.

The way local candidates were selected was also changing. Becoming a candidate often followed months of planning and bargaining with the influential constituency. Before the gentry had handpicked the candidates; by 1799, the party leaders were beginning to choose.

What altered only slightly was the kind of candidate selected. Now the gentry were likely to be lawyer-planters with political aspirations instead of gentleman planters who were consenting to governmental duty as part of their community service. In any case the gentry still dominated. The reasons for this were purely practical. Campaigning required time, since travel was difficult and required patience, physical endurance and, on occasion, ingenuity and luck (one congressman drowned while crossing the Potomac on his way to Washington). Money was also a factor. Elected officials had to be able to afford to be away from home for extended periods. If no one was available to tend the crops or take care of the livestock, a political career was impossible. But many men were still drawn to public office by patriotism and the prestige of public service. (However, senators throughout the states were often unopposed—the six-year term meant being away from family and livelihood for most of that period, and many found this overly burdensome.)

As in colonial days, gauging one's chances of victory was an important part of the precandidacy process. Ways to sound out one's popularity included newspaper articles or speeches announcing "If they want me to serve . . ."; sometimes an informal poll was taken. Estimates could be fairly accurate as voter participation was predictable, and, based on one's friends, a candidate could assess the strength of his support. Some contenders even asked the county clerk for lists of freeholders, which were sent with addresses and how a voter had balloted in previous elections. Others asked storekeepers to take informal polls and advise them of their popularity.

To announce one's candidacy, the tradition of having one's friends "make known among our neighbors my having offered my services" was still used, but now printed announcements, known as broadsides and circulars, were also employed. Broadsides were single-page campaign sheets; circulars were longer documents serving the same aim and one form or the other might be mailed to voters in the district, typically one to two months prior to the polling. Incumbents tended to announce candidacy in their regular letters: "The period when my fellow citizens will be again called upon to exercise the inestimable right of suffrage is not far distant. Permit me once more to make you a tender of my services, and to request you to consider me as a Candidate at the ensuing election of a member of Congress . . ."[8]

Despite the fact that electioneering was looked down upon, a good deal of it necessarily took place. The written word and formal speeches were used. Speeches, which were sometimes made by proxy, consisted of reasons for running, biographical highlights, pledges and sometimes discussions of the issues.

In 1791, when James Madison was in Philadelphia serving in Congress but was up for re-election, he sent letters to his father and brothers reviewing activities of Congress, excusing his absence from the district and asking that they send the letters on to friends and contacts in his behalf.

Friends of the candidate were expected to act as campaign committee and sponsor parades, barbecues, celebrations and bonfires, particularly in communities where the candidate could appear only briefly. They also circulated literature and sponsored campaign meetings.

A primary way to develop identification was to tie in with a popular cause. Revolutionary War injuries always garnered sympathy and respect, and taking into account local sentiment on issues such as tariffs, canals or Jay's Treaty was a sure way to win votes.

The practice of kissing babies in order to win votes started early. One candidate reported that he gained support by "jollying the men, hugging the ladies, and giving red stick candy to the children," and was said to have "kissed more babies than any other in Southwestern Virginia."[9]

As a group, politicians hated making direct appeals for votes, and they would undoubtedly have identified strongly with the fictional candidate, "Wou'dbe," from a popular period play:

> "Must I again be subject to the humours of a fickle crowd: Must I again resign my reason, and be nought but what each voter pleases? Must I cajole, fawn, and wheedle, for a place that brings so little profit?"[10]

On election day itself, candidates were expected to appear at as many polling places as possible, making for an arduous travel schedule.

To the people casting votes in the 1790s, the procedure was similar to that used before, but the method of nomination had changed. Instead of making nominations orally at the polls on election day, nominations were submitted to the county clerk in advance because of the expanded election districts. County clerks then compiled lists of candidates and transmitted them to town clerks who were to advertise in advance the names of the candidates and the time and place of the election.

New Jersey law, which would have been typical, provided that the election began annually at 10:00 A.M. at the usual place of holding town meetings and ended at 6:00 P.M. the following day. (Though elections of the past continued for up to three weeks, now the tendency was to specify that they last no longer than two to five days.) Voting regulations were read at the opening of the polls, and the election judge, assessor and collector presided to assess the qualifications of voters, maintain order, count votes and prepare the certificate of election.

In those counties where voting was by ballot, the county clerk was responsible for providing each township with a ballot box. Some state laws specified that special sealing wax and tape were to be provided; others specified that a ballot box should be a hinged wooden box, often with two locks and keys.

Oral voting was still practiced in many places, but when ballots were used they consisted of a single paper ticket (some would have been preprinted; others would have been prepared by the voter at home) that the voter handed to one of the election officials, who announced the voter's name and—if there was no objection—placed the ballot in the box. Some districts checked names against an alphabetical tax list as a way of verifying a voter's eligibility. Inspectors were to check to be certain that only one ballot was submitted, but at no time were they to look at a ballot before placing it in a box. At the end of the day ballots were counted. Local winners would be announced as soon as possible; county, district or state election tallies would be sent on to the official responsible for tabulating the total vote.

Fraud was possible, and indeed, the increasing rivalry between the two parties drove some to attempt rigged elections. In Delaware, as a contemporary writer describes, expert confidence men were known to specialize in throwing elections:

> slight [sic] of hand men . . . are stationed near the inspectors, and when such votes come up as they can make so free with as to ask a sight of their ticket, if granted (they with that skill that belongs to their art) dexterously exchange the ticket, if not one belonging to their own party, and to such perfection is this juggling reduced, that I heard one of these characters the evening of the last election, boast that he could produce for his share more than seventy exchanged tickets . . . If his associates were equally industrious, what conclusion are we to draw?[11]

Despite the fact that election day antidrinking laws had been on the books from colonial days (though generally disregarded), there were still attempts to silence the "voice of grog." In 1798, Delaware passed a law that levied a $20 fine on anyone setting up a booth or stall to sell spirits within two miles of the polls on election day or the days before and after the election. Justices of the peace or constables were "to prostrate, beat down, and remove all and every booth . . ." The officials would be fined if they failed to take action.[12]

## Suffrage Requirements

Of continuing importance, of course, was the issue of voter eligibility. As the country neared the end of the 18th century, the state constitutions were becoming much more specific about age, sex and residence requirements, though citizenship was not an important factor at this time, and the property requirement was becoming less so. Vermont, which became a state in 1791, was the most liberal in the country—it was the only state where full manhood suffrage prevailed. Vermont's only voting requirement was one year's residence in the state and "quiet and peaceable behavior." Showing that liberalism of this kind wasn't purely regional, Kentucky, joining the Union in 1792, allowed all free males who had lived in the state two years, and in their county one year, to vote. But that system was not yet acceptable to all. Tennessee entered the Union in 1796 and a property qualification was part of its suffrage law.

The early American concept of equality was different from ours today. At that time, Americans seemed to have no problem with resolving that all elections ought to be "free," and all should have an equal right to elect officers, and then resolving to exclude from the vote blacks, Indians, women, servants and people who lacked the right property qualifications. (Though many states prevented "undesirables" from voting, Kentucky in 1799 was the first to exclude specific groups—blacks, mulattos and American Indians—in a state constitution.) In some states taxpayers insisted on getting the ballot, and that raised the issue of whether or not the hard-working rent-payer—

who contributed to the community but did not pay taxes—had the right to vote. Officials in several states also wrestled with whether or not nonproperty-owning soldiers who had fought alongside Washington should be given the franchise. Even the property qualification caused its share of problems. How could voting inspectors determine the worth of voters' estates? Federalist William Griffith, who favored dropping the property qualifications said: "Every citizen has [besides his property] his liberty, his life, and his just rights in society to be protected; and these are equally important, and common to all members of the community."[13]

Although many small farmers were enfranchised in Virginia after the Revolution, most played little part in local politics other than voting on local issues in town meetings, says Daniel P. Jordan in *Political Leadership in Jefferson's Virginia*. Generally they were content to follow the advice of the minister or the squire. Not all of them even attended town meetings regularly, and deferred to the citizens with "larnin'" to control the issues.[14] Only in difficult economic circumstances were the farmers likely to rebel against the wishes of the rich.

## Getting the Results

As one might expect, once elections became more than local, getting votes sent out to be added to state or district totals was a time-consuming and difficult task. In Delaware's Sussex County in the 1790s, the people celebrated Return Day, which had its roots in colonial practice and is still celebrated today. After polls were closed, election results were brought to Georgetown (the central location for the county) by election officials who raced to arrive before representatives from other communities. Proud of their speedy horses, the officials arrived in the square with an air of importance, delivering their slips to the Board of Canvassers. This official board, with the sheriff presiding, sat at Georgetown at twelve noon on Thursday after the election on Tuesday. Results of local elections as well as many federal returns as were obtainable were hastily recopied and displayed in large figures on a huge white sheet that partially veiled the front of the old courthouse. They were also announced in a loud voice from the courthouse steps to the assembled throng in the public square ("the Green"). After the returns were announced, the winning party held a parade.[15]

As people began to adapt to a national political system, politics broadened its appeal and became even more fun. The rise of political parties added zest to local happenings, and though the early presidential elections were essentially "power-brokered" at the highest level, plenty of election day activity took place in all the states to prepare the machinery for the election system to come.

By the turn of the century, the Federalist party was weakening, and it was by no means assured that the federal system could survive a transition to a party with such a different ideology. A peaceful transition from one leader to his second-in-command was one thing, but if the leading forces in the current government were voted down, could another party build upon the ashes?

# Election Days in Jeffersonian America 5

Despite political agitation within Delaware, New York and New Jersey for selecting presidential electors by popular vote, the legislatures were still holding on to control— or, in some cases retaking control—of the electoral votes for Election Day 1800. That year, only five (Virginia, Rhode Island, Maryland, Kentucky and North Carolina) of the 16 states had popular elections.

While the country wrestled with the flaws in its electoral system, a battle for party dominance between the two newly formed political parties caused the final selection of the president in 1800 to be made, not by the people, but by the House of Representatives.

The players in 1800 were the same as they had been in 1796, but they were campaigning from very different vantage points now. Adams was running on his presidential record of four years. He had not won over the people, despite having done an admirable job of keeping the United States out of a war with France by maneuvering in the treacherous political waters of what became known as the "XYZ Affair"—an effort by three French agents (Adams's report to Congress referred to them as Mr. X, Mr. Y and Mr. Z) to extort money from American diplomats whom Adams had sent to negotiate a treaty of peace. Adams had become enormously unpopular at home because of the Alien and Sedition Acts. This legislation, passed by the Federalists, forbade "insurrection, riot, and unlawful assembly" and prescribed fines and jail terms for "false, scandalous and malicious writing" about the president, Congress or the nation. These Acts, which Jefferson, serving as vice president, and the Republicans considered highly unconstitutional, motivated Jefferson to work actively toward his own successful election.

Party nominations for president took place in Congressional caucuses held in the nation's capital—most likely during the first quarter of 1800. (According to historian Edward Stanwood, no records or exact information about the meetings exists.) [1] Adams and South Carolina's Charles Cotesworth Pinckney, whose brother Thomas had been a candidate in 1796, were the Federalist candidates; Thomas Jefferson was the Democratic–Republicans' choice. Though caucus members may have discussed options for the second spot, it must have been left negotiable, for New York, as we shall see, was ultimately offered the honor of making the final selection.

In the Federalist camp, the split that had festered since Adams first took office had widened and come into the open. Taking advantage of the loophole presented by double balloting, Hamilton again covertly sabotaged Adams's candidacy by working to help Charles Pinckney win the nomination. (Though people were aware that Adams and Jefferson were intended as the presidential contenders, the double balloting system did not so specify, meaning that, if popular enough, any one of the four could be elected president.) But with a little "help" from opponent Aaron Burr, word of Hamilton's doings leaked out, toughening the stance of Adams's Federalists, but otherwise weakening party unity.

The major challenge for each party was to maneuver the electoral vote to its favor. The existing electoral college requirements allowed the states to choose from three basic kinds of elections, with many variations of each. The first, of course, was choice by the legislators. Sometimes the two state houses made appointment by joint vote, sometimes they voted concurrently and compromised on the final selection. Occasionally the electoral choices required approval by the governor.

If a state chose to hold a popular election, voting was by district or by general ticket. With the district method, sometimes the people voted in equal districts (the districting was decided upon by the legislature), each district choosing one elector; but sometimes the districts were unequal and irregular. Some states required a plurality for victory, others a majority. An extreme example of the vagaries of the districting system was set by Massachusetts in 1792 when the legislature divided the state into four districts, two of which were to vote for five electors each, and two for three electors each, with a majority vote required. If a district failed to give a majority to the number of electors for which it was voting, the legislature was to fill the vacancies by voting on the candidates with the highest standing. As things turned out in 1792, only five electors were chosen by popular vote; the legislature was left to choose 11. [2]

With the general ticket system, every voter balloted for all the state's electors. A party ticket became very helpful to voters who, with the limited communication methods of the early 19th century, had little hope of being able to form individual opinions about a long list of possible electors.

Typically, states did not choose one system and refine it. They kept switching methods (often to gain political advantage), and the fact that each election year featured a different voting method simply added to the muddle of what was already a very confusing election system.

The art—and it was still an undeveloped one—of political dominance was for the party in power to select the system most favorable to itself. Federalist legislators with party control of the legislature would likely choose to retain control of the electoral votes rather than chance a popular election. In the election of 1800, fear that the people no longer favored the party in power led the legislatures in New Hampshire, Pennsylvania and Massachusetts to retake control of voting from the people; on the other hand Rhode Island moved the vote from the legislature to the people.

The setting of state election days was also under experimentation and was also a legislative prerogative that could be used to political advantage. While federal election days had to be held during a particular period of time as specified by the first U.S. Congress, state elections could be held whenever the state wished, often not at the same time as the federal election. One candidate in Virginia candidly explained that since some candidates wanted to run for both state legislature and for Congress, they could not do both if those elections were held on the same day. However, as William Paterson, one of the framers of the Constitution whose career included service as governor of New Jersey and as a member of the United States Supreme Court, explained, the moving around was for "the local interests and the conveniences of parties."[3]

For the first few elections, the electoral candidates were chosen (sometimes against their wishes) by the local political leaders, but were eventually selected at their party's state convention (at first this only happened in states where there was a well-developed two-party system). Then the slate of electors was championed by the appropriate area newspaper, all of which were partisan. From the time of the state's publication— though there were occasional exceptions, it was assumed that electors would vote only for their party's candidate.

For the election of 1800, Republicans knew that because so many electors were chosen by state legislatures, the battle for party control would begin at the local level. State elections would be vital, because they would determine which party controlled electoral votes. (1800 was the first time when almost all legislators and congressmen had party affiliations. Up until then, a good number of candidates had still been elected on personal renown alone.)

As the aggressors, the Republicans saw the need for unity and organization, and Virginia led the way in development of a workable party system for the state. In January 1800, Republicans held a party caucus creating a statewide central committee of five members as well as committees for each county. The central committee was to coordinate the campaign, publicize the slate and keep up regular correspondence with the county committees. Other states built on the Virginia model, though none achieved the degree of coordination reached by Virginia for this election year.

New York's state election day fell in April and—because of the large number of electors the New York legislature would appoint—it was a closely watched election. This was also Hamilton territory, but if there was a Republican equal to meeting him on home turf, it was Republican politician Aaron Burr—a New Yorker and an early "boss" of the famous New York political machine, Tammany Hall, which was already several years old in 1800.

Burr was a good political strategist, and his drive for power and his hatred of Alexander Hamilton led him to learn how to play the political game early. He developed a technique still used today by well-managed party organizations. He maintained an elaborate index system of voters with their political histories, their idiosyncrasies, and how to make sure they arrived at the polls. He used this knowledge to control the vote. Burr also was a leading proponent of helping to create voters. Early on, he found public money that he used to help the poorer constituency become landowners.[4] Tammany in the Burr era was well on its way to building a strong machine that would play a major role in hundreds of elections to come.

In preparation for Election Day 1800, Burr lined up many important people statewide to buttress the national ticket. The polls opened in New York City, and throughout all three days of the April voting, Burr prodded Tammany aides to turn out the vote, while Hamilton tried to nullify the effect by galloping between polling places trying to turn out the Federalists. The presence of Hamilton and Burr made known to all the national significance of this election. It was reported that informal public debates took place between the two when they accidentally met at the polling places.

By midnight of the third day, the Republicans were able to send word to Philadelphia that they had victory in New York City, and it meant victory in the state. As a reward, Republican congressmen responded with an invitation for New York to choose the vice presidential candidate. The nomination ultimately went to Aaron Burr.

Elsewhere, the campaign was also active. In Maryland, one could overhear discussion of politics at any gathering—from a cockfight to a church meeting. Would-be officeholders were losing their feelings of modesty, and one observer noted that candidates, including potential presidential electors and members of the state assembly "mount the Rostrum, made out of an empty barrel or hogshead, [and] Harange the Sovereign people—praise and recommend themselves at the expense of their adversary's character and pretensions."[5]

To avoid providing the opposition with ammunition, candidates were careful about what they wrote as well as what they said. In fear of his personal letters falling into the wrong hands, presidential contender Jefferson tended to avoid political subjects except when his mail would be sent by private conveyance; other letters he simply didn't sign.

The Republicans campaigned with a platform of sorts, and the issues they promoted most were states' rights, discharge of the public debt, resistance to alliance with a foreign power and opposition to military buildup. They also were very vocal about their disgust at the Alien and Sedition Acts.

Despite the fact that some substantive issues were discussed, at times the campaign slipped into personal vilification. Jefferson's Deist religious views, his French leanings and the likely dismantling of Hamilton's financial system were the main issues. He was also accused of fathering numerous children by his slaves. Said the *Connecticut Courant* of his possible election: "There is scarcely a chance we will escape a Civil War. Murder, robbery, rape, adultery, and incest will be openly taught and practiced . . ."[6]

When a slave at Monticello named Thomas Jefferson died, the Federalists had a grand time spreading the word that it was the vice president who had died.

The Federalists were not alone in their personal smear campaign. Adams was accused of wanting to reunite with Britain and start a dynasty. Adams was also supposed to have sent General Pinckney to England to procure four mistresses—two for each of them. When Adams heard this, he answered: "If this be true General Pinckney has kept them all for himself and cheated me out of my two."[7]

In early November, the states began selection of electors, and, on December 3, when early reports began leaking out, the Republicans felt sure of a victory. Celebration parties were held, and by December 14, though not all the returns were in, Jefferson began making a few select cabinet appointments.

But as the month wore on, it became clear there was a problem. None of the Republican electors had withheld any votes from Burr (a necessary strategy because of the double balloting system whereby electors did not differentiate between votes for president and vice president), and the Republicans had garnered equal support for both their candidates—Jefferson and Burr had tied with 73 electoral votes apiece, meaning that the House of Representatives, dominated by lame-duck Federalists, would break the tie. (At the time, most states selected congressmen a year or more before they took office, causing a sizable portion of any given Congress to be members who were on their way out of office.)[8]

Congress had provided a system for cases where an electoral tie vote needed to be resolved by the House: As soon as the House returned from the Senate Chamber where the electoral votes were counted, it was to ascertain that all states were represented and immediately begin to vote, continuing without adjournment until a president was chosen. Each state had one vote, and representatives were to ballot among themselves to determine how the state would cast its one vote. States divided on the issue were to cast blanks. Two identical ballots were prepared by each state and put into separate ballot boxes—each box to be tallied separately. If there was an agreement between the two countings, then results were announced. If there was disagreement, then a new ballot was taken until a majority of votes was received.[9]

Despite Hamilton's warnings that Burr was unscrupulous, many Federalists chose to back him, feeling it would disorganize the Republicans and that Burr's background made him more readily disposed to Federalist needs. Indeed, if each representative had voted, the Federalist wishes easily would have predominated, since each state was only allowed one vote.

As the second Tuesday in February (February 11), the established day for the official electoral count, neared, Washington hotels and boarding houses filled with people who wanted to know the election outcome. Demonstrations for Jefferson took place outside the unfinished Capitol where the House of Representatives was to vote.

On the first ballot, eight states voted for Jefferson, six for Burr and the rest voted blank. Voting continued; the House balloted 19 times on the first day with no resolve. The balloting continued during the next seven days. Joseph Nicholson, a representative from Maryland, a divided state, had a high fever so he had a bed fixed for himself in a committee room in order to stay for the balloting and keep Maryland from voting for Burr. Other representatives sent for pillows and nightcaps, and, wrapped in blankets and coats, they napped while awaiting the next ballot.

As the voting continued, Congress was becoming disturbed. There was real fear for what would happen to the country if a decision was not reached by March 4, Inauguration Day. The governors of Pennsylvania and Virginia were talking of calling out the militia to prevent a Federalist usurpation of the presidency.

Amidst this tension, there was finally movement toward breaking the deadlock. On the 36th ballot—taken on February 17—a Vermont Federalist was purposely absent. The Maryland and South Carolina Federalists voted blanks as did a Delaware representative. Jefferson had, at last, achieved 10 of the 16 states, one more than the required majority of nine.

"I hope you will have the cannon out to announce the news,"[10] read a message sent from the nation's capital to Richmond.

In New England, where the Federalists were strongest, there was talk of secession, but Jefferson's low-key style and his inaugural speech stating, "If there be any among us who would wish to dissolve this Union or to change its republican form, let them stand undisturbed as monument of the safety with which error of opinion may be tolerated where reason is left free to combat it."[11] His early actions helped calm the country, and the relatively smooth transition of power helped the people take one more step toward feeling more and more like Americans.

Now, not only had the United States demonstrated a peaceful transfer of power from one man to another, it had shown that the country was strong enough, and the belief in overall mutual aims tough enough, to withstand the transfer of power from one political party to another.

## Preparing for 1804

In a day when a fence was needed around the White House to keep the cows from straying on to the lawn, visitors enjoyed the twice-yearly White House receptions Jefferson held. Ice cream and apple pie were served and all were invited to come in and shake the president's hand. Indian chiefs were as likely as dignitaries to be found chatting with Jefferson.

It was also a day when security protection was not what it is today. One local Washington editor wrote that he visited the White House, found no one home and was able to walk right in to browse over Jefferson's collection of oddities, including the skeleton of a mammoth and Indian paintings on buffalo hide.[12]

Amidst this atmosphere, Jefferson's first administration ended. It had been a good one. The country entered 1804 with the national debt paid off, and a president who had just made the land deal of the nation's lifetime. Jefferson sent representatives to France to try to buy New Orleans from Napoleon for $2 million and ended up with an agreement for the U.S. to buy the entire Louisiana Territory for $16 million.

Despite all this good news, one troublesome piece of business had to be resolved before the next election day—the constitutional matter of the double balloting system. The tie vote between Burr and Jefferson had been the last straw in tolerating the "fatal flaw." In 1797 and 1798 amendments had been put forth to no avail, and even after the troubled election of 1800, amendments offered in 1801 and 1802 failed to pass. Finally, at the eleventh hour, in September of 1804, the 12th amendment was ratified. All constitutional requirements remained the same, but now electors were to vote separately for one man as president and one as vice president. In each case, the elected person needed to have a majority of the whole number of electors appointed. If no candidates had the majority, then the House was to vote by state from among the top three. The Senate was to make the selection for vice president if no candidate received a majority.

## The Election of 1804

Jefferson was renominated at a formal caucus of Republican senators and representatives held in Washington in February 1804, in preparation for the spring elections of some of the legislatures. After the fiasco of 1800, the Republicans were ready to dump Burr, so George Clinton was nominated as the vice presidential candidate.

The Federalists, with less than one-third of the seats in Congress and terribly weakened after Adams's defeat in 1800 and Hamilton's resignation from the government, waited much longer to decide on their candidate, and eventually simply came to an informal understanding that Charles Cotesworth Pinckney and Rufus King would be their choices.

In 1804 political activities generally took place on patriotic days. While dates such as July 4 were celebrated by both parties, dates such as March 4, the anniversary of Jefferson's inauguration, were celebrated only by the Republicans. Militia units often had party affiliations, and some celebrations took place on muster and militia days. Generally, the celebrations would begin with a parade, led by the appropriate military unit and followed by local and state politicians. Sometimes benevolent societies and organizations of professional men would join in. Such parades often concluded with a high-spirited dinner with perhaps 25 toasts; Republican toasts would begin with one to Jefferson, followed by toasts to leading issues of the day, such as the economy, peace or the Louisiana Purchase.

At this time, most states were grappling with the issue of the ballot. While some voting was still done orally, more and more states were switching to the written ballot. Customarily, political organizations prepared their own ballots, and the voters' real choice was whether to accept a Federalist or Republican ticket. (Initially, ballots were to be handwritten, not printed, but as this became more and more laborious, legislatures soon permitted both.) On a typical party-supplied ballot, one could not write in other names, but names could be scratched out. It is reported that this was generally more of an effort than most voters cared to exert—thus straight ticket voting began early on.

Political parties soon learned how to outwit the system. Sometimes the ballot heading would be for one party, but candidates listed would all be from the other party; the voter accepted what he thought was the Federalist ticket, for example, only to end up casting his vote for a list of Republicans. This was an early voting scam used in all areas where printed ballots were employed and was used equally by both parties.

Political parties also sometimes got control of election officials who helped sway the vote one way or the other. In a New Jersey election in 1808, the losers complained about the way the ballots were counted: "The Federal ones were not taken down by the clerk or handed by the Judge to the other Inspector, but were put away in his pocket, thrown behind him, or dropt on the floor, and the number supplied by democratic ones."[13]

As America gained new settlers, election officials had more and more difficulty keeping track of who the voters were, and, in areas where there were property or tax-paying qualifications, whether or not they were truly eligible. Voter registration of some kind seemed to be the answer. Early attempts at registration involved checking off voter names against the tax registry (helpful in states once the voting requirement became a tax-paying one). However, people who claimed to have been "overlooked" by the assessors were able to get their names entered at the polls by paying a small tax. Sometimes there were many voters who paid at the last minute, and there were frequent accusations that the political parties paid their tax bills.

The partisan press continued to be very important, and with the move of the capital to Washington, Jefferson needed a local mouthpiece. He persuaded Samuel Harrison Smith to move from Philadelphia, the former capital, to Washington to establish the *National Intelligencer*, which spoke to the common man and favored the administration. The pro-Republican articles published in the *Intelligencer* were extremely important because they were then reprinted in other Republican newspapers from Georgia to Maine.

During this period of peace and prosperity, the Federalists could no longer muster votes. Even when citizens were warned that Jefferson's Louisiana Purchase had cost them $4 apiece, few seemed to object. Jefferson won by a landslide. He and Clinton received 162 of the electoral votes and carried 14 states. Pinckney and King carried only two.

In this election, seven states (Vermont, Connecticut, New York, Delaware, South Carolina, Georgia and Tennessee) used the legislature to choose presidential electors, three (Maryland, North Carolina and Kentucky) held a popular vote by district, while the remaining seven provided for a statewide popular vote by general ticket. More than ever, it had been an election by the people.

## Women and the Vote

If time travel were possible, a state that historians would likely want to visit on election day would be turn-of-the-century New Jersey, where, until 1807, voters included blacks and women (widows and single women, that is; if the state followed the letter of the law, wives were excluded on a technicality of property requirements).

In 1776, when New Jersey drew up its state constitution, the framers failed to exclude blacks and women from voting. This was in keeping with the liberal views of the area given that the state was heavily settled by Quakers who gave women a high degree of—though not complete—equality.

Historians doubt that blacks or women voted in any overwhelming numbers most of the time, but seeing women and blacks at the polls was not uncommon.[14] Rural voters sometimes even complained that city gentlemen had the advantage in the vote because it was so much easier for them to transport their women to the polls, while rural men often found it was difficult even to make the journey by themselves.

In 1806 a political fight over the location of a county courthouse finally resulted in suffrage change in New Jersey. Newark had been the original seat of the Essex County courthouse, but Elizabethtown wanted to house the new one that was to be built. A vote was to be held on the matter; the county was alive with excitement over the issue. Passions ran so high that it was unsafe for residents of one town to visit the other—assaults were not unheard of.

On February 10, 1806, voting began at a poll on Day's Hill, where Elizabethtown residents wanted the courthouse to be. Election activities proceeded calmly for a time, but with the opening of the poll on the second day, irregularities began to appear. By the third day, with the opening of a poll near Newark, fraud became rampant, with no effort to conceal what was going on. Men and boys voted unchallenged as they went from poll to poll casting repeated votes. Vehicles were used to transport the voters more quickly. Newark sent spies to Elizabethtown to find out how many votes were needed to win. Women—black, white, married and single—also voted again and again, and finally men and boys disguised as women voted once more.[15]

The largest number of votes ever before cast in the county had been 4,500; for this election, nearly 14,000 votes were cast. The township of Acquacknonk, said to contain about 350 voters, polled nearly 1,900. Newark had won, but the election was finally declared void.[16]

The episode brought attention to the suffrage law and the irregularities it made possible.

Because New Jersey differed from other states in opening the franchise to "all inhabitants,"

> New Jersey legislators reacted to the scandal by an effort to restrict the vote. Although women and blacks were no more active (and maybe less so) than the "free white males" who also voted again and again, they were the victims of the legislature's attempt to reduce fraud by bringing New Jersey more in line with the laws of the other states. In 1807, a bill was introduced limiting the franchise to free white male citizens. It passed by heavy majorities.

Little reaction from women was reported. There was not much follow-up in the press, nor did there seem to be any public outcry. The women of the day seemed to be indifferent to their loss of rights, leaving it to their grandchildren's generation to begin a fight for suffrage that would last 80 years. As for blacks, not even a civil war completely solved their problems, and it would be many years before they, too, could freely vote again.

## Election of 1808

Despite the triumphant return in 1806 of Lewis and Clark from their explorations of the Louisiana Purchase and the presence on the White House lawn of the grizzly bears they had brought back, Jefferson's second administration was in trouble.

As the election year approached, tensions with Britain and France had increased; those nations continued interfering with American fleets and, in the case of the British, "impressing" or seizing American sailors. Jefferson intended to avoid war at all costs and had hoped trade embargoes would pressure other countries into leaving the U.S. alone, but the sole result of the embargo was to damage the American economy. Businessmen and farmers were upset, and other citizens were angered at the thought that America was not acting to protect herself against these insults. When the British ship *Leopard* attacked the American *Chesapeake*, killing three and injuring 18, Jefferson tightened the embargo, which made things even worse.

In addition, the Republican Party stumbled. James Madison, Jefferson's secretary of state, had long been expected to succeed Jefferson, but Virginian John Randolph, deposed by Jefferson from his position as White House spokesman, opted to vent his frustration on Jefferson by backing James Monroe, also a Virginian, instead of Madison. In the meantime, New York Republicans, tired of the prospect of the continuation of the Virginia dynasty controlling the presidency, united behind Vice President George Clinton, who also had presidential aspirations. Supporters sought a way to back him without his declaring an open candidacy, an act for which he would have been criticized. This threw the party into chaos as Republicans and the press jockeyed to support one candidate or the other.

But to Republicans, the most alarming occurrence of the election year was the resurgence of the Federalist Party. Federalism had been virtually stilled during Jefferson's days, and the re-emergence of this Party was unwelcome in a time when politicians felt that total party dominance would one day be possible. After briefly considering backing Clinton in order to defeat Madison, the Federalists again put forth Charles Cotesworth Pinckney and Rufus King.

In late November, early electoral results began to trickle in, and by mid-December, as struggling horses arrived carrying the electoral votes, a final estimate was possible. With one elector uncounted, the results were 122 electoral votes for Madison; 47 for Pinckney and six for New York candidate George Clinton.

Though the ultimate result with Madison taking the presidency were what Jefferson hoped, the victory of Election Day 1808 did not come to Madison and the Republican Party without effort and pain.

The decade closed with the resurgence of a very young two-party system. In addition, a problem within the electoral system—the method of double-balloting had been solved by the 12th Amendment. A foundation was set upon which new election day traditions could begin to build.

# The End of the
# Virginia Dynasty _____ 6

"A scene worthy only of Hottentots and savages" are the words a "Traveller" used in *The Delaware Gazette* to describe the city of Wilmington at election time. Describing bonfires set in many parts of the town on election night, the writer notes that "a number of writched and many barefoot beings, some blacks, whooped and hollowed" in merriment as they threw on "great amounts of furniture" from the surrounding buildings.[1]

Typical of election time doings throughout the country, bonfires, barbecues and parades were beginning to involve citizens of all ranks. Along with the aforementioned "writched and barefoot beings," John Marshall, who would become one of the best known chief justices, was even reported to have attended an election day bonfire.

The increasing involvement of all Americans in the celebratory aspects of election day mirrored what was happening on the political front. The period between 1810–1824 was to see a breakdown in the property-holding requirement of the suffrage laws, making more and more Americans eligible to vote. Dead, too, by the end of the Virginia dynasty's reign over the presidency was the Congressional caucus nominating system that had kept party leaders in control of the selection of national candidates. Nominations by state conventions or legislatures were more acceptable to the people, and, by the election of 1824, these methods had replaced what was known as "King Caucus."

## The Election of 1812

Election Day 1812 was the last hurrah for the two-party system for a time. Britain's continued interference with United States trade and her impressment of American sailors into the Royal Navy pushed the United States to the point where President Madison, who never intended to lead the country into war, felt that armed response was unavoidable. The controversy over the wisdom of going to war against the mightiest naval and military power in the world breathed enough life into the pro-British Federalist party that it was able to muster broad support for the election. As a result, interest in the election was comparatively high. In states where the results were expected to be close, the number of voters often approached 60–80% of the adult male population.

One political tactic the Federalists found necessary was a name change. Madison's supporters had continued calling themselves Republicans, finding that the image of "supporters of the Republic" was a positive one. However, the Republican electioneering of the early 1800s had sufficiently connected "Federalist" with the image of aristocracy and elitism, so that for this election year, the Federalists took to calling themselves "Federal Republicans" and sometimes just "Republicans." Supposedly to alleviate confusion, they began calling their opponents "Democrats," which in the early 19th century carried the connotation of demagoguery and mob rule. And at times when the Federalists found it advantageous to be against the war, they called themselves the Peace Party, making Madison's party, of course, the War Party.

Locally, political systems were refining their methods and putting together loose confederations of regional groups. Lacking control of state legislatures and needing a way to gather support, Republicans in New England led the way for state nominating conventions. People were told of county meetings through newspaper notices and, at these meetings, nominated assembly candidates and elected delegates to the state

*German-born painter John Lewis Krimmel depicts a citywide election in Philadelphia in 1815. At the Central Building, later known as Independence Hall, voters are lining up to hand their ballots to clerks inside (each ward would have had a different window). In the center of the painting, an infirm voter has taken advantage of a carriage supplied by politicians in order to come to vote. To the left of center, a wagon full of cheering voters travels along Chestnut Street; others, who have already voted, fight, drink and eat roasted oysters. The hotel at the extreme left served as Republican Party headquarters. (Courtesy tNhe Henry Francis du Pont Winterthur Museum.)*

conferences that chose Congressional candidates and presidential electors. The idea
soon spread, and, to keep up in states where political contests were close, the
Federalists soon had to follow suit.

Bringing the polls closer to the people was another local movement of this era.
Throughout colonial times and into the early 19th century, traveling to the polls was
impossible or a serious hardship for many, and districting—breaking the counties into
election districts—was a way to bring the polls closer to more of the voters. Delaware
Governor Joseph Haslet, a Republican elected in 1810, clearly outlined the humanitarian and proper reasons for this:

> "Can it be said that elections are free to all having the qualifications of electors,
> when many are prevented from attending the elections by the distances they live
> from the places of holding them? . . . Or can electors be said to be equal, when
> to give their votes, some voters need to travel only one mile and some must
> travel sixty."[2]

Districts were established by the state legislature and were decided upon based on
an evaluation of population, land area and, usually, partisan voting. The Republicans,
particularly, stood to benefit from this. Larger towns, likely to be the seat of county
voting, were the stronghold of the gentry and the business class who tended to be
Federalists. By moving the polls to the outlying areas, Republicans were likely to pick
up more votes, thus they pushed hard for districting the states.

In 1812, while Elbridge Gerry was governor, Massachusetts Republicans outdid
themselves in their efforts to redistrict the state and deprive the Federalists of control
of the state senate. In carving up the state so that each area had a predominant number
of Republicans, Massachusetts ended up with one district so uniquely shaped, that on
a map it looked like a salamander. The Federalists soon took to calling the districting
a "gerrymander." The name stuck and is still used today to describe a biased system
of districting. Massachusetts was not alone in this practice, and other states rivalled
Massachusetts for imagination. One part of New Jersey was carved into a horseshoe-
shaped district to accomplish this same purpose.

On the national front, foreign tensions put the campaigning off schedule in 1812,
and Madison was not nominated until May (as opposed to February or March) of 1812.
Only a few more than half the Republican congressmen met in caucus to nominate
Madison and Massachusetts Governor Elbridge Gerry for vice president.

DeWitt Clinton was determined to challenge Madison as an antiadministration
candidate. With New York's backing (and nomination via state legislative caucus),
he persuaded many of the Federalists to unite in an effort to defeat the incumbent.
(Philadelphia lawyer Jared Ingersoll ran as vice president.) Not all party members felt
this feasible. The Virginia Federalist contingent went ahead with the nomination of
Rufus King, nevertheless Clinton mounted a strong challenge to Madison. Gaining
the support of all of New England except Vermont, he added New York, New Jersey
and Delaware, and gained five of Maryland's 11 electoral votes. The final tally was

89 electoral votes for Clinton to Madison's 128—figures strong enough to make clear that the country was not entirely supportive of "Mr. Madison's War."

And Mr. Madison was in for a bit of a siege. Opposed to the war from the beginning, the Federalists gained control of the New England legislatures, and, at the Hartford Convention—a meeting secretly called for and attended by five New England states—secession from the United States was threatened. What was more, the war was not going well. As Madison and the Republicans viewed Election Day 1816, it must have been with sinking hearts.

But the Republicans were destined to be saved. A surprise turnabout in the war and announcement of efforts toward a peace treaty whereby the U.S. neither gained nor lost anything coupled with Andrew Jackson's stunning victory over the British in New Orleans created a different atmosphere for the campaign of 1816. Nationalism and patriotism reigned, and the Republicans relished their good fortune. Now they—not the Federalists—were the party of nationalism and centralization.

As Election Day 1816 approached, Madison prepared to step down, hoping that friend and fellow Virginian James Monroe would succeed him. However, when it came time for the nomination, the continuation of the Virginia dynasty was not automatic. James Monroe had been waiting in the wings as secretary of state, trusting that he would be able to follow Madison, but another strong contender for the Democratic–Republican nomination appeared. Senator William H. Crawford, a highly competent Georgian, was very well liked and had worked closely with a powerful and popular group of young Congressmen known as the "War Hawks" (political leaders including Henry Clay, John Calhoun and Daniel Webster who gained that name because they had been adamant that war was the only solution to the international problems of 1812).

Only Crawford's reluctance to run saved Monroe from stiff intraparty competition. When Crawford denied interest in the presidency, his local backers avoided the March 16 caucus. But even without their presence at the caucus, Crawford had 54 votes to Monroe's 65. Had Crawford evinced interest, he probably could have had the nomination. Daniel Tompkins, governor of New York, was put forth for vice president.

Criticism of the caucus system continued and numerous meetings were held in various parts of the country to express dissatisfaction with the method. It was, after all, a method to which the framers of the Constitution would take great exception as it made the country's chief executive beholden to Congress. Until then, one had to admit, it had perpetuated a state dynasty with Virginia providing all but one of the nation's presidents—another situation that the Founding Fathers would likely have viewed as flawed.

Though the politicians of the time didn't realize it, the mechanics for a new system were being readied. First in 1808, when backers of Madison and Monroe worried that the national Congressional caucus would not be in their candidates' favor, each group held its own state legislative caucus to nominate its own candidate. That year the Monroe supporters were to be disappointed, nevertheless a new nominating system was being tried. In 1812, DeWitt Clinton had made a very respectable run for the presidency based on a nomination by a New York state legislative caucus he controlled, and by 1816 states were often meeting in caucus or convention groups to endorse the candidates nominated by the national caucus. Methodology was changing, and in a few short years the congressional caucus system would be obsolete.

Dissatisfaction with Virginia's domination of the presidency was also growing. John Adams had strong hopes that his son John Quincy would one day be president, but after nomination of Monroe the elder Adams noted that John Quincy would be forgotten "till all Virginians shall be extinct."

By this time, the Federalists were almost nonexistent. There is no documentation of any Federalist caucus, and there was no agreement in the Federalist press. Rufus King, senator from New York, received 34 electoral votes for president, but no united organization had been behind him.

By 1816, 10 of the 19 states chose electors by popular vote, but seven of these states did so by general ticket, with only three voting by district. The remainder of the electors were chosen by the state legislatures. With 183 electoral votes, Monroe won handily.

## Voting on the Frontier in the Early 1800s

Curiosity, the desire to explore and the increasing need for unclaimed lands led America's newcomers to leave the eastern seaboard and push the frontier farther and farther west in the 19th century. Early in the 1800s, areas such as Missouri and Indiana were on the edge of civilized territory.

Political parties were slow in coming to the early frontier, so local candidates campaigned on personal attributes, rather than party allegiance. Campaign methods in Indiana harked back to the methods used by the colonists where candidates announced themselves in the newspapers or by handbills that were distributed from house to house. Typically, these announcements became more and more praiseworthy as the campaign neared. Here's what voters read on the eve of one early election:

CITIZENS OF KNOX

An American, a child of your State, and a friend of your rights, now offers his services to represent you in the legislature. His qualifications are so well known they need no comment. His principles both religious and political have been tested and passed the Rubison [sic]. Such a one now solicits your suffrages and if he becomes the object of your choice, promises that he will serve you faithfully and render an account of his conduct.

Vincennes, Aug. 4th, 1817.

GENERAL W. JOHNSTON[3]

Campaign travel was fraught with difficulties. Writes one candidate for office in Indiana about the conditions in 1826: "No roads, nothing but Indian paths, sleep in

Indian huts, swim ponies over streams, use Indian guides, build canoes, sleep in woods with wolves howling, make one speech and return home."[4]

Drinking was an integral part of election day in some parts of Indiana. The old-timers prided themselves on the fact that they wouldn't take bribes for a vote, but "treating" by the local politician was regularly practiced. The hard part was getting men to the polls before "Old King Alcohol" had paralyzed them.

Elsewhere in the state, the Puritan ethic had set in, and one young politician made the most of it. When it looked as if he wouldn't win the election, he decided to demonstrate his worthiness by entering a saloon (called a grocery in those days) and destroying it. He broke bottles and took the faucet out of the whiskey barrel, then paid the grocer for his property. The news spread like wildfire, and the young man won the election.[5]

Fights were regularly scheduled for election day, too, as it was the one time of the year when the principals could have their seconds near at hand. Deadly weapons were rarely used to settle a dispute.

To prepare for a fight, combatants had their heads shaved and soaped; they stripped to the waist, tied their suspenders around their bodies and entered the ring while the crowd stood around the pen to witness the fight. Sometimes the drama of this moment was great enough that friends of the fighters could bring about a reconciliation between the two men, in which case the fighters washed off the soap, dressed, and the crowd adjourned to the courthouse to vote. If the fight did transpire, it might be a fierce one, but those who stood by were quick to pull off the victor when the "underdog" had had enough.[6]

The scene at the courthouse was always a lively one. Men pushed ahead, giving their tickets to the inspector faster than he could write down the names of those who voted. As votes were cast for the various candidates, the crowd would hoot or hiss depending on their allegiances. By common consent, fighting was not permitted near the polls; however, if the polls were so crowded that it hindered the progress of the voting, sometimes a sham fight would be staged in order to disperse most of the crowd and allow the election board time to breathe.[7]

In Missouri, another new territory, one of the first significant elections of opposing forces was the election of 1816 for territorial delegate to the U.S. Congress.

Created in 1813, Missouri Territory was an area where fur trade had dominated, but as the farmers arrived, they needed customs and laws that could govern the new society. William Clark, who had been serving as the area's Indian agent after his and Meriwether Lewis's landmark expedition to the Louisiana Territory, was appointed the territory's first governor.

The candidates, John Scott representing the old guard (French families and government employees who had been there for a time), and Rufus Easton representing the new (lawyers, land speculators and farmers coming in to settle the area), both ran on pro-statehood platforms, but the battle was a bitter one revolving around personal issues.

As governor, Clark presided over the election, but his actions did not aid the democratic process. Before all the votes were counted and with Scott running a bit behind, Clark declared Scott, the candidate he favored, the winner. The outcry that followed went all the way to Washington, D.C., where Congress ultimately voided the election and stipulated that a new one be held in 1817.

In 1817, the people were ready for another election. Soldiers stationed in the area were prepared to enjoy the festivities, and election day became a time of particular merriment with much music and parading. The military favored the election of John Scott and wore labels or tickets in their caps printed with "John Scott." Near the door of the poll, "John Scott" was printed on the side of a large shed, and under it were spread tables covered with food and drink.[8] Voters were sometimes escorted to the polling place with fife and drum.[9]

But Clark further upset Missourians by his failure to observe local customs. Upon emerging from the polling place, Clark reportedly announced in a loud voice that he had voted for John Scott. This had been the custom in his native Virginia but stirred anger in Missouri.[10]

Despite these missteps, the rescheduled election favored Scott, and this time he was the winner by a majority of almost 400 votes.


## The "Era of Good Feelings"

The period following Monroe's election was viewed by the country as a halcyon time. Delighted by the decline of the Federalist party evidenced in 1816, Monroe set out on a triumphal 13-state tour shortly after his 1816 victory, and the New Englanders, who had never personally seen Jefferson or Madison, were very excited about a visit by a president. The high spirits of Bostonians, and of the country as a whole, led the Boston *Columbian Sentinel* to deem it the "era of good feelings."

Amidst this period of contentment, a quiet revolution regarding suffrage rights had taken place. In all but three states (Rhode Island, Virginia and Louisiana) property- or tax-paying requirements had been eliminated. New western states like Indiana, Illinois and Missouri all entered the union between 1815–1820 with liberal suffrage laws. Because settlers in the frontier states had to work so strenuously for survival, they were a more homogeneous group in their values; the land did not attract aristocratic types nor did it attract the "less desirables" who found life easier in the cities. Westerners seemed to feel much the same as the very first colonists—that almost everyone should be eligible to participate in government.

In states that were already part of the Union, suffrage requirements were discussed at each state's constitutional convention, and, in some states, the property qualification was hotly debated. Many at the New York convention in 1821 favored keeping it, given that the history of long and large holdings resulted in a strong class with special privileges. One legislator, however, argued for broader suffrage noting: "It is said that our wealth builds our churches, establishes our schools, endows our colleges, and erects our hospitals. But have these institutions been raised without the hands of labor?"[11] One final purpose that kept the property qualification alive in some states was the growing prejudice against foreigners. Some delegates to state conventions felt that the property test would protect the state "against the tumultuous, disorderly Irishmen in the cities and the Germans in the country."[12]

The states were also wrestling with other suffrage issues. Interestingly, major discussions occurred about whether or not military men could vote. Most states did not want men who were only temporarily stationed in their state influencing local politics, but whether or not members of the military deserved special privilege in their own state (since many of them might not be property owners or taxpayers) was questioned. In New York, an attempt was made to give the vote to veterans but not to militiamen. Most felt it to be unjust that the men who fought the nation's battles should be shut out at the polls, but they didn't necessarily want to give the vote to those soldiers who had not been in battle and did not otherwise qualify to vote as taxpayers. (The result of the vote in New York was to exclude both the veterans and the militiamen from special privileges.)

Maine legislators debated about whether or not to exclude convicted criminals from the polls (as many other states had done), but ultimately they declined to do so, feeling, as one delegate summed up, "evidence of the conviction was not easy to have on hand, and no man should be burdened with such a stigma for the rest of his days."[13] However, like many other states, paupers, soldiers, sailors and students were not allowed to vote. These restrictions were the beginning of laws that would come into being as the property test was dropped but means were still sought to control who could vote.

Suffrage for blacks was another issue discussed in constitutional conventions in the North in the 1820s, and the results followed a predictable pattern. Free blacks were rarely prevented from voting in states where they were few in numbers. In border states, where a good number of free or escaped slaves had settled, the states tended to draw careful restrictions.[14]

In 1820, sentiment was so strongly in favor of the president that he was never officially nominated and ran without opposition. Monroe won the presidency by default with 231 electoral votes; John Quincy Adams received one.

That lone vote that kept Monroe from sharing with George Washington the distinction of having received 100% of the possible electoral votes has received great attention. Originally, the interpretation was that William H. Plumer of New Hampshire voted as he did simply to preserve the honor of a unanimous vote of the electoral college for George Washington. Today, revisionist historians point out that Plumer couldn't possibly have known that he was casting the lone dissenting vote in 1820, and his own writings buttress this interpretation. Plumer's written observations are also of interest because they reveal what it was like to be an elector at that time. He writes of the December 5 meeting of New Hampshire electors:

At ten o'clock in the morning I met all the other electors two of whom, Ezra Barlet and Samuel Dinsmore, hold offices (collectors of taxes) under the United States, and are therefore ineligible to the office of electors; but as there is not provision for the board or any other tribunal to settle that question, I was silent and they took their seats and acted as electors.[15]

Chosen as elector against his will, Plumer felt bound to accept. He was elected president from among the group of other electors and set about taking care of business, including selecting the messenger, from among 36 applicants, to carry the votes to Washington. The first afternoon they met, Plumer led a discussion of how each intended to ballot. He presented well-formed thoughts on why he favored John Quincy Adams and Richard Rush for president and vice president, and later wrote: "I made this statement with great calmness, and fully illustrated every idea in a very particular manner, taking half an hour. The board listened with fixt attention, but appeared surprized, and were perfectly silent."[16]

On December 6, the electors met with William Plumer casting the lone dissenting vote. He noted: "I have acted according to my own judgement; and shall have no cause to regret it tho no other elector should vote for the same men."[17]

That year, 163 of 235 electors were chosen by the direct vote of the people. One hundred and five of them in nine states by general ticket, and in six states by districts, leaving only nine states choosing by legislature.

In spite of increased opportunity for the voter, this particular election brought about little excitement, simply because there was no contest. In Richmond, Virginia, only 17 men bothered to vote, and it is estimated that less than 1% of the male population went to the polls in 1820.

But the story of 1820 isn't quite over. When the votes were counted, Congress had difficulty deciding whether or not to count Missouri's electoral votes. Because at the time of the vote its constitution was not yet in line with Congress's requirements on the slavery issue, Missouri had not yet been admitted to the Union. After bickering over whether or not to include Missouri's votes, a decision was finally reached to announce the electoral vote in two ways—with and without the Missouri vote. Even after this agreement was reached, Virginia's John Randolph insisted on making an issue of it, but the group was weary of all of the discussion and left him to rant alone.

## 1824: The "Stolen" Election

As Americans looked toward 1824, they saw change all about them. The nation had grown significantly during the past few years, and sectional interests were coming to the fore. What was good for one part of the country wasn't right for another. Funds for internal improvements and a protective tariff were two of the primary national issues. New England was shifting its primary business from foreign trade to manufacturing, opposed spending federal money on any internal improvements such as canals and roadways and supported the tariff. The South was against both the tariff and spending on internal improvements, while the Middle States favored both. The isolated West favored spending money to improve transportation.

Though the country was still operating with only one political party, the varying needs of the different states were beginning to seek other answers. Many candidates were ready to make themselves available to help. In Washington, John Quincy Adams, secretary of state, hoped that now that the Virginia dynasty had died out, his turn for the presidency had come at last. But he faced stiff competition from the very popular secretary of the treasury, William H. Crawford, who had the backing of old-line party leaders including the Albany Regency (New York politicians who dominated politics in that state), ably headed by Martin Van Buren. Henry Clay, speaker of the House, represented the West and also proved to be a worthy candidate. Also hopeful was John C. Calhoun, secretary of war.

The method of nominating the candidates was a problem politicians had to consider. In 1816, widespread opposition to the caucus nomination system for being an arbitrary decision by a few politicians emerged. Because there had not been much of a race in 1816, and no nominations at all in 1820, little had been done to change the caucus system, but by 1824 it was a prime campaign issue. Supporters of William Crawford, the secretary of the treasury and the president's choice for successor, thought that the caucus system was still viable as a way to gain a national consensus on a candidate. They opted to hold a congressional caucus, but when only 66 members attended (about one-quarter), Crawford was badly tarnished by being associated with it.

Because of this reaction, the other candidates—Secretary of State John Quincy Adams, General Andrew Jackson and former Speaker of the House Henry Clay—and their supporters looked to the state legislatures as a way to get a body of people to put a candidate's name in nomination. Adams was nominated by the legislatures of most of the New England states; Clay was named by the Kentucky legislature and several other state legislatures.

The Tennessee legislature nominated a western candidate whom no one, including himself, took seriously at first. But when Andrew Jackson, a self-made military man and Indian fighter from Tennessee who had also served in the House and the Senate, was put forth as the "people's candidate," his growing popularity caused everyone to give him a second look.

Perhaps the most significant news event of 1824 was General Lafayette's visit to America. The country was nearing its 50th birthday, and many of the heroes—upon whom the nation had relied—were gone. Lafayette, with his status as a Revolutionary War hero, brought nostalgia for what had been. Upon his arrival in New York City, newspapers throughout the country declared GENERAL LA FAYETTE ARRIVED![18] He visited every state, and everywhere he was greeted with warmth.

As people contemplated election day in light of Lafayette's arrival, one thing was obvious. The nation would soon be without its war heroes to lead the government. Gone were the men who had been at the forefront of the Revolution. One Kentuckian noted, "My invariable rule has been, in regard to elections and appointments, always to prefer the candidate, if equal to the necessary duties, who had been actively engaged in the Revolutionary war."[19] A New Yorker noted that since what the country sought was the nearest approximation to a man with the republicanism of the Revolution, then the next electoral college should be made up of veterans of 1776 who could select the next president with this criterion in mind.

For this reason, candidates tied themselves to the Revolution in any way they could. Though Jackson had played a rather insignificant role, his backers made much of the fact that he was the only candidate who had participated in the Revolutionary War at all. John Quincy Adams's supporters stressed the fact that Adams had grown up amidst men who espoused the principles of the new Republic. Since Crawford, Clay and Calhoun were really only "boys" at the time of the Revolution, they had a more difficult time, though Calhoun's supporters were adept at stressing the young South Carolinian's resemblance to the men of Washington's day.

Typical of many of the new states that were wrestling with the electoral system was Indiana, which had achieved statehood in 1816. In both 1816 and 1820, its electors were chosen by the state legislature. By 1824, the people were given the right to choose their own electors, but like in other states, the procedure for nominating a slate was problematical. One difficulty surrounded communication. In 1810, Indiana had one newspaper, and by 1828 there were still only 15 for the whole state. Daily mail did not arrive in the area until 1836, and the existing postal service required recipients to pay for delivery. As rates were quite high, many letters were left unclaimed at the post office.[20] How best could a statewide consensus be reached on electors (who might not be well known)? And if they were nominated for reasons of political allegiance, were they bound to vote for the candidate they originally intended? Neither state laws nor party machinery provided any means for selecting a ticket. The method settled on was a system whereby various newspapers advocated certain individuals (or sometimes candidates for state legislature trumpeted a certain group and that was picked up by one of the newspapers favoring that candidate). This was the method older states had been using for several years and was to become the answer to the difficulty in gaining a majority for a group of unknowns.

Eighteen of the 24 states were now able to choose electors by popular vote; only six (Vermont, New York, Delaware, South Carolina, Georgia and Louisiana) still selected them through the legislature. Nevertheless, it is estimated that only about one-quarter of the eligible voters cast ballots in 1824.

As the states' various electors began to be known, it became clear that Jackson and Adams were the leading candidates (Crawford was a distant third, and Henry Clay received backing as well). In February when the count was official, Jackson emerged with 99 electoral votes and 153,544 popular votes to Adams's 84 votes in the electoral college and 108,740 popular votes. Despite a decisive win in the popular vote, Jackson lacked the required majority in the electoral college—meaning that the election would have to be settled in the House. (Because of all the excitement over the presidential contenders that year, the vice presidential spot had been largely ignored. Adams at one point expressed interest in having Jackson as his running mate (to remove him from the presidential field), but when Jackson didn't rise to the bait, Adams never sought out anyone else. Jackson had linked up for a joint ticket with Secretary of War John C. Calhoun, and Jackson electors, as well as many Adams electors, voted for him—giving Calhoun an easy and clear-cut victory.)

Amid rumors that a deal had been cut between Adams and Clay (as speaker, Henry Clay had tremendous influence in the House), and that Clay was to become the administration's secretary of state in return for his support of Adams, the House vote took place. Only one ballot was necessary. Thirteen states declared for Adams, seven voted for Jackson and four favored Crawford. Adams voiced regret that the vote could not be submitted to the people again, and Jackson fumed at the inanity of the system.

Three days later, when Adams made Clay secretary of state (what some historians feel was a natural progression of events, not a precut deal), Jackson saw red, asking: "Was there ever such bare-faced corruption in any country before?"

Certainly the wishes of the people had been defied, and Jackson did not doubt that the election had been "stolen" from them and from him.

Jackson resigned from the Senate and went back to Tennessee. In October of 1825, the Tennessee legislature nominated Andrew Jackson for president for the campaign of 1828. Only a year after the election of 1824, the next election day campaign had begun.

# The Common People
# Get the Vote _____ 7

"To the Polls! Let every man go to the Polls!" cried the newspapers in 1828. It was a time of political awakening, and public interest and activity were increasing. The fact that Jacksonians had begun the campaign in 1825 , shortly after their candidate's bitter defeat, certainly added to the year's anticipation, but changes in voter qualifications made a difference, too. Property- and tax-paying restrictions were lessening, and alterations in the methods by which electors were chosen (all but two states—South Carolina and Delaware—now chose presidential electors by popular vote) meant that many people who had never been permitted to vote in a presidential election now had the opportunity to do so.

The political formation of the country was changing, too. No longer did one political party divide itself into temporary factions for the duration of an election as had been done for the last decade or so. Jacksonian politics hit with such force that some of the reaction, inevitably, was strong opposition to Jacksonians. That was given vent through the development of the anti-Jacksonians who soon came to call themselves National Republicans. Of course, "King Caucus" had died in 1824, so for the first time, mass meetings for nominations replaced caucusing.

The feel of the country was changing as well. The East and South were losing some of their power as more and more Americans moved to the West (still east of the Mississippi) to find more land and better opportunities. The people of the western states had more liberal views, and the working class and frontier farmers were gaining in power.

With this blooming of the pursuit of the American Dream, many people were turning to the perfect candidate for the day: a man who was born into a poor family in the Carolinas, who participated in the Revolutionary War when he was only 13, and who grew up to distinguish himself in law, politics and many post-Revolutionary military battles. With a strong belief in the spirit of the people, Andrew Jackson had little trouble convincing many people that from such stock presidents could be made.

His opponent, presidential incumbent John Quincy Adams, represented the Old Guard and refused to electioneer for himself. Throughout his four years in office, he had also refused to play politics with patronage, making only a few changes in appointees and refusing to punish political disloyalty. This won him few friends, especially when pitted against Andrew Jackson, the most popular military hero since George Washington. Jackson represented change and was supported by a well-oiled political machine, which was ably operated by Martin Van Buren, who had gained his skill as leader of the Albany Regency, the New York State political machine begun by Alexander Hamilton.

To Jacksonians, the administration was fair game within the walls of Congress as well as without. Adams began his term with a strong vision, but despite the merit of his plans (internal improvements including a network of roads and canals, a department of interior to regulate the use of natural resources, expeditions to map the country, government aid to education, etc.) and the fact that they would have benefitted the common people, Jacksonians in Congress vehemently rejected the programs, often as a way to express anti-Adams feelings. Every item eventually became a reality, but not under Adams.

Van Buren had three main goals for the Jackson campaign: 1. Voters needed to be convinced that Adams achieved the presidency through a corrupt bargain; 2. The people were to be shown that they needed Jackson in order to have a true democracy; 3. Campaign workers had to be well organized nationally. Van Buren's accomplishments set the pattern for future elections, including our elections today. To coordinate the campaign a central correspondence committee was organized in Washington; it was the model for current national committees. The central committee orchestrated local activities, which included frequently held political meetings in every village, town and city. The organization also collected money, printed pamphlets and biographies, and supplied newspapers and the electorate with campaign literature.

While every state in the U.S. witnessed a great deal of activity in the campaign for the presidency, it is interesting to take a look at a few of the specific local happenings. Documentation from Missouri offers us one glimpse:

Meeting almost a full year before the presidential election, the first Missouri county meeting supporting Jackson enacted the following resolution and set the tone for the campaign: "Resolved that John Quincy Adams does not hold his present office by the voice of the people; and that the possession and exercise of power without their consent is an open usurpation, which should be peacefully and constitutionally resisted."[1]

As Van Buren had hoped, Adams supporters spent much of the following year defending their candidate from the "corrupt bargain" charge.

Jacksonians liked gatherings, and they held many county conventions. To publicize the first one in the state, handbills were scattered "as thick as the plagues of Egypt," noted the proadministration St. Louis *Missouri Republican* on December 6, 1827.

Missourians would have welcomed a commitment by either candidate to internal improvements since they were hoping for a turnpike that would connect Jefferson City to the leading cities throughout the nation. But since both Adams and Jackson hedged on many campaign issues, the local campaign—like the national one—resorted to personal attacks. However, a few campaign toasts at an Adams meeting on the Fourth of July show that the issues may have been largely ignored, but they weren't forgotten:

"Internal Improvement, by roads and canals—the sure and legitimate means to render us truly one people. 7 cheers."

"Domestic Manufacturers. Essential in peace—indispensable in war—they form the true basis of the National Independence. 7 cheers."

"Our free and happy institutions—let them remain uncontaminated by political demagogues."

"The Agriculture of the West: may it receive equal legislative encouragement, and make equal progress with the manufacturers of the East."[2]

There were plenty of festivities for Jackson as well, accompanied by a good deal of libation, leading the *Missouri Intelligencer* to comment: "Nearly all who attended, went with their mouths so full of *Jackson*, that when they were opened the *Hero's* name would *pop* out with the noise and fermentation of a *beer* bottle, when the cork is extracted."[3]

During the national campaign, issues were largely set aside, and personal accusations predominated. The Democratic–Republicans, later called the Jacksonian Democrats, accused Adams of living in "kingly pomp and splendor" in the "presidential palace." When he bought a billiard table and some chessmen with his own money, he

# Jackson Men,
## *Look out for the*
# SPURIOUS TICKET.
## The Democratic Electoral Ticket, with *Forty Three* names on it, is circulated by the Opposition.
## If you vote that Ticket, your Vote is lost to the Good Cause.

*The poster above was used during the campaign of 1828 to warn voters that false ballots were in circulation. Of course, this was not the first time trickery was used at the polls, nor would it be the last. Falsifying of prepared ballots was a practice that was to continue until late in the 19th century when the introduction of the Australian ballot finally put an end to this and some other kinds of deceit. (Courtesy Tennessee State Library and Archives)* was accused of installing "gaming tables and gambling furniture" in the White House at public expense; he was accused of having premarital relations with his wife, but the basic charge was that at heart he was a monarchist like his father (he was referred to as "King John the Second").[4]

While Adams supporters levied numerous accusations at Jackson, two caused him the most trouble. The first was an adultery charge. This stemmed from the fact that Jackson's wife, Rachel, had been married previously. Though she was told that her divorce had been complete, two years later it became known that it had not. Jackson remarried her immediately, but the opposition wouldn't let up. Causing both Jackson and his wife personal grief and anguish, the issue continued to be put forth time and again.

What became known as the "Coffin Handbill" was equally damaging. It detailed in words and pictures the executions ordered by Jackson of six Tennessee militiamen, mutineers during a war in Alabama with the Creek Indians. Jacksonians explained that the executions were justified. During a time when the Indians were getting the better of Jackson and his men, the militiamen tried to stir up mutiny among the soldiers, stole supplies, burned a bakehouse and then deserted. In fact, when apprehended, the mutineers had a fair trial but since the result was death, Adamsites still called Jackson a murderer.

Campaigners also had a good deal of fun. They made up slogans, popularized political songs and organized barbecues, dinners and street rallies. In honor of "Old Hickory" (a name Jackson acquired during the War of 1812 when he proved to be "as tough as hickory"), many campaign activities included the use of hickory brooms, canes and sticks. A particularly colorful account of this is contained in this boyhood reminiscence written in the "log cabin" days of 1840:

". . . in the section of country where I then resided, there was as great a rage for *Hickory sticks*, and *Hickory clubs*, as there now is for Log Cabins. I recollect that my father, who was then a thoroughgoing Jackson man, carried a *Hickory stick* almost as large as my wrist; . . . and every other Jackson man did the same thing."[5]

Recalling another "hickory" experience, the fellow added: "A party of Jackson men in Philadelphia sent into the country and procured a large Hickory Tree; after having placed the Tree in the ground they poured a barrel of Beer upon its roots, and then each Jackson man present drank beer from the roots of the *Hickory Tree*."

At the polls, there was every sign that America was still a frontier country. Men with whiskey bottles protruding from their coats bribed voters at the polling places while hired toughs beat up illegal voters and those inclined to vote more than once.[7]

In the election of 1828, three times as many voters cast ballots as had done so in 1824; this represented approximately 56% of eligible voters. When these votes were tallied, Jackson had 178 electoral votes to John Quincy Adams's 83. Since only two states of the 24 chose through the legislature, the results were as close as possible to a true popular verdict. The total popular vote for Jackson was 647,286, and Adams 508,064. John C. Calhoun won the vice presidency.

## The People and Jackson's Inauguration

Jackson's inauguration so well depicts the spirit of the day that it is difficult to discuss his election without mentioning it. When it came time to inaugurate the "People's President," the Jacksonian-organized Washington Central Committee was beside itself with joy. Here was a chance to create a giant spectacle unrivaled in American political development. The only problem was exactly what to do. Some committee members advocated whisking Jackson to Philadelphia quickly in order to avoid the worsening road conditions of late winter and letting him take up residency there until it was time to make a triumphal journey to the capital. Crowds would be gathered along the route, and cannon salutes would welcome him to Washington. Others advocated an early count of the electoral ballots so that a prominent group of congressmen could go to Tennessee, inform Jackson of the results and then escort him back. In the meantime, the committee was flooded with invitations from towns who wanted him to "stop in" on his way to Washington.

On December 22, in the midst of all this planning, Rachel Jackson died. All planning ceased immediately out of deference to Jackson, and in mid-January, the future president finally boarded a steamboat to begin the journey to Washington. As it started up the river, Jackson's boat was surrounded by other ships, packed with people, and as the crowd saluted their hero and shouted their huzzas, Jackson came out on deck and graciously returned the greeting.

For the inauguration on March 4, the excitement was palpable. Thousands of people had come as far as 500 miles to see the new president and visit their nation's capital. They had been arriving for days, sleeping on everything from inn beds to billiard tables.

For the first time in presidential history, the swearing-in ceremony took place outdoors, giving the estimated 15,000 to 20,000 onlookers the chance to witness it. The crowd was so large that the dignitaries had difficulty reaching their proper places, and finally a ship's cable was strung to keep the crowds back. When Jackson appeared from between the columns of the portico, he was greeted with great shouts and applause. Following Chief Justice John Marshall's swearing in of Jackson and his 10-minute softly spoken speech (which few would have heard), there came a cannon salute and the people charged forward to shake the new president's hand. With difficulty, he was escorted to the White House where an informal reception for the people had been planned.[8] The crowd followed, and the events that ensued topped anything the Washington Central Committee could have imagined. One guest noted that so many people came that "The President, after having been literally nearly pressed to death and almost suffocated and torn to pieces by the people in their eagerness to shake hands with Old Hickory, had retreated . . . to his lodgings at Gadsby's. . . . punch and other articles had been carried out in tubs and buckets, but had it been in hogsheads, it would have been insufficient."[9] Confusion was such that ladies fainted and fistfights broke out, and "those who got in could not get out by the door again but had to scramble out the windows."[10]

## The Rules for Voting Begin to Change

After Jackson took office, there was a general awakening of civic consciousness and a continued breakdown in the property requirement for suffrage. The government was coming to be viewed as a "vast and mighty engine" belonging to the people, and everyone wanted to participate. Jackson had proven that a common man could become president, and it was becoming harder and harder to tolerate suffrage restriction. White manhood suffrage was the ideal, and the men of the West viewed with disdain those in the East who favored restrictions.

Virginia was one state that held on to a property requirement, but residents soon began to see its negative effect on the state's development. Because landholders held almost all legislative and official positions, small landholders and worthy men who held no property avoided settling in Virginia. Despite Virginia's need for pioneers to develop the land to help keep pace with other states, the property requirement remained, and new settlers moved to more hospitable states like Illinois, Indiana and Wisconsin. At the 1829 state constitutional convention, the delegates still didn't seem to understand that for the sake of state development they needed to rethink their position, and the property requirement was defended by such noteworthy men as James Madison, James Monroe, John Marshall and Edmund Randolph. Instead of questioning the wisdom of the restriction, the convention focused—not on whether there should be a suffrage requirement—but on how to establish what the requirement would be. The state had expanded, and sectional differences arose in land worth and holdings. The westerner's land was less valuable, but he tended to own more of it; the easterner could own a small amount of land, and yet possess an estate of considerable value. With the backdrop of these differences, a discussion continued about whether to require a certain size of landholding (favoring westerners who could own more for less) or whether to require a certain value (favoring easterners whose land was worth more).

The result was a requirement stipulating that to vote, a man must possess an estate or freehold worth $25 or be in occupation of a house worth $20 rent yearly, or be the father of a family and pay taxes.

A delegate complained:

"I have seen respectable young men of the country, the mechanic, the merchant, the farmer of mature age, with intelligence superior to that of one-half the freeholders, and glowing with a patriotism that would make them laugh at death in defense of their country; I have seen such commanded to stand back from the polls, to give way to the owner of a petty freehold."[11]

Those who were disfranchised in Virginia were crimedoers, the insane, paupers, soldiers and sailors. Blacks were not specifically barred from voting at the time, because it was accepted that they would never even try to vote in the Old Dominion.

In Rhode Island, the property requirement became an increasing source of discontent as political interest revived during the campaign of 1828. A major rally was held in Pawtucket, a densely populated mill village, on March 14, 1829. Three hundred demonstrators met "to propose and adopt a memorial to the General Assembly" for the extension of suffrage. They hoped other towns would hold similar meetings and that a suffrage convention would meet in Newport to coincide with the next June session of the legislature. As taxpayers, they questioned why the vote was denied to those taxed to support the government.[12] But Rhode Islanders were to battle long and hard to open up the vote. In 1829, they had only just begun a fight that would not end until the 1840s. (North Carolina had the distinction of being the last state in the Union to abandon the property test, which it finally did in 1856.[13])

During the 1830s six states—all northern—permitted blacks to vote: Maine, Massachusetts, New Hampshire New York, Rhode Island and Vermont.[14] Many states had never addressed the issue one way or the other but found that as the slavery issue heated up and the number of free blacks increased, it was a topic that they needed to address, although there is little indication that blacks were ever numerous enough at the polls to be particularly noticeable.

In Tennessee, those in favor of letting blacks vote argued that free blacks did military service and paid taxes. As a result, it was decided to exempt blacks from military service and taxes in order that there be no *quid pro quo*. Those against letting blacks vote argued successfully that because people of color weren't represented at the constitutional convention, they shouldn't participate now. For some reason, this helped make disfranchisement more palatable.

In North Carolina, state constitutional convention delegates who wanted to exclude blacks and mulattoes argued that "they were socially inferior," and since public sentiment would exclude them from most important social and political activities, it would be foolish to bring equality where it couldn't, in fact, exist.[15] Those in favor suggested that higher requirements for free blacks than for whites might be appropriate; some recommended a $250 property requirement; others felt they should not ever have been convicted of a crime. In the end, it was a 64 to 55 vote to completely exclude the free black man.

In Pennsylvania, arguments about the issue followed similar patterns. Those against allowing blacks to vote suggested that they were discriminated against no more than were minors, women and nontaxpayers. (A point well-made.) Those in favor argued that blacks had no control over their color and it shouldn't be held against them—suffrage qualification should be something that any man could attain. The property requirement, the taxpaying test, long residence, age and literacy, were all qualifications one could attain, while color meant that these men were hopelessly disfranchised. Ultimately, suffrage was denied Pennsylvania blacks in 1837 by a vote of 77 to 45. This was the last change nationwide until 29 years later when the 14th Amendment was passed.[16] Though blacks had to wait until 1869 and the passage of the 15th Amendment to be given the legal right to vote, the prior amendment did provide for black citizenship and equal protection under the law.

## Voting Methods Become More Sophisticated

While voice voting was still used in some communities, the method increasingly being used was a ticket system where the political parties provided their own preprinted tickets. Each party printed its ticket on a separate color so that it was easy for anyone to distinguish one party from another. Political workers stood at the polls with boxes of tickets (this was known as "boxing" a district), and they provided them for voters who had not yet picked up a ticket. Tickets were also available at the newspaper offices (since the press was partisan, each paper provided only its own party's ticket). Occasionally, tickets were distributed with the purchase of newspapers. If a person did not wish to vote a straight party ticket, he could "scratch" a name (cross out the name of the person for whom he did not want to vote and usually, though not always, he was permitted to write in the name of the person for whom he did wish to vote). Parties sometimes provided "pasters"— strips of paper with a candidate's name that could be used to vote in favor of a particular candidate. Some men wrote the entire ticket with a pen and would vote half a sheet of paper.

Voting by paper ballot had practical advantages. In Indiana, one particularly impatient voter became known for his unusual way of getting around the crowd at the polls on election day: He traditionally "Split a long stick, inserted the ballot in the split, and hoisted it in the window over the heads of the bystanders . . ."[17]

## Growth of a Convention System

By the early 1800s—to replace the haphazard methods of self-nomination used in the South and the nomination by the candidates' friends in the North—the convention method was being used for choosing candidates for local offices. Small states like Delaware and New Jersey had also used conventions for state offices. (That residents of these geographically small states could more easily travel to a central spot for a gathering undoubtedly made the difference.)

Accounts of politics in Alabama provide background as to how the convention system began. In that state in the 1830s and 1840s, it was the custom to put a notice in the local party press stating the time and place at which the meeting was to be held, and anyone who then showed up was considered a delegate.[18]

At the convention, sometimes candidates had been agreed upon in advance, and their names were simply presented to the body for formal approval. Other times, the convention empowered the chairman to select the nominees. But most frequently a nominating committee was appointed; it then withdrew from the meeting and returned later with the slate that would be accepted by acclamation.

Conventions were particularly important for their role as barometers of the times. Customarily, the conventions considered national and state issues that were important at the time. After delegates argued out issues on which they disagreed, they concluded by passing a resolution on an issue. These debates were the modern equivalent of the public opinion poll, and politicians followed them closely, adjusting their actions accordingly.

Large delegations were more common than not, and in Alabama nine men were to split Coosa county's one vote at the Democratic convention of 1840; 12 were chosen from Tallapoosa, which had one vote; 15 were to help cast Bibb County's two votes, and 23 men where chosen to represent Autauga's three votes. Probably these large delegations were chosen to address the possibility of absenteeism because of difficult travel, but they also offered the opportunity to placate the numerous factions found within the counties.[19]

## 1832 and the Advent of National Nominating Conventions

The election of 1832 was particularly significant because it was the first election where national nominating conventions had decided on the choice of candidates. The Anti-Masonic Party, a third party that grew out of bitter opposition to the secrecy of fraternal orders, was the first to use the national convention system when it met in September of 1831, but that meeting was followed shortly by the National Republicans, who met in December with 156 delegates from 17 states; and finally, the Democratic–Republicans met in May of 1832 with 334 delegates representing every state except Missouri. All three nominating conventions were held in Baltimore. With the downfall of the Congressional caucus system, this nominating method grew up to take its place.

Delegates were chosen in a variety of ways—by state convention, district convention, local meeting or informal caucus. If a state had no representatives, occasionally a visitor was asked to vote.

Distance and lack of interest kept some states from sending delegations early on. And though some of the delegations sent were very large (Maryland sent 181 delegates to a Democratic convention in May of 1835), states were generally limited to the voting strength of their electoral vote.

Conventions, which necessitated the development of committees to run the conventions, were the beginning of party organizations and created a place for party professionals seeking power.

As for the results of the conventions that year, Jackson's Democratic–Republicans (soon to be known simply as the Democratic Party) met in May of 1832, but Jackson had already been nominated by various state legislatures and conventions, so the national convention's main purpose was to select a vice president. Jackson's choice, Martin Van Buren, was nominated on the first ballot. Since "Little Van" was not overwhelmingly popular, this was indicative of very strong support of Jackson.

The Anti-Masonic Party nominated William Wirt, and the old Adams–Clay party took on the name National Republicans and made Henry Clay its nominee with John Sergeant of Pennsylvania as his running mate.

Jackson's powerful personality and strong measures brought out emotions both for and against him. Manufacturers disliked his tariff policy (the 1828 policy known as the "tariff of abominations"); and when South Carolina voted to nullify the Tariff of 1828, Jackson's threats to use force were politically risky, but important in building the Union.

His stands made him unpopular with big business, which used coercion to harm Jackson. Manufacturers threatened workers with loss of their jobs if Jackson were elected. A Cincinnati packer told farmers he would pay $2.50 a hundred for pork if Clay were elected, but only $1.50 if Jackson were elected.[20]

The populace was still very much involved in the election of 1832, and there were enormous processions with people on horseback waving flags, branches and banners. In some cases, men left home, as if leaving for war, and rode from one political meeting to another for weeks at a time. Large gatherings were held in groves where speakers addressed the people and denounced "the Monster" and the "Corporation" and Jacksonians called upon Americans to "stand by their Hero."[21]

As people began taking great pleasure in politics, they found many ways to express preference. In the register of the Union Inn, near Indianapolis, guests entered not only their names, but the names of presidential candidates whom they supported—or did not support. Some entries had only the names, such as "Harrison" or "Van Buren" on the same line as the guest's name. Others had humorous remarks such as "anti-Van" or "anything but Van Buren," etc. Supportive remarks such as "William H. Harrison for ever," were included as well.[22]

Jackson won the 1832 election by a smaller margin in popular votes than previously, but this time he had more electoral votes; he had 687,502 to Clay's 530,189. In the electoral voting, he garnered 219 to Clay's 49. South Carolina cast all her eleven votes for her favorite son, John C. Calhoun.

## Election Predictions of the Day

Today many criticize the electronic media for making election predictions as polls in the East close and final results begin to take shape. Many feel that westerners should have the opportunity to vote without being influenced by early predictions. The situation wasn't so different 150 years ago. Until 1844, election day was held at various times in the various states (still according to the timetable set by the first United States Congress), and the Newport, Rhode Island *Mercury* provides a good illustration of what Rhode Islanders knew before voting.

In 1832, Rhode Island held the election for presidential electors on Wednesday, November 21, and so the newspaper of Saturday morning, November 17 ran the slate of the electors for the National Republican, the Administration, and the Anti- Masonic tickets. Yet in that same paper, only an inch and a half away, there is an article entitled "Election of President," and *The Mercury* includes return news from many of the states including New Hampshire, Maine, Massachusetts, Connecticut, New York, Pennsylvania, New Jersey, Ohio and Virginia and notes: "From the returns which we give below, it will be seen, that Gen. Jackson will obtain an immense majority of the Electoral Votes."

## 1836: The Election of Jackson's Man, "Little Van"

Ironically, the 1836 election of Martin Van Buren, who was also referred to as the "Red Fox of Kinderhook" (his hometown), "Little Van" and the "Little Magician," had less to do with his ability to campaign for himself, and more to do with the power of the political structure he had built for Andrew Jackson under whom he had served as secretary of state, vice president and all-around advisor.

Some major issues that would figure prominently in elections to come were beginning to brew at about this time. Abolition—a movement among northerners who felt slavery should be abolished—was becoming a major political issue and the intense wish of southerners to maintain the status quo caused a great deal of friction. Threatened slave revolts in the early 1830s and the "Murrell Conspiracy," an insurrection planned in Mississippi, threw all the South into a panic, and during the winter of 1835–36 various southern legislatures passed resolutions defending slavery and denouncing the abolitionists. In December 1835, slavery became a Congressional issue when the abolitionists petitioned Congress demanding the abolition of slavery in the District of Columbia. In his annual message, Jackson asked for legislation to ban incendiary literature from the mails, and from then on the issue of slavery in various guises dominated national politics.[23]

Politically, the Jacksonian period had had such an effect on American politics and elicited such strong emotions from the people that the only possible way to defeat the Jackson machine was to build a party based on anti-Jackson sentiment. Jackson's tyrannical actions against the Bank of the United States had led to his detractors referring to him as "King Andrew." Since it was the Whig party that had opposed royal tyranny in England, a new party arose calling themselves Whigs. Made up of a group of National–Republicans, Anti-Masons, bank Democrats (former members of Jackson's party who favored the national bank system he so strongly opposed) and states' rights men.

As it happened, the Whigs were not well enough organized by 1836 to settle on just one candidate, so they opted for regional candidates. There was no national convention, and each area candidate was nominated either by state legislatures or popular conventions. Massachusetts nominated Senator Daniel Webster, who was expected to take the New England votes; Tennessee Senator Hugh L. White was expected to carry the South, and Ohio's William Henry Harrison was to appeal to the West. They decided that by running "favorite sons" they might split up enough of the votes to throw the election into the House where Harrison or White might win.

Although the strategy was good enough to throw fear into the Democrats, it ultimately failed. Jackson's strength behind Van Buren was too powerful, and the final tally was 170 electoral votes for Van Buren; Harrison, 73; White, 26; and Webster, 14. In the popular vote it ran 764,176 for Van Buren; 550,816 for Harrison; 146,107 for White; and 41,201 for Daniel Webster.

What the Whigs had discovered with their "favorite son" campaign was a candidate worth grooming for another race. General William Henry Harrison had made a good showing, and he looked like a strong contender for the following election.

## Reporting 1836-Style

Newspapers, with their strong political loyalties, were a vital factor in campaigns. Aside from their immediate value in publicizing rallies, speeches, conventions and the like, they played an invaluable role in keeping up the spirit of the campaign throughout the election. The reports on the 1836 election offered up by a St. Louis paper provide a good example.

The pro-Harrison *Republican*, (the first news page—which was page two, page one traditionally featured advertising—carried a banner headline promoting Harrison for president and Tyler for vice president) offered close coverage of the election of 1836. Sending people out to the polls for what would be a two-day election, it reported:

> This day is the anniversary of the battle of Tippecanoe. Our friends should bear it in mind. The veteran Harrison never lost a battle—if his friends charge manfully at the polls, a victory will still perch on his banner. "At the tap of the drum," let us all be ready for the onset.[24]

On the second day of the election, *The Republican* strongly urged voters (specifically those for Harrison) to make their way to the polls, and went on to describe the casting of the first vote for Harrison:

> We were present, yesterday, at the opening of the polls and it gives us great pleasure to state that the first vote cast, was given to GEN. HARRISON—the Whig candidate—by an aged and venerable townsman—one of the original French settlers of St. Louis. This venerable man had known Gen. Harrison, as the Governor of the North Western Territory, and subsequently as the Commander of our army and an able representative of the West in Congress. The tribute of such a man is above all price, and we hope his example will be imitated.[25]

On Wednesday, November 9, the newspaper was sorely disappointed in the fact that its party's—the Whigs—victory had been so small. After reporting the results, the newspaper rebuked the readership: "The vote is much larger than we anticipated. The two days have passed off very quietly. We give our opponents much credit for their zeal in inducing people to vote with them. Had our friends done as much, we could have added several hundred to our majority."[26]

Unlike today when voting returns are known almost instantly, the people of St. Louis had to wait a long time for national results since the newspaper received the returns by mail. Initial frustration began on Thursday, November 10 when *The Republican* reported: "We had an entire failure of the Eastern mail yesterday."[27]

By Saturday, November 12, the editors were getting edgy. In a story, still placed under a banner reading FOR PRESIDENT, WILLIAM HENRY HARRISON, OF OHIO, FOR VICE PRESIDENT, JOHN TYLER OF VIRGINIA, ran this story: "THE MAILS—The incessant rains for the few past days, have rendered the roads almost impassable. Nothing was received from the East, yesterday, beyond Belleville. The mails from Illinois and the different parts of this State likewise failed."[28]

Of course, eventually the national results came in, but waiting was obviously trying.


## Abuses Lead to Election Reform

Many instances of abuse of the election system occurred during the 1830s, but one incident in 1838 is particularly worth noting. While it took place during a state election in Millville, New Jersey, the contest had national repercussions. At the close of the election, the judge of elections and two inspectors, who were Democrats, reported that the Democrats had a better than two-to-one majority. Historian Richard McCormick, in *The History of Voting in New Jersey* continues the account:

> The town clerk, a Whig, failed to affix his seal to this return, whether from design or neglect can only be surmised. This informal document, addressed to the county clerk, was then entrusted for delivery to a young man who at midnight gave it to another person at a public inn, who in turn passed it along to the county clerk's son, in whose hat the clerk accidentally found it on the following morning![29]

At the time when all township returns were due, the county clerk, a Whig, had only this informal return, and so he chose to disregard it. Totaling the votes from all the reporting townships but Millville gave the Whigs a slight majority. Later that evening, he received Millville's official return, but did not redo his figures.

The Assembly, with a Whig majority, agreed to seat the Whig claimants, on the basis of the partial return made by the Whig county clerk. The Democrats, of course, contested, and it was referred to the Committee on Election, which was dominated by Whigs.

Once an investigation was opened, it was also revealed that between 30 and 40 acknowledged foreigners had voted in Millville, a practice that had been followed for several years. Eighteen Germans, who worked in a nearby factory and spoke no English, were herded to the polls by Democratic leaders, given white Democratic tickets (Whig tickets were yellow and white) and allowed to vote. Several Irish laborers were similarly enfranchised. Their votes went unchallenged by both parties.[30]

Ultimately the committee ruled that the clerk's functions were not purely ministerial, but that he had an obligation to determine whether or not certain votes were legal. The Whig-dominated committee eventually determined that instead of a Whig slate being elected, actually two Democrats and one Whig had been legally elected.[31]

This affair was followed almost immediately by the famous "Broad Seal War," which took place in the New Jersey congressional election of 1838. Fraud on the part of the Whig governor and his council, caused Democratic votes from two townships to be uncounted, and the final count favored the Whigs. The governor provided the respective six Whig congressmen-elect with commissions to which he affixed the state's "Broad Seal," but when they arrived in Washington, the House of Representatives refused to seat the Whig claimants. After finding signs of impropriety, the Congressional Committee on Elections insisted upon including the votes from the other two townships, resulting in the election of five Democrats and one Whig. Largely because of the national disgrace at having its representatives rejected by Congress, New Jersey set about developing methods of reform that went into effect in 1839. Reforms elsewhere in the nation followed.

The Jacksonian era ushered in a new kind of politics. The dropping of the property ownership requirement in many states increased interest in elections and got more people to the polls than ever before. With the heightening of political organization and the coming of national parties and major nominating conventions replacing caucuses, there were more and more events in which to participate, and Americans happily complied. Election day was coming of age.

# A Holiday Is Born _____ 8

The increases in public participation during the election days of the 1830s were mere warm-ups for what was to come. By 1840, an ever-greater number of people were eligible to vote, and even those who weren't, including women, were politically active anyway. Much of this spirit was engendered by Jackson's "people's government"; not surprisingly, election day and the events surrounding it also belonged to the common people more than ever before, and included rallies, parades, stump speaking, barbecues, songfests, fist fights and lots of liquor.

As politics and elections continued to expand in scope and significance, opportunities for fraud increased. While underhanded methods of balloting or counting the votes had been around since colonial times and before, the broadening of the franchise, the increasing influence of the elections and the growth of political parties opened the door for ingenious ways to beat the system.

Election day did not become an oficial national holiday with a uniform date until a Congressional Act in 1845, so 1848 was the first presidential election where all Americans voted on the same day. But if one wants to talk of a "holiday" in the popular sense, then surely, Election Day 1840 ushered in a new era.

## 1840: The Log Cabin and Hard Cider Campaign

The contest in 1840 featured incumbent Democrat Martin Van Buren, who had failed to win much respect while in office. (His administration had been plagued by the Panic of '37 and the resulting economic depression.) To challenge him, the Whigs—passing over two brilliant and well-respected candidates, Henry Clay and Daniel Webster—turned to the candidate who had shown the most promise in 1836, military hero General William Henry Harrison. John Tyler of Virginia was chosen as his running mate. A third party entry in the field at this time was the Liberty Party, which was the first antislavery ticket. James G. Birney of Kentucky was the candidate.

The Whigs had learned a few tricks from the Jacksonians and intended to portray Harrison as a military hero and a man of the people. (This was an interesting image for the well-born Harrison whose military achievements had been slight and whose father had been among the signers of the Declaration of Independence.) Ironically, the famous symbols for which Harrison was known then and remembered now were actually inspired by the opposition. In a Jacksonian newspaper, alluding to Harrison's lack of intellectual depth, it was suggested that "upon condition of his receiving a pension of $2,000 and a barrel of cider, General Harrison would no doubt consent to withdraw his pretensions [of running for president], and spend his days in a log cabin on the banks of the Ohio."[1] Instead of taking it as an insult, the Whigs took the image and ran with it. They affixed the log cabin image to floats, handkerchiefs, flags, hats and campaign literature. A network of log cabin headquarters were created across the states with 17 Hard Cider Tippecanoe Clubs in New York City alone. Log cabin songbooks and log cabin cider were dispensed freely.[2] Harrison's military status was equally embellished. As governor of the Indiana Territory, the general had been working to solve the "Indian problem," and finally used force in 1811 in an uneventful battle at Tippecanoe. However, 29 years later, the telling of the events at Tippecanoe bathed Harrison in glory.

The participation of the people was overwhelming. At Whig rallies, crowds sometimes ranged from 1,000 to 100,000—sometimes the numbers were so vast they were assessed in acreage. One-mile parades soon became 10-mile parades, and rallies lasted three to five hours.[3]

A look at the festivities in a few states provides a wonderful vision of the pageantry and celebration involved. In Indiana, the Whigs opened their 1840 campaign on May 29 with a mass meeting at Battleground, in the northwestern part of the state, attracting delegations from nearby Ohio, Illinois, Michigan, Kentucky and Tennessee. Michigan City's delegation led their procession with a full-rigged ship, *The Constitution*, drawn by six white horses. On the masthead flew a pennant for Harrison and Tyler. In Indianapolis groups from the southern part of the state met up and departed for the meeting in squadrons of 200. Those on horseback led the column, followed by the carriages and the men on foot. Three days of rain slowed their progress, and those who walked slogged barefoot through the black mud, carrying their shoes. The column was said to extend along the road 25 miles. The men slept by the wayside in barns, corn cribs or around hay and straw stacks. Once gathered at the Battleground, the crowd was estimated at 40,000. Three tables, each 100 yards long, were filled again and again for the hungry multitude.[4]

Tennessee was also the site of great festivities. In Nashville, the Democrats kicked off a campaign rally with the firing of cannons and a parade of citizens that lasted 12 hours during which 15 speeches were made and two preambles and 24 resolutions adopted.

The Whigs countered in May with a gigantic festival. At 8:00 A.M. the steamer *Gallatin* pulled into Clarksville laden with 250 delegates. A mile-long procession soon formed. At the head were the speakers and distinguished guests. Bands, military companies and cavalry were interspersed among the marching county delegations, each of which carried a banner or escorted a float.[5]

One of the floats was described by the Nashville *Whig* as a log cabin drawn by four horses. The cabin had several coonskins nailed about the door, and a live coon playing upon the bark roof. Inside was a barrel of "hard cider."[6] Flags featuring a bust of Washington, the American Eagle and pro-Harrison slogans flew from the cabin, and the horses sported decorative banners. The *Whig* continued: "The drummer at the head of the delegation was taken prisoner at the Battle of the Thames by General Harrison. He says that 'General Harrison saved him from one Monarchy and is about to save him from another.'"[7]

In Arkansas, both parties held rallies throughout the state. The Whigs used canoes, log cabins, cider barrels, live raccoons and humorous songs to stir enthusiasm. One Whig parade in Little Rock turned out more than 4,000 marchers.[8]

One Democrat described a Whig meeting in Dover, Delaware as a "desperate effort to humbug the people of Kent with music, coonskins and hard cider." The Democrats also accused the Whigs of "infamous acts at their *bachanalian* [sic] clubs, besides drinking hard cider and singing Tippecanoe songs." A statewide invitation to all voters to attend a roast beef dinner on election day was also part of the Whig campaign of that year.[9]

Singing campaign songs became a popular pastime, and budding lyricists throughout the nation worked on ditties they hoped would catch on.

Another local campaign tool that gained national importance was what came to be known as the Whig Ball. Built by ardent Whig William Johnson of Dresden, Ohio, in honor of a Thomas Ewing, who was campaigning for the Senate, the ball was 13 feet in diameter (for the original 13 states) and was made of poplar board bent into shape and covered with muslin. On the muslin were painted the various states, rivers, mountains and Whig political slogans.

The ball was so popular that it was displayed throughout Ohio and then went on a tour of other cities, stopping in Boston, New York, Philadelphia and Washington. Everywhere it drew huge crowds, and Whigs made copies of their own out of paper, leather or tin and rolled them through the streets.

To counter Whig momentum, Democrats came up with various nicknames for Harrison ranging from "Granny Harrison, the Petticoat General" (Harrison was 67 when nominated) to "General Mum."

As for the outcome, the people had their own way of prophesying it. Gauging whether or not the White House was laying in stores for another term was one form of political prognostication. Said a St. Louis newspaper: "A correspondent of the *Boston Atlas* says: 'The ladies of Washington consider the question of the Presidency settled, for they say Mr. Van Buren has given directions to his housekeeper to lay in no pickels [sic] for the next session, which is thought to be a most significant symptom of an intention to remove from that city."[10]

For election day, the partisan press was the first to strongly encourage people to vote. In the *Daily Missouri Republican*, a St. Louis Whig newspaper, for Monday,

*The original Whig Ball was 13 feet in diameter (for the original 13 states) and was made of poplar board covered by muslin. The states and various rivers and mountain ranges as well as political slogans were written on the covering. Whether the ball depicted was the original or one of the copies it inspired is not clear. The original Ball was preserved until 1844 when it was awarded to the convention delegation with the most visitors at the Baltimore convention. Delaware was the victor. (Courtesy Library of Congress)*

November 2, 1840, there was a banner for Harrison and Tyler, and numerous calls to vote: "DO YOUR DUTY. Will the merchants remain in their stores, the mechanics in their workshops, the lawyers, and the doctors at their professions and the laborers at their various duties TO-DAY and TO-MORROW, and let the election go by default? . . . It will be seen to-day how sincere many men are in their outcry against the misrule of the past administration by the effort they make and the time they give to reform it."

Store owners were encouraged to close their shops for the day and "give the day to the cause of the country."

No political party wanted their voters to have difficulty getting to the polls, and so they went to extraordinary ends to help out. In the *Daily Missouri Republican*, just under the banner displaying whom the newspaper supported for office (Harrison and Tyler), in larger than average type with a steamboat pictured above, it said: "A steamboat will leave the wharf at 9 o'clock this morning [for Carondelet], and will convey any Whig, free of charge. The boat may be known by the fact that it will have a Log Cabin on the bow. As it will be impossible to poll all the votes in the city today, it would be well for all who can to avail themselves of this opportunity."

Just below an announcement of a Whig rally, under a TO THE POLLS headline, ran the following: "As it is now evident that all the votes in the City cannot be polled to-day, every one who can should go to other precincts. Central and Carondelet are near enough for those who have the means to go to them.

"We would remind our friends that any who vote out of the City, will not thereby lose the opportunity to vote for township officers, and when they return, if the polls are not crowded, they can still vote and should do so."[11]

A particularly interesting aspect of the above announcements is that the system advocated could certainly have encouraged fraud. If voters travel to Carondelet on the first election day to cast votes in the national election and then returned to their own polls to vote on local matters on the second day, surely it would have been very hard for some voters to resist voting for the national ticket twice. Registration systems, when they existed, were inadequate, and many voters certainly must have figured, "What's the harm?"

Voter turnout in 1840 superseded all other national elections. Population growth and the lessening of suffrage restrictions combined with the irresistible excitement of the campaign led to more men than ever going to the polls. In 1824, 356,000 people voted; 1836—1,500,000; 1840—2,400,000—seven times as many as 16 years earlier.

*The Delaware Gazette* wrote: "It is very possible that many persons have voted at the late election who are not in the habit of so doing; we have heard of a few instances in which one or two individuals voted, who have not exercised this privilege for 14 years."[12] No doubt— politics had become an important part of people's lives.

Harrison, who was the first presidential candidate to take to the stump for himself, won easily. Though in the popular vote he polled only 145,000 more than Van Buren, his electoral margin was 234 to 60. And while the Liberty Party attracted only a little more than 7,000 votes, it was the forerunner of a very important movement and would eventually lead to the creation of the Republican Party in the 1850s.

As for the Democrats, they were furious that they had been "sung" out of office, and the Jacksonian New York *Evening Post* wrote: "We could meet the Whigs on the field of argument and beat them without effort. But when they lay down the weapons of argument and attack us with musical notes, what can we do?"[13]

Despite the pleasure the people had derived from the election of William Henry Harrison, his presidency was ill- fated. He took office on March 4, and on March 27 he came down with pneumonia; on April 4 he died, leaving John Tyler to assume the reins of leadership.

## The 1840s and '50s: Expanding Upon the Past

The 1840s and 1850s brought about two campaign practices that were especially important. The first was stump speaking (referring to the old tradition of candidates using a tree stump as a handy place to stand to address a rural audience). The party would send out stump speakers to spread the word in as many locations as possible. Preceded by a local speaker who would talk for about an hour, the stump speaker would then talk for approximately two hours and then set off for the next town. (At major gatherings, stump speakers would sometimes stay and make several speeches in different locations around the area.) Traveling was by horseback, and, from all accounts, schedules were arduous. In the 1840s the death of an otherwise healthy Indiana gubernatorial candidate was blamed on the taxing schedule he followed stump speaking.

When future president James K. Polk ran for governor of Tennessee in 1839, he and his opponent traveled the state together, speaking to joint meetings. In another election, one of Polk's competitors had a way with humor, and stump speaking with "Lean Jimmy" Jones, a 6'2" one hundred and twenty-five-pounder took on a burlesque quality as "Lean Jimmy" regaled crowds for three to four hours with mimicry, joke-telling, wisecracks and taunts.[14]

A letter in the library of the Indiana Historical Society from Joseph Masterson to his grandmother and aunt mentions attendance at a Democratic political rally where there was stump speaking. He noted that while the Democrats had approximately 24,000 people in attendance, the Whigs' meeting (he referred to it as a "journey-cake log-cabin fandango,") in the area was attended by no more than 50.[15]

Barbecues had become a much-enjoyed part of campaigning by the 1840s and '50s. Generally several speakers were assigned by a given party's state committee to each barbecue. Two to 10 oxen would be barbecued for the event (in the South, hundreds of slaves would help prepare a table for the thousands of participants). The festivities generally lasted two days, during which two to five speakers, stationed on convenient stumps in the grove, would speak to the multitude. In an account of politics in Indiana, it is noted: "It was not uncommon for a speaker to talk from one stump two hours then go to another stump and speak two hours, making as many as four such speeches in the course of the day at the same meeting. The evidence is unmistakable that the people in general came as much to hear the great speakers as to eat the roasted beef."[16] While music was very much a part of these events, many a person listened intently to the speakers, "gnawing meantime at his beef and bread and washing it down with good cider or corn whisky."[17]

In locations no longer voting orally, ballots, printed up by each party with the names of that party's candidates, were now frequently used. However, not all parts of the country used a written ballot. For example, until 1874, most voters in Arkansas did not have to register (or pay any sort of poll tax), and they would simply enter the polling place and tell the clerks how they wished to vote. The clerk would then record the vote in a public poll book. In 1846, the [Arkansas] General Assembly provided for a secret ballot, but returned to the voice method in 1850 because so many voters could not read and write. Ballot voting revived again in 1854 to be followed in 1864 by a state constitution that returned to voice voting. Not until the adoption of the state constitution of 1874 did the use of ballots in Arkansas come to stay.[18]

The 1840s were also a time when states began to examine the advantages and disadvantages of the multiple-day election system. Many felt that in large townships it helped reduce congestion at the polls, but when it was discussed in New Jersey, many advocated a single day as a way to help reduce expenses and eliminate the opportunity for fraud. "The night of the first day of elections is always a scene of much evil," declared one delegate. "Persons take advantage of that night to make their calculations as to the prospects of their party and what influence they can bring to bear for their own benefit."[19] But change comes hard, and states that had converted to the one-day election method were sometimes criticized for not giving the people ample time to vote: ". . . The election in Illinois only continues *one* day.—Those who neglected to go yesterday may save themselves the labor of going today," sarcastically remarked the *Daily Missouri Republican* on November 3, 1840.

Congestion and disorderliness at the polls were very real problems. Arrests for preventing citizens from voting were frequent. And while the young at heart would go to the voting place as part of the day's celebration, it was not viewed as a pleasurable activity by the old or infirm. Writes one victim of election day crowding in St. Louis in 1840 to the newspaper editor:

> I heartily respond as a freeman and voter, to your call to the polls on Monday next. But must we approach at the price of loss of *apparel, life or limb*? I am a feeble old man . . . ; Cannot something be done by this enlightened city to make the passage to the polls *safe*, and free from *terror*? Cannot a fence, for instance, be erected so as to admit voters at one door and give egress at an opposite one—with protection afforded by a strong police?
>
> At the last election I tried in vain to approach the Hayscales, Fourth ward—I saw the fate of many who persevered—and hearing that the Grove was not crowded, I hastened there—where, however, I had to wait, pushing and striving for two hours, and at last was admited [sic] by the *humanity* of some bystanders, who said "*Let the old man vote, he has been long waiting.*"[20]

In larger cities congestion at the polls led to the expansion of the number of places where people could vote. Some cities were divided into wards or districts with a polling place for each section.

Though efforts were being made to run more orderly, businesslike elections, slip-ups did occur. Less populated areas were most likely to be affected. In Wilmington, Delaware in 1842 the local court had neglected to appoint election inspectors for a western district, so, rather than deny the people the opportunity to vote, a "standing out" was called for instead. (A "standing out" would have referred to voting as they sometimes did in colonial times with those in favor of one candidate standing to one side, and those in favor of the other candidate standing to the other.) Gathering in front of City Hall, both parties brought in as many people as they could to be counted. The Democrats won by 50 votes, but there was extreme friction over the local election.[21]

## Getting Election Results

Waiting for the national returns was not easy, at least for the editorial staff of the newspaper. Relying on slow methods of transportation, the editors made frequent appeals for people to bring in any news they should receive via personal correspondence: "We ask this favor not merely on our own account, but as a favor to the public generally. Every hour of the day there are persons in the Reading Room seeking intelligence. All returns sent to us will be spread on the Bulletin Board."[22]

Election gossip from stagecoach travelers and from mail boat workers was also greatly appreciated. This word appeared in the anti-Whig *Louisville Daily Journal* on November 8 following the election of 1844 (the Whig candidate that year was Henry Clay; James K. Polk ran on the Democratic ticket): "The clerk on the mail-boat informs us, that, just as he was leaving Cincinnati, he saw the clerk of the *Clipper*, direct from Pittsburg [sic], who told him that the very latest news from Pennsylvania was not as bad as that previously received, yet still we have little or no hope for the State."

## Election Day Fraud and Deceit

No longer cozy small-town affairs, elections were now typically a mass of people all trying to participate. With the increase in numbers, the opportunities for fraud multiplied, and creative minds were at work.

Bogus tickets were one common form of fraud. Either party would create a ticket featuring a slate of candidates from their own party, but the ticket would look like that of the opposition. If the Whig ticket were blue in a certain locale, then Democrats might issue blue tickets with Democratic names printed on it. The unwary or illiterate voter might unknowingly accept the proffered blue ticket, little realizing that in dropping it in the ballot box, he was, in fact, voting against his candidates.

Publicizing the wrong date of election was another tactic parties would use to confuse the electorate. The Democrats might ride through Whig territory in any given state and tell potential Whig voters to come to vote on what would end up being the wrong day. Since newspapers were sometimes not available in rural areas, and then published only weekly, this was a ruse that could sometimes work.

In Delaware in the early 1840s, it was the Democrats, as the underdogs, who complained of dishonest elections. In this Wilmington election, officials may have participated in the fraud. The Democratic *Delaware Gazette* accused Whig inspectors of turning away Democratic voters:

From the manner in which they [the Whigs] acted at the election in the city [Wilmington] Tuesday last, one would have supposed that they were as perfectly organized as a band of robbers or pirates as they had certain *signs* by which the Inspector could determine when a voter presented himself at the polls whether he was a democrat or a whig; and if the former he was rejected, and if the latter, his vote was received, and no questions asked.[23]

In places where there was a tax-paying qualification to vote, many kinds of fraud developed. Assessors were accused of giving certain party members lower assessments so that they could afford the tax; members of the opposition were supposedly assessed at a higher rate to make it more difficult for them to qualify for the vote. Delinquent individuals who were supporters of the wrong party were sometimes not informed of their delinquency until too late. Allowing voters to pay—or not pay—their taxes on election day was another way of helping one party qualify more voters.

Ironically, there were even a few reported instances of black landlords and merchants (in states where some blacks were free) of using their position to coerce white voters. In St. Louis some blacks owned homes that they rented to white voters; others were merchants who traded extensively with white dealers:

It is an easy matter for them to say to their tenants, "Mr. Blair and Mr. Brown are our friends—vote this ticket or seek another place of abode." It is no less easy for them to tell the merchant that, unless he votes for certain men, he will lose a large custom; and no one acquainted with human nature will deny that such requests are usually complied with.[24]

Importing people, called "floaters," to vote was another method of fraud. In Delaware, there was a complaint that the Whig hotels were packed with ruffians ready to earn some money by going to the polls the following day. Evidently all social levels were involved—merchants to pipe layers would come in to help out their party in a town. Sometimes the opposition party would pay the expenses of "poll watchers" who were used to help prevent the floaters from voting.[25]

Naturalizing foreigners quickly was another favorite way of finding extra voting bodies. In Philadelphia in 1838, it was found that many of the naturalization papers had been forged in order to help the people register to vote. *The Newark Advertiser* also reported several instances of fraud in its state. After admitting that he had resided out of state during the year, one voter took the oath in New Jersey, voted and then announced his intention to go to New York to vote. Another person was challenged, but even after admitting he didn't live in the township, took the oath and voted. Yet another individual was challenged for nonresidence, and a witness testified that the voter had told him he was going to New York one or two months ago. One of the inspectors read the oath, and explained it. The "possible New Yorker" agreed to take the New Jersey oath, twice drew back but finally kissed the book. His vote was received.[26]

In the 1840s and '50s, New York City Tammany politicians refined the city machine tactics for which New York would become so well known. In 1844, 55,000 votes were cast for Polk and Clay—10,000 more than the total number of qualified voters in the city. These additional voters were produced in several ways. Some were convicts. Prisoners from Blackwell's Island were brought to the city the night before the election. They were lodged and well fed, sent out to vote and then permitted to escape. Some were even entrusted with electioneering in various wards.[27] Repeaters were also used, and election clerks and police looked the other way.

In 1856, when the temper of the times meant that many towns experienced disorder and riot on election day, New York City was no exception. Wrote a reporter for *The Times*: "As Charles Jonas, a Fillmore voter in the employ of Hoppock, Mooney and Company, No. 138 Liberty Street, visited the poll of the Second District, First Ward this morning, he was asked by Wood's men to show his ticket, which he declined. They then forcibly took his ticket from him, tore it up and tendered him a Buchanan and Wood ticket, saying he must vote it or none. He again declined, when he was immediately felled by a blow, was beaten, and dragged out."[28]

Jones returned later with his employer who promised to help him vote his own preference, but the two fared no better: "Immediately after Jonas had cast his vote, he was hit a blow in the mouth. Mr. Mooney ordered a policeman standing by to arrest the offender; the policeman wished to know of Mr. Mooney if he (Mr. Mooney) would appear against him. Mr. Mooney said he would. The policeman then disappeared and Mr. Mooney was attacked by a gang of ruffians, knocked down, kicked in the face, head, sides, etc."[29]

In reaction to the many forms of election abuse, legislatures nationwide began to respond. In New Jersey, Governor William Pennington called the improprieties a direct threat to the system. "Every guard in your power should be thrown around this most sacred right of freemen [the vote]."[30] His legislature responded by passing a comprehensive statute regulating elections. It provided that taxes must be paid *prior* to the first day of the election to put a stop to enrolling voters on the day of election, and, if challenged, aliens had to produce naturalization papers. (Formerly, the burden of proof had been on the challenger.) In other locations, heavy fines were levied for false swearing, bribery, intimidation, multiple voting and similar offenses. Penalties were also established for misdeeds by election officials. Inspectors were to be fined for accepting fraudulent votes. If a justice of the peace failed to keep order at a polling place, he was to be fined. The enforcement of these laws in the various states waxed and waned depending on local politics, and though Americans were far from having corruption-free elections, an awareness of the nature of the problem led to attempts to solve it.

## Through a Child's Eyes: Election Day in Newport

In Newport, Rhode Island in the 1840s and '50s, election day was a grand occasion. The day's events were very family-oriented and heavy drinking was rare. In a 1913 reminiscence for the Newport Historical Society, one Miss M. E. Powell recalls the election days of her childhood during midcentury: "... On the morning before Election [a school holiday] no lazy boy snoozed abed; no little girl begged for one more nap. No warhooping [sic], no playing with the kittens—but rush and scramble and with slides and leaps fly down the short flights of the spatterdashed staircase to the rest of the family gathered at a hasty breakfast in a fine old paneled room."[31]

For election day, the household dressed in their best, including a "best bandanna" worn by the cook. No matter what the temperature, everyone wore their summer finery. The ladies came out in full attire with fans, pagoda parasols, and veils, while the men sported white duck or nankin trousers with brimmed straw hats. Breakfast was barely touched in order that the children could go out to watch the visitors (including the legislature and governor) arrive—mostly by carriage.

Later, people visited from home to home or walked along the parade route. Black women sat along the parade selling bread, election buns, popcorn balls, candies, peanuts and cocoanuts. Children saved up their spending money to buy special treats on that day. Young ladies, generally dressed in special, showy bonnets from Providence, gathered on the Mall where young people of both sexes perched along the flat-topped whitewashed fence to watch the goings-on. For public amusement, a sideshow, complete with giant and fortuneteller set up their tents nearby.

At last, along came the procession of the governor and the legislature. After watching the procession and, presumably voting (this reminiscence of childhood is understandably lacking in voting details), people retired to drawing rooms to enjoy election cakes and egg nog while awaiting the returns. Generally before the children's bedtime, a gentleman would come out on the balcony of the State House to announce the state victors.

Then everybody huzzared and shouted and backed away from the Mall . . . [T]he cannons roared out the loudest salute ever fired. All the windows rattled awfully though they were open. The smoke was thicker than fog in Quaker Meeting week. The Governor and everybody came down the steps, the procession re-formed, and the crowd began slowly to dwindle, as it vanished from the Parade.[32]

The side shows and booths packed up, the giant came out of his tent, and the wagons set out for the other Island towns. Most teenaged boys, instead of going up to the governor's headquarters on the hill to see the Artillery fire, raced down to the wharf to watch the fights. "The parade was just litter, egg shells and mess from end to end!"[33]

Included with Miss Powell's reminiscences are a sampling of recipes from the day of which this is one:

---

### ELECTION CAKE

*To be baked in big round pans, three or four inches deep, and when cold to be very thinly iced so that the cake shows through.*

*Ten cups of flour, two of sugar, one of home made yeast or two-thirds of a cup of distiller's yeast, omitting a little to use in the morning. Beat the batter well. Let rise over night. Take two cups of sugar, three of butter, two eggs and the rest of the yeast, add to this first batter, beat very hard and let it rise again. When very light add half an ounce of nutmeg and one-fourth ounce of mace, two pounds of raisins, one pound of citron, one teaspoonful of soda, two teaspoonfuls of cream of tartar, one wine glass of brandy. Let the cake rise again in the pans before putting it into the oven. Bake in a moderate oven (and pray reduce the spice.)*[34]

---

Oddly enough, Mrs Powell would seem to have forgotten to include milk in her recipe, and a contemporary recipe suggests a half pint for the same size of cake.

## 1844: James "All of Oregon, All of Texas" Polk

The 1844 presidential campaign revolved around issues. Whether or not there should be a national bank was one hotly contested subject; another was whether or not the U.S. should take over the entire continent. Still to be claimed were the Oregon territory and Texas. Obtaining Oregon could require sensitive negotiations with Great Britain, and taking over Texas might mean war with Mexico. Whether or not such a huge slave territory as Texas should be added to the U.S was also often discussed.

When it came time for nominations, President John Tyler had so alienated the Whig Party he was supposed to represent that Henry Clay became the Whig candidate with the second spot taken by Senator Theodore Frelinghuysen of New Jersey. The Democrats finally settled on the man who would be the first "dark horse" candidate, James K. Polk of Tennessee. George M. Dallas of Pennsylvania became his running mate. (The Democratic convention was the first ever to be reported by telegraph—on the original line connecting Washington and Baltimore.)

Tyler pulled together a party of his own making and ran with a "Tyler and Texas" slogan. However, when the Democrats promised to press for annexation of Texas, he ultimately dropped out and threw his support behind Polk.

Running on an "All of Oregon, all of Texas" slogan, Polk was hounded by Whigs who played up his dark horse status by asking, "Who is James K. Polk?" Clay, a brilliant politician with an active after-hours life, was accused of moral unfitness because of spending his "days at the gaming table and his nights at the brothel."[35]

Though the election was close in popular votes (Polk received 1,338,464 to Clay's 1,300,097), the electoral vote was decisive with 170 for Polk and 105 for Clay. The Liberty Party was growing stronger. With James G. Birney running on an antislavery platform, the party won 62,300 votes, about nine times the number it had received in the previous election.

Tyler took Polk's election to be a mandate for the annexation of Texas, so he pushed through a joint Congressional resolution calling for the admission of Texas as a state. On March 1, with less than three days left in his term, Tyler signed the bill.

Polk intended to be president for one term and took the office with four goals in mind. He wanted to reduce a burdensome tariff, set up an independent treasury, settle the Oregon boundary question and acquire California as a territory of the United States. In four short years, he accomplished all these goals and added a million square miles of territory to the United States in the process.

## Early Elections in Oregon

In Oregon Country, the first election was held as early as 1841 to select members of court and to elect people to draft a code of laws. By 1843 voters in the May 2 election concerning the establishment of a provisional government in Champoeg expressed their preference by standing on one side or another of a line. By 1844, general elections were held regularly and became particularly meaningful in 1846 when it was determined that the region belonged to the U.S. (The campaign slogan of 1844, "Fifty-four Forty or Fight," referred to this dispute.) Statehood came in 1859.

Political information was spread primarily by word of mouth. Farmers read little, and the weekly newspapers available were very partisan, like all newspapers at that time.

As in all communities, the local issues were often the most pressing. In Oregon, school elections were followed particularly closely because "rate bills" were part of the package—each family paid according to the number of children sent to school, so discussions were very heated and neighborly feelings disappeared for the duration of the election.

Families took political affiliation very seriously, and forecasting votes was aided by the practice of the son always voting as the father voted. ". . . For a son to vote differently from his father would have been a family scandal."[36]

By the latter part of the 19th century, paper ballots were used. Typically both parties used tickets that were the same size, about 4 inches wide and about 16–20 inches in length. As voters came to the poll they were handed either the Democratic ticket, which was a plain strip of white paper, or a Republican ticket, which had a form of a woman holding the American flag. Voters would then fold the ticket and place it through the slit in the top of the ballot box. Most people voted straight tickets without scratching. Repeat voting was common. Since there was no registration, voters who decided to vote more than once were limited only by their method of transportation and how many polls they could visit on election day.[37]

*In* County Election, *George Caleb Bingham shows voters waiting in line to cast their ballots. To the left of the voter are the candidates, dressed in their finest, taking advantage of a final opportunity to ask for each person's vote. On the left side of the painting, one fellow is enjoying the refreshments (which would have been provided by the candidates or their parties), and one gentleman seems to have had a bit too much to drink—his friend seems to be carrying him to the voting line. (Courtesy The Boatmen's National Bank of St. Louis)*

Openly buying and selling votes was also common. Writes a former principal who recorded events of that time: "On one occasion I saw a man vote for a side of bacon. I saw a man walking up and down the street of a village with a generous supply of five dollar gold coins in a shot-bag, shouting out openly, 'Five dollars for any ___ who will vote the ___ ticket.' There were several who changed their votes as desired and received the promised money.[38] Many state and national elections were very close, and a vote for one side by a man who would have voted against it counted as two votes.

## Election Day Quilting in Texas

Texas entered the Union in 1845, and election day there was sometimes called the poor man's Christmas because of the large quantities of food and drink available on that day. Drunkenness and gambling were common.[40] Noted one Adolphus Sterne in his diary: "Much Beaf [sic] and Port were devoured at political gatherings, and dancing and serenading were very much a part of the day."[41]

Earlier, evidently, election day was a quieter affair. Writes a lady of the election for president of the Republic of Texas in September of 1836: "There was no drinking or fighting. The ladies spent the day quilting. The young people began dancing at three o'clock and kept it up till next morning . . . That was my last ball at an election. After that there was too much whisky drunk for ladies to be present."[42]

Crucial to the settling of the frontier was the development of a government to keep order, and like the settlers of the original colonies, the people of the West enjoyed their election days as a time of coming together. Some frontier election days embodied the democratic process at its best; others were tarnished by too much liquor or by the greed of one party that felt it imperative to get the votes at any cost. But, as elsewhere, the local governments managed to survive and thrive well enough to withstand what was necessary until the coming of national reforms. In the meantime, election day continued to play an important role in the successful opening of the West.

## The Whig Ball Tradition Continues

People had such fun with the original Whig Ball during the Log Cabin and hard cider campaign of 1840 that it continued to inspire replicas. In 1844, the Whigs in Cincinnati decided to make a huge political ball to use in helping turn out the vote. It left Cincinnati by steamboat, and in Alabama it stopped in Mobile and Montgomery: An Alabama man wrote: "Of course, it attracted much attention and was visited by almost the entire population, especially elating the Whigs."[43] The name of each State with a motto was placed on the ball. Under Massachusetts were the words, "Ever Faithful"; under Vermont, "The Star that Never Sets"; under South Carolina, "Hemp for Traitors." The account notes that this last inscription was so insulting to some South Carolinians in the city that they were "hardly restrained from cutting the ball to pieces with their knives."[44] After a stay in South Carolina, it started on its next journey where a public road had to be enlarged in order for it to pass. (A colonel in the area, an ardent Whig, used his slaves to widen the road.) It finally reached Columbus, Georgia where it was allowed to go to pieces.

## The (Original) Whig Ball Continued

The original ball's last visit was to Tennessee in 1840, where it was put in storage, only to be brought out again in 1844 with the announcement that it would be awarded to the state with the most visitors at the Baltimore convention. (Maryland was excluded since it was hosting the convention.)

Delaware set out to win the ball; Whigs sent horsemen throughout the counties calling on people to urge them to travel to Baltimore, and a large steamer was chartered to take them to the city, though many traveled by other means.

The contest was held at a Baltimore sports field the day after the nominations, and the chief of police was designated to "count noses." Great cheers went up from the Delawareans when they were announced as the winner. Daniel Webster made the presentation of the ball. The Delaware delegation had some difficulty getting the huge ball through the streets of Baltimore to the wharf as several losing delegations attempted to take it away. Taken by steamboat to Delaware, it was then loaded on a large wagon and pulled by four horses to Georgetown, and a Whig rally was held several days later so that more people could see the state's prize.

After the ball was used for a final time on Return Day (the day when the election results were announced in Delaware), it was placed in storage in a carriage house on a farm just outside Georgetown. Sometime later when some Whigs stopped to check on it, they were dismayed to find the carriage house broken into and the ball destroyed. They assured everyone it was the work of Democrats, but that was never proven.[45]

## Establishing the Holiday

During Polk's tenure, something very important happened to election day. Perhaps a diary entry from President James K. Polk himself says it best:

> Tuesday, 7th November, 1848.—This is the day appointed by law for the election of President and Vice-President of the United States. Heretofore the people of the several States have by State laws fixed the period of holding the election in each State. Since the last Presidential election Congress for the first time exercised the power vested in them by the Constitution, and fixed the same day for holding the election in all the States. There will probably be not less than three millions of votes polled in this election.[46]

This Congressional Act had been a long time coming. The federal government had been concerned about encroaching on states' rights by stipulating a specific timetable. (It was feared that if a date when legislatures were not in session should be inadvertently selected, it would give the impression that the federal government favored the popular vote for electors over legislative selection.)

But finally, the following schedule was set: On the first Tuesday after the first Monday in November of every fourth year, the qualified voters of the United States are to indicate how their states are to represent them that year. Then on the first Monday after the second Wednesday in December, the electors cast their votes for president.

The process was to end on January 6 when the electoral votes were to be counted in the presence of Congress, and the results announced. If there is no clear winner, then part two of the Constitutional plan takes over, and the House of Representatives selects who is to be president. Though the day of the counting of the electoral votes has been changed occasionally throughout the years, the day specified for citizens to vote is still the same.

## 1848: The "Free Soil" Party Gains Strength

In 1848, for the first time ever, all Americans went to the polls on the same day. Perhaps it was only fitting that the man for whom the majority cast their votes was a very popular president. Zachary Taylor had become a military hero during the Mexican War. An unlikely politician, he had never before even voted in a presidential election, so it was only through great persuasion that he registered as a Whig and allowed his name to be submitted for president. Millard Fillmore, comptroller of New York and a former congressman, was selected to run with him.

The Democratic nominee was expansionist Lewis Cass of Michigan who believed in squatter sovereignty, which gave settlers in new U.S. territory the right to decide for themselves about slavery. (War of 1812 veteran General William O. Butler was nominated for vice president.) The slavery issue caused so much dissension among New York Democrats that it split the party in two—the Hunkers, who "hunkered" after office and supported Cass, and the Barnburners (the free- soil—antislavery—Democrats who would "burn down the barn to get rid of a few rats.") Eventually the Barnburners split off from the party and, joining with abolitionists and some Whigs, met in a big tent in Buffalo in August to organize the Free Soil Party, which was the beginning of the Republican Party we know today. Van Buren was their nominee with Charles Francis Adams as his running mate.

The issues of the election were territorial expansion and slavery. The Wilmot Proviso had recently been introduced in Congress and forbade slavery in any territory obtained from Mexico. It passed the House, failed in the Senate, but firmly established sectional feelings for 1848. (The southerners were violently opposed to any curtailment of their right to bring their property—slaves—into new territory.) The political parties chafed against the slavery issue as it sectionalized the country and made it difficult to unite behind one candidate.

On election day, the Free Soil Party made quite a showing. Holding the balance of power in 11 states, it split the Democratic vote and contributed to a Whig victory with

Taylor garnering 163 electoral votes to Cass's 127; Taylor's popular vote was 1,360,967, Cass's 1,222,342.

Sixteen months after Taylor's triumphant arrival in Washington, the very popular president died on July 4, 1850, after a sudden illness. A very surprised Vice President Millard Fillmore was left to assume the presidency and prepare for the next election.

Verdict of the People *by George Caleb Bingham depicts election day in a Missouri town in the 1850s. The votes have been counted and the results have just been announced. While the majority of the crowd seem pleased with the announcement, Bingham's painting also shows those who obviously backed a losing candidate. (Courtesy The Boatmen's National Bank of St. Louis)*

## The Nativist Movement

As more and more immigrants arrived in more and more parts of the United States, it led to a "native American" reaction of wanting to limit voting rights to prevent foreign domination at the polls.

In the East, particularly, the Irish had gained a bad reputation as "hoodlums" who caused riots. The press reported that they beat respectable citizens, insulted public dignitaries, fought openly with the police and raised general havoc. An election was considered an occasion for a grand uproar.[47]

Evidence exists that mass naturalizations took place on election eves and that both parties had a hand in it. A resident of New Brunswick, New Jersey notes: "The simple truth is that the honest men of the County are tired of being voted down by the seven hundred foreigners in this city, a vast majority of whom were ten years ago the ignorant serfs of Ireland, and are now simply the tools of designing demagogues who use them like cattle."[48] At a price, blank naturalization papers bearing court seals were also easily available.

To keep foreigners from voting, some states tried a literacy test, and it was maintained in states like Connecticut and Massachusetts, which required that voters be able to read the constitution and write their names; to pacify natives, this requirement wasn't applied to anyone over age 60 or to anyone who had voted before. (Most states didn't opt for the literacy test because it prevented illiterate natives from voting as well.)

In other states naturalized citizens faced a longer residency requirement; other areas required a special oath of allegiance from foreigners. In Rhode Island, naturalized citizens were still required to satisfy the property requirement.

At the height of the nativist movement, the Know Nothing Party emerged, so called because members, who were initiated and then sworn to secrecy, answered all questions about the organization by saying, "I know nothing about it." In 1856, now calling themselves the American Party, their platform called for limiting officeholding to native-born Americans; requiring 21 years' residence for naturalization; denying political station to anyone recognizing allegiance to a foreign power; and endorsing popular sovereignty in the territories.

Ironically, at the same time as the growth of the Know Nothing Party, part of the country was eager for foreigners. Large tracts of land awaited cultivation, and the states sought people to come and develop them to add to population and thus achieve greater representation in Congress. One of the ways they tried to attract foreigners was through greater participation in government. In Wisconsin, foreigners were allowed to vote before they had actually become citizens, permitting immigrants to vote three years into the five-year citizenship process. Iowa provided similarly.[49]

## 1852: Slavery Settled by Compromise?

As the country passed the midcentury mark, sectional tensions overshadowed most campaign activity. Still believing that compromise on slavery was possible, Henry Clay put forth the Compromise of 1850, which initiated what was the last and possibly the greatest Congressional debate involving the highly esteemed statesmen, Henry Clay, Daniel Webster and John Calhoun. The plan proposed that California be admitted as a free state, that New Mexico and Utah be organized as territories without legislation either for or against slavery, that a more efficient system be set up for returning fugitive slaves to their masters, that the slave trade be abolished in the District of Columbia and that Texas be compensated for some territory ceded to New Mexico.

President Taylor strongly opposed the compromise and was prepared to back his feelings with military force. Had he lived, there almost certainly would have been a minor version of the civil war in the Southwest. However, Taylor's death sent Vice President Millard Fillmore, a supporter of the Compromise, into the White House, and within five months the bill had passed. At least in the short term the country breathed a sigh of relief. The campaign of 1852 began with most people trying to believe that the slavery issue had been settled by compromise.

In the wake of such heated political feelings, however, both parties had difficulty rallying around one candidate. Meeting in Baltimore, the Democrats were deadlocked for 49 ballots before finally turning to dark horse Franklin Pierce of New Hampshire. Senator William R. King of Alabama was selected to run with him.

The Whigs had an equally difficult time. Their convention was held in mid-June, also in Baltimore. Daniel Webster and President Fillmore were contenders for the nomination, but finally, on the 53rd ballot, the nod went to General Winfield Scott with the hope that a war hero would lead the party to victory. The vice presidential nomination went to William A. Graham, secretary of the navy.

Guided by wishful thinking, both parties continued to advance the belief that the slavery question had been settled, and both platforms endorsed the compromise. (Scott refused to say anything at all on the compromise, making his party fearful that he might in some way betray it. As a result, the campaign focused largely on personalities rather than issues. Both candidates were political unknowns. A logical question, used as a campaign snipe by the Whigs, was "Who is Franklin Pierce?" The public could see that he was handsome, and they learned that this politician from New Hampshire had served in both houses of Congress and fought in the Mexican War, had passed out during one of the battles (probably because of the seriousness of his injuries), had had a drinking problem (the Whigs pointed out), but that he was now temperate (stressed by the Democrats). He was called "Handsome Frank," and the Democrats tried to refer to him as "Young Hickory of the Granite State," hoping that the name would conjure up Democratic successes of old.

Although General Scott was a military hero with a distinguished record, very little was known about him politically, and, during the campaign, voters learned little from the candidate himself—who remained tight-lipped on the issues. He prided himself on his fine appearance in his military uniforms, and the opposition made the most of his nickname, "Old Fuss and Feathers," which he had been given by his fellow army officers.

The "Barnburner" Democrats who had split off to join the Free Soil Party in '48 had folded back into the Democratic Party for '52, making the party difficult to beat. Pierce won a handsdown victory. With 1,601,117 popular and 254 electoral votes to Scott's 1,385,453 popular and 42 electoral votes, the margin was huge. (The Free Soil Party did make an appearance. It had nominated John Parker Hale of New Hampshire for president and George W. Julian of Indiana for vice president, but they obtained only 156,000 out of almost three million votes.) The days of the Whig Party were numbered and this was the last election in which it made a respectable showing.

## 1856: Tensions Mount

While campaign activity—parades, mass meetings, songs, picnics and many hand-outs—was very much a part of the election of 1856, the air of gaiety was misleading, for the Compromise of 1850 that was to have pulled the country together was, instead, tearing it apart. Several new developments had occurred.

Slavery in the territories had become an issue again. Southerners were furious that they could not take all of their property (slaves) into the newly opened Western land. This was particularly problematic as the lands were very fertile.

The Kansas–Nebraska Act, introduced by Illinois Senator Stephen A. Douglas, solved the southerners' problem by creating the two territories of Kansas and Nebraska, establishing popular sovereignty for the area and allowing settlers to choose whether or not slavery would be allowed. Unfortunately, the Act led to "Bleeding Kansas," so called because of the amount of bloodshed in struggles between pro- and antislavery settlers.

Reaction to the Act in the North was fury. Because the northerners felt that this new act violated both the Missouri Compromise and the Compromise of 1850, they even more openly refused to comply with the Fugitive Slave Act, and the underground railroad for helping slaves escape began transporting even more fugitives. Douglas was burned in effigy Imany times and denounced in mass meetings.

It was a time of high emotion and violence everywhere. When a proslavery mob that included a former senator from Missouri plundered the town of Lawrence, Kansas, other acts of brutality resulted, and these deeds led to violence in faraway Washington, D.C. In 1856, Massachusetts Senator Charles Sumner gave a speech on "The Crime Against Kansas," denouncing the Kansas–Nebraska Act and singling out Senator Andrew Butler for favoring slavery. While sitting at his desk in the Senate two days later, Sumner was beaten senseless by Congressman Preston Brooks, a relative of Butler's. So serious were his injuries, that Sumner was not fully active again for three years.

The Kansas–Nebraska Act split both Whigs and Democrats into pro- and antislavery groups; because of this split the Republican Party arose. Meeting in Ripon, Wisconsin in 1854, antislavery Whigs, Free Soilers and Democrats against the Kansas–Nebraska Act formed the party and within months had begun to build very strong grass-roots support. By the fall of 1854, Republican organizations had been established throughout the west and in some of the eastern states; by the following year the Republicans had bases from which to operate in all except the southern states. What had started as a sectional party had become a major force for the campaign of 1856.

Two years after its inception, the Republican Party met in Philadelphia and nominated "Pathfinder" John C. Fremont of California, who had achieved fame in his exploration of the West. (Fremont was selected because he was known to the public, and it was thought that he would increase party appeal.) Former Senator William L. Dayton of New Jersey was selected for the ticket's second spot. Running with the slogan, "Free Soil, Free Speech, Free Men, Fremont" and promising to prohibit in the Territories the "twin relics of barbarism—polygamy and slavery," the party gathered support from abolitionists, Free Soilers and from northeastern business interests that didn't want Congress dominated by slave states as well as from western farmers who didn't want to compete with slaveowners.

*To prevent immigrants from voting, squads of Know-Nothing party members rampaged through Baltimore on election day in 1856. The city had a nationwide reputation for political violence. (Courtesy, Maryland Historical Society, Baltimore)*

President Franklin Pierce misread the mood of the country and soon lost political control of his party. When 1856 neared, Pierce couldn't get the votes for the nomination. Instead the Democrats turned to what would be the last of the presidents to stand for compromise on slavery, bachelor James Buchanan, a statesman whose assignment to Britain during the Kansas-Nebraska fray made him the least controversial nominee. Congressman John C. Breckinridge of Kentucky was nominated for vice president in order to attract the southern vote.

The American Party (the Know Nothings) nominated former President Millard Fillmore and Tennessee newspaper editor Andrew J. Donelson and ran them with the slogan, "America Must Rule America."

Only Buchanan and Fillmore appeared on the ballots in the South. (Southern states opted not to allow their residents to consider a Republican.) There, the campaign activity was sluggish. The "Free Soil" men with their moral crusade against slavery provided liveliness to the campaign that year. Using songs, parades and mass meetings, the Republicans made great efforts to spread the word about the new party. Political clubs played an active part in the campaign throughout the North and West, and marching groups were organized and made reciprocal visits to one another. The Republicans also brought something new to the campaign trail—orator/poets. William Cullen Bryant, Henry Wadsworth Longfellow and Ralph Waldo Emerson all stumped for the Republicans.

The Democrats countered by calling the opposition "Black Republicans," and they threatened that the South would secede if Fremont won. The antiforeign, anti-Catholic American Party labeled Fremont a Catholic because he had been married by a priest (there were extenuating circumstances; Fremont was Episcopalian), and used that as a hammer against him politically.

When the vote came in, the people supported the Democratic Party, which offered no solutions but promised stability through continuity of the Union. In the electoral college, Buchanan received 174 votes to Fremont's 114 and Fillmore's 8. Buchanan had 1,832,955 popular votes; Fremont 1,339,932; and Fillmore 871,731. Buchanan had won with only 45% of the popular votes; the Republicans had shown surprising strength for a new party.

## The Vote of the Colorado Mountaineers

The first election day in Colorado was held shortly after the first settlers arrived in the Cherry Creek region of what is now Denver. Leaving Iowa on September 20, a group traveled up the Platte River, sometimes with some 500 Indians accompanying them. They arrived at the mouth of the Cherry Creek on October 23, 1858. With snow in the mountains the night they arrived, the "Colorado '58ers" took time to build cabins for protection, and shortly after that, an election was held to select the first territorial representative to go to Washington to stand up for what was then considered the Pikes Peak region. Writes '58er, Milo Fellows: "About this time the first excitement since our arrival occurred, all over an election to send a delegate to Washington."[50] It seems a group of heavy drinkers among the pioneers wanted to send one William Clancy of Omaha to the post. The author and his more sober companions favored Hiram J. Graham from Pacific City, Iowa. Before 9:00 A.M. of the day set for the election, a blizzard started, complicating the prospect of people leaving their cabins to cast their votes. Fellows took a cigar box and created a ballot box, "a good one—as good as there was in Colorado at that time."[51]

The method of swearing in the election board was discussed. Some felt it didn't make any difference; others felt it did. The men finally chose Fellows to administer the oath, so he did so, using the one that qualified town officers in the state of Michigan.

> Most of the others were laughing at us, but we went through with it straight as a string, opened the polls, and voted every man who would put in his ticket. After supper, in the midst of the blizzard we wrapped up our books and ballot box and started out to different cabins for more votes from those who failed to brave the storm, and by nine o'clock we had enough votes to beat Mr. Clancy. I think it was about seven majority. At all events we sent Mr. Graham to Congress armed with the strangest and first election credentials Colorado ever sent to Washington, D.C.[52]

In the mountain region where rich mineral deposits lured many, early government began within "claim clubs," which were the first organized method in the area for keeping order and maintaining ownership within the mining districts. The club organizers took on governmental duties and established rules concerning boundaries and the terms for owning mining claims and a system for resolving disputes. As an outgrowth of these clubs came an effort to organize a state or territorial government to provide a stronger structure for preserving interests and property.

One of the early Denver election descriptions from the *Rocky Mountain News* indicated crowds at the polls that were so great that people didn't like entering, and voting declined: "We believe we have never before seen, at one time, in the streets of Denver, as many drunken men, as many fights, or as much boisterous rioting as were witnessed at this election. Yet, we have heard of no one seriously hurt. Black eyes, bruised faces and bloody noses were about the extent of the affray."[53]

## Halfway Around the World . . .

Ironically, while the rest of the country was trying to ignore the slavery issue, the "fire bell in the night" so specifically warned of by Thomas Jefferson, and while threats of secession had been in the offing for more than 10 years, in far-off Hawaii in the 1850s there was great excitement and appreciation for America's election day. Appearing in the *Pacific Commercial Advertiser* of August 18, 1856 were these words:

A plan is about being started among the American residents of these Islands to hold an Election for President, the 10th [sic] of November, the same day that the election takes place in the U.S. The idea is a novel one, and it would be interesting to know the political sentiments of Americans . . .[54]

The paper reported that never before had there been so much excitement in Honolulu as upon the arrival of the *Yankee* on December 19, 1856, 14 days from San Francisco. The December 25, 1856 edition of the *Advertiser* said this about the election of James Buchanan and John C. Breckinridge:

There gathered at the American Club an assemblage of over six hundred Americans. Led by "Rowe's American Brass Band," the procession moved to the residence of United States Commissioner David L. Gregg where he and Alex

*New York Ciy's famed Tammany Hall was shown in* Frank Leslie's Illustrated Newspaper *as it looked on election day 1856 with members gathering to discuss strategy and swap news. In the early part of the century, the Society of St. Tammany held its meetings in taverns, but in 1812, members decided they wanted an official hall. Shares of stock were issued to build what was officially the Tammany Hotel at the corner of Nassau and Frankfort Streets. This was Tammany headquarters until 1868. (*Frank Leslie's Illustrated Newspaper, *November 8, 1856)*

C. Campbell made speeches. Nine rousing cheers for Buchanan and Breckin-ridge were followed by the Band playing *Hail Columbia*. The parade proceeded [on] . . . By this time the procession, with the addition of many native Hawaiians, was about one thousand strong . . . The *Advertiser's* Office was the next location visited. Three gallant cheers were shouted for the Freedom of the Press, after which the Band played the *Star Spangled Banner.*[55]

# A Country Divided _____ 9

Could slavery be settled by a vote? In Kansas, where bloodshed wasn't working, it was time to give it a try. The Kansas–Nebraska Act of 1854 provided that states entering the Union would decide for themselves whether to be a slave state or free. In the fall of 1856, Kansas was due to elect a territorial delegate to the United States Congress, members of a territorial legislature and delegates to a convention to write a state constitution. Whether pro- or antislavery forces gained control of these elective posts might foretell Kansas's (and the country's) future.

Like other heated elections of the day, no stone was left unturned while the opposing sides explored how to turn out the vote, and people were brought in from miles around to cast the "right" votes. Wrote one participant from Atchison in a letter dated Thursday, October 2, 1856, to the *Daily Missouri Democrat*:

> . . . Our leading men here . . . think the pro-slavery vote will be by far the largest. This may be, if Missouri will come forward as she ought. She, in fact, controls the fate of Kansas—being just on the border, and separated only by a narrow river. She can send, at a moment's notice, men enough either to control the ballot-box or repel an invasion; and why can we not with justice apply to Missouri for aid now, when we know hundreds of men are entering the Territory under the leadership of the notorious Jim Lane, for the sole purpose of voting.[1]

The vote, which took place October 6, gave control to the proslavery forces, but when fraudulent votes from two areas were thrown out and the antislavery party took over, more fighting occurred. Kansas was not to be settled easily. As tensions mounted, it affected the mood of the country—in Washington, congressmen began to attend sessions bearing arms.

In taking office, President James Buchanan stepped into this quagmire, and the situation steadily worsened. Two days after Buchanan's term began, the Supreme Court handed down the Dred Scott decision, shaking antislavery people to the core. The court had ruled that a slave who was taken from a slave state into a free territory (in this case, Wisconsin) was still a slave; the ruling violated the Missouri Compromise, which forbade slavery north of the Mason–Dixon line. The court also ruled that Congress could not legislate concerning slavery in a territory, and it implied that

106

neither could Congressionally created territorial governments. This would have meant that all territories were open to slavery and could exclude it only when they became states. Instead of solving a problem, the Dred Scott ruling created a bigger one. The Republicans started angling for a reversal, and the southern Democrats wanted to push through legislation for federal protection of slavery in the territories.

When abolitionist John Brown seized the federal arsenal in Harpers Ferry in an effort to start a black insurrection, emotions were at an all-time high. Continuing trouble in Kansas further fanned the flames of hatred. The delegates who gathered to write the state constitution ultimately decided that they really only wanted the territory residents' opinion on one issue: slavery. In a referendum vote on the constitution with or without slavery, Kansans voted in favor of slavery 6,226 to 569. (The Free Soil men had opted not to vote and intended to get the election declared invalid.) More blood was shed and other constitutions were written—one constitutional group relied on a military guard to protect it until the document was written. The issue just would not disappear. Southerners became more and more convinced that secession was the only means to preserve their way of life.

In the meantime, two Illinois senatorial contenders were traveling the state in 1858 conducting a series of debates "amidst banners, brass bands, raucous crowds, and sweating reporters."[2] Stephen A. Douglas, a Democrat sometimes called the "Little Giant," had been in politics for years and was already well known. Abraham Lincoln, a Republican, was a relative newcomer, but the debates drew such great attention (at one stop, 12,000 people attended) that, though Lincoln lost the senatorial seat through gerrymandering, he was catapulted into the national spotlight.

## The Election Nears

The Democratic Party, embodying the last remaining sign of any sort of North–South cooperation, held its nominating convention in Charleston in April of 1860, and all the country waited with heightened anticipation. Would the party be able to devise a way for North and South to pull together? Not unexpectedly, arguments over slavery were bitter. The southern Democrats wanted to put federal power behind the Dred Scott decision by supporting passage of a law protecting slavery in all the territories, but when Stephen A. Douglas's followers, the northern Democrats, refused to agree to this proslavery measure, eight southern states withdrew, breaking the last North-South link and making it impossible for Douglas to get the needed two-thirds majority vote necessary for the party's nomination. After two weeks of argument and attempts at getting the required votes, the convention delegates who remained voted to adjourn and made plans to meet in Baltimore in June.

The next political party to meet was a spirited group who called themselves the Constitutional Union Party. They met for their first and only convention in May of 1860—also in Baltimore. Made up primarily of former Whigs, the new party intended to campaign for preservation of the Union. They selected veteran Whig John Bell of

Tennessee to run for the presidency; Edward Everett of Massachusetts was chosen for the ticket's second spot.

On May 16—three weeks after the first Democratic convention had to be adjourned with nothing resolved and one week after the Constitutional Union Party had met, the eyes of Americans turned to Chicago where the Republican Party convention was to be held. (A location this far West was made possible by the completion of the railroad to the Midwest in the 1850s.) Meetings were held in a large structure called the "Wigwam," which had a capacity of 10,000. After considering William H. Seward and Salmon P. Chase, whom they decided were too radical to win, the party opted for Abraham Lincoln, who was nominated on the third ballot. (This was not by accident. Lincoln had remained at home in Springfield, but his campaign managers had gone to Chicago with the intent of seeing Lincoln nominated and campaigned hard to see it become a reality.) Senator Hannibal Hamlin of Maine, a former Democrat who had turned Republican, was chosen to run as vice president. The party supported liberty for the territories, free homesteading for farmers, a protective tariff and the construction of a Pacific railroad.

Once they reassembled in June, the Democrats continued to haggle over which delegates would be seated. Again, a group withdrew. When those delegates who were accepted finally settled down to business, Stephen A. Douglas received the nomination. The convention selected Alabama Senator Benjamin Fitzpatrick for vice president, but when he later declined, the national committee asked Herschel V. Johnson, former governor of Georgia, to be Douglas's running mate.

With great interest, Americans awaited news of what the other Democrats would do; they hadn't long to wait. Those states that had walked out of the Democratic convention soon held their own convention, also in Baltimore. The so-called Dixiecrats nominated John C. Breckinridge of Kentucky and Senator Joseph Lane of Oregon to run for president and vice president respectively. They mounted a campaign promising federal protection of slave property in the territories and received the support of President Buchanan as well as former Presidents John Tyler and Franklin Pierce.

Although there were four major candidates in the election, each section of the country really only acknowledged two. Lincoln and Douglas were the two serious contenders in the North, and Bell and Breckinridge in the South. (Nine slave states refused to put Lincoln on the ballot.)

With the Democratic Party split in half and with neither side able to dominate, Republican excitement was mounting. Unless the two Democratic factions united to work together before November, the Democratic Party split meant almost certain victory for the Republicans.

Once the campaign was underway, it followed the pattern begun in 1840; there were processions, torchlight parades, stump speakers and mass meetings. Stephen Douglas, whose small stature but large girth and high energy level soon gained him the nickname, the "Little Giant," took to the stump himself—the first time a presidential candidate traveled to campaign for himself. To add to political festivities, fat boys were recruited to march as "Little Giants."

John Bell's campaign symbol was the bell—his name obviously inspired the idea, but parades and rallies in his honor usually featured one large bell that party leaders explained was ringing to sound an alarm to the people to do what they could to preserve the Union. Followers of the Union Party responded by attending campaign events with bells of their own to ring as a sign of unity. As for Breckinridge, his campaign featured the standard political efforts of the day but there were no particularly colorful touches.

Abraham Lincoln did not travel to campaign, but he did receive visitors at his office in Springfield. Lincoln had several nicknames including "High Old Abe" (in reference to his size) and "Honest Abe" (because he had a reputation for honesty and integrity). He was also called the "Rail-Splitter" candidate, a nickname he acquired when his cousin appeared at the state party convention in Illinois carrying two fence rails, supposedly split by Lincoln. The campaign joke ran that Lincoln split rails while the Democrats split their party.

Because Lincoln was particularly popular with young men, the Republicans had no problem putting together groups to campaign. They had battalions of men who carried fence rails; there were other campaign processions featuring men who were 6'4"— Lincoln's height. In addition, the Republicans soon saw the birth of a political phenomenon that became known as the Wide Awakes.

## The Wide Awakes

Perhaps it was the enthusiasm for the new Republican Party, or perhaps it was the common man's way of taking some sort of united action at a time when the country was being torn apart. Whatever the reason, when the spring campaign of 1860 got under way in Hartford, Connecticut, the time was ripe for the birth of the "Wide Awakes," a marching group of "common men" known for their uniforms of capes and hats. As it happened, the group came about quite by accident.

After campaign speeches in an immense hall in Hartford, a torchlight procession had been arranged to escort the speaker, Republican Cassius M. Clay of Kentucky to his quarters. When the torches were taken out, the men discovered that many of them leaked. Several marchers worked at a local dry goods store, so they led some of the group to the store and tore off squares of black cambric and hooked the material over their shoulders with tape, making capes that protected their clothing from the drip of the torches. Their leader liked the look of the capes and put the men wearing them at the head of the line where the novelty of their dress helped attract attention.

At the end of the evening, it was decided that a company should be organized to wear glazed capes and caps and carry swinging torches at political events. The name "Wide Awake" was adopted by the group after *a Hartford Courant* headline concerning party activities read: REPUBLICANS WIDE AWAKE!

Money was raised to build a meeting spot, and the idea of the club soon spread to many parts of the country. Adopting the same uniform, all the clubs performed essentially the same duties—escorting speakers, keeping order at rallies, canvassing voters, guarding ballot boxes and distributing campaign literature as well as participating in many, many parades. It was quite common for Wide Awake Clubs in one state to journey to another state to participate in local events. A gathering of clubs from several states in New York resulted in a parade that was five miles long. By August, there were more than 400 organizations in existence, and by election day, there were more than 500,000 uniformed Wide Awakes in the northern states.[3] When the war began, the military drilling and regimental aspects of the Wide Awakes were credited with helping make the North slightly better prepared.

People all over the country participated in many rallies prior to the election, and on election eve in St. Louis, there was what was called the "Last Grand Rally." Representatives of all the candidates were on hand, and huge crowds attended:

> . . . At an early hour the streets were alive with processions, marching and countermarching, and musical with the sweet melody of many bands. Until a late hour the shouts of interested and excited partisans, in favor of their respective candidates.[4]

*In the spring of 1860, a marching group of Lincoln-supporters in Hartford, Connecticut, first donned black cambric capes to protect themselves from the dripping torches they were using for a torchlight parade. They became known as the Wide Awakes. Their attire caught on and soon Wide Awake groups spread throughout the northern states. The various groups' duties were to escort political speakers, keep order at rallies, guard ballot boxes, distribute campaign literature and participate in parades, many of which were several miles long. (Courtesy The Bettmann Archive)*

A huge bonfire illuminated the area where the speeches took place, and the Wide Awakes and other groups took part in what was a very long and raucous evening.

## Election Diary Notes from an Illinois Farmer

While most modern day diarists would be hard-pressed to pen more than a sentence or two about their political activities and voting experiences during an election year, it is interesting to note that the diaries of this period have much to report. While the cities certainly would have been centers of political activity, that did not mean that people from outlying areas did not enjoy the festivities. In his journal, John Edward Young, an Illinois farmer who lived in the southeast part of the state near Athens, gives a detailed account of pre-election festivities as well as of election day itself (the spelling is as it was in the diary).

His entries concerning the election begin on August 8 when he attended the Republican mass meeting in Springfield. Describing it as "unforgettable," he notes "It would be impossible to convey an adequate idea of the appearance and splendor of the scene."[5] With an estimated 100,000 in attendance and a procession nearly eight miles long, Young takes time to note down some of the more impressive sights: "A log cabin. A rail pen. A platform seventy feet long drawen by twenty two yoke of oxen on which a number of occupations was practically represented. A blacksmith a tinner a carpenter a saddler a waggonmaker a spinner and weaver a shoemaker a tailor a school teacher and lastly a rail splitter was all at work at there several vocations."[6]

Many other floats and wagons were described in his writings, the efforts of the campaign organizers were not lost on Young.

By one o'clock, Young noted that the grounds were full to overflowing, and speakers had taken up talking in four different places and kept at it until evening when people drifted back to town for the torchlight procession of 4,000 Wide Awakes who were accompanied by bands. There was a fireworks display, then more speeches and by midnight the crowd dispersed to their homes or to stay with friends.

## The Election's "Lost Boy"

The election year 1860 was a time of great import to the country, so it is interesting to note that there was still time for some levity. Stephen Douglas had broken with tradition by traveling nationwide campaigning for himself. The press considered it vote-begging, and he took great criticism for it. When Douglas was heading north he came up with a way to fend off some of the criticism and announced that he was really on his way to visit his mother in Clifton Springs, New York. But as the trip dragged on and Douglas's path wandered, the Republicans produced a handbill that read:

A Boy Lost! Left Washington, D.C. some time in July, to go home to his mother. He has not yet reached his mother, who is very anxious about him. He has been seen in Philadelphia, New York City, Hartford, Conn., at a clambake in Rhode Island. He has been heard from at Boston Portland, August, and Bangor, Me. . . . He is about five feet nothing in height and about the same in diameter the other way. He has a red face, short legs, and a large belly. Answers to the name of Little Giant, talks a great deal, very loud, always about himself. He has an idea that he is a candidate for President.[7]

As November neared and Democratic hopes waned, Douglas abandoned any concern he had about what the press or the public thought of his stumping, and he took off for a swing through the South. No longer campaigning for his own cause, he traveled from town to town imploring people to realize the importance of preserving the Union. Despite often being pelted with eggs and tomatoes as he spoke, he continued pleading for loyalty to the next president right until election day.

## Election Day 1860

A description of election day in Springfield, Illinois, where Lincoln lived, presents a very vivid picture of what the polling was like in 1860.

The polls were held in the courthouse, up two flights of stairs, where there were two windows for voting. Outside the building an immense crowd gathered, waiting their turn to cast their ballots. On the steps, the ticket peddlars passed out party ballots, and bands playing music paraded the streets in wagons, labeled with various political slogans. Their appearance in front of the polls now and then was a signal for increased hurrahing, yells and cheers. The Republicans, however, had a greater show of strength than did the Democrats. Whenever the smaller group became a little too clamorous, the Wide Awakes commenced singing:

"Ain't I glad I've joined the Republicans.
    Joined the Republicans, joined the Republicans,"

The refrain, taken up by the crowd, soon swelled into a chorus that squelched the Democratic cheers quite effectively.

The bitterness of feeling among the party rivals led to a good number of fights around the polls. Describing an outburst between Charles H. [sic] Lanphier, proprietor of the *Register*, and E. L. Gross, a Republican lawyer, a newspaper reporter noted:

I happened to be an eye-witness to the whole affair and can testify that Lanphier was the party in fault. Mr. Gross was standing by the railing, talking, when a Democrat remarked in a loud tone, "Look out for bogus tickets." Mr. Gross said in a sarcastic way, "The bogus tickets were printed at the *Register* office."

Lanphier was standing near by and leaning over said, "What's that you say?" Mr. Gross repeated in a half joking manner, "The bogus tickets were printed at the *Register* office," whereupon Lanphier almost sticking his nose in Gross's face, said, "That's a lie," emphasizing the word "lie" as loudly as he could. Mr. Gross instantly struck him on the head with his cane. The two clinched, and while Lanphier was trying in vain to throw Gross down, the latter gave him several excellent whacks with the stick. A crowd interfered and the combatants separated . . .[8]

Lincoln himself voted at 3:30 P.M. amid considerable excitement. His friends almost lifted him off the ground and would have carried him to the polls if there hadn't been some interference. Once at the polls, each person wanted to have the privilege of handing Lincoln his ballot. One fellow yelled out: "You ought to vote for Douglas, Uncle Abe, he has done all he could for you."[9] The cheers of "Old Abe," "Uncle Abe," "Honest Abe" and "Giant Killer" were deafening. The populace was thrilled to have him among them.

As for election day for the Illinois farmer, John Edward Young wrote:

A most beautiful day with a white frost this morning. I halled some pomekins the forenoon and went to Athens in the evening and voted the Republican ticket throughout. This is one of our Countries memorable days. Its events will fill a page in its history that will remain as long as there is a lover of liberty or a friend of freedom on earth. Today this great nation is to say whether it is for freedom or slavery. The contest between the parties is fierce and determined but the right will prevail. The election has passed off quietly.[10]

Throughout the country, fraudulent voting tactics continued. Newspapers warned voters to beware the bogus tickets and to watch for the arrival of repeaters who were being imported to vote again. In Springfield, amusement and indignation greeted a scam pulled on the Democrats. Knowing that the Republicans had copies of the prior election year's Democratic ballot, the Democrats had new tickets designed for 1860 and chuckled at how smart they were to change to a new, secret ticket design to prevent voters from being tricked into taking the wrong ticket. The Democratic newspaper ran warnings against bogus tickets that might be printed with Republican candidates substituted. But ultimately, the joke was on the Democrats. A Republican had somehow obtained a copy of the real Democratic ticket and sent it to St. Louis to have 50,000 copies made—with Republican candidates substituted. On election day the city was flooded with the imitation, and it was estimated that 500 were voted in before Democrats discovered the change in the names.[11]

When the final votes were in, Lincoln's opponents had 60% of the popular vote, but Lincoln carried all 18 of the free states, giving him 180 out of 303 electoral votes. Breckinridge had 72 of the electoral votes, and Bell, 39. Douglas came in with only 12. The popular vote was 1,865,593 for Lincoln; 848,356 for Breckinridge; 592,906 for Bell; and 1,382,713 for Douglas. The key to Lincoln's victory lay in the split of the Democratic Party.

News of Lincoln's election was carried by the Pony Express across the plains from Fort Kearny, Nebraska to Fort Churchill, Nevada in six days—the fastest time ever made by the Pony Express. It was the first and last time the Pony Express carried such news—the development of the telegraph soon made overland relay obsolete.

Distance from the nation's capital and lack of statehood status did little to dampen political enthusiasm in parts as far west as Washington Territory. In 1860, Washington was only a territory and had no votes for the presidential election, but a brand new paper, the Olympia *Washington Standard*, took great interest in national political doings, and its first issues were devoted to the presidential election.[12]

Although more than a week passed until the results were obtained, there was unrestrained celebrating once the news was known. Guns were fired and parades were held in even the smallest localities. Republicans in the small town of Tumwater fired a 100-gun salute, then marched to Olympia, ringing bells, blowing horns and cheering. One Republican in the mining area of eastern Washington Territory, where news of the election was slow in arriving, wrote, "Old Abe must certainly be elected President, for the air is as clear as a bell—we have not had a cloudy day for the past week."[13]

## Election Reaction in the South

In the South, the reaction to Lincoln's victory could not have been more extreme. The Atlanta *Confederacy* wrote: "Whether . . . Pennsylvania Avenue is paved ten fathoms deep with mangled bodies, the South will never submit to . . . the inauguration of Abraham Lincoln."[14]

On December 20, the southern storm broke. Meeting at Charleston, the state of South Carolina declared that "the union now subsisting between South Carolina and other states under the name of the United States of America is hereby dissolved." And on February 4, 1861, seven southern states (South Carolina, Mississippi, Florida, Alabama, Georgia, Louisiana and Texas) met at Montgomery to proclaim the Confederate States of America.

## The Election of Jefferson Davis

When the seceding southern states, represented by delegates selected by each state's secession convention, met in Montgomery, they were concerned that the situation might worsen once Lincoln was inaugurated on March 4, and they felt that they had just one month to form a new government. As a result, the day Jefferson Davis was elected was not an actual election day for the people.

The s outhern states were very concerned that the vote for president and vice president be definitive, so they established a system whereby each state had one vote.

No candidate would be formally nominated, so each state's delegation would have to agree on the one person whom they wanted for the office. The states—all edgy over what candidate the other states might favor—seemed, almost by default, to move toward Jefferson Davis, the compromise candidate. Though better leaders were available, they were controversial, and it would have been difficult to come to rapid agreement about anyone else. So it happened that, on February 9, Jefferson Davis was unanimously elected to a one- year term as head of the provisional government of the Confederacy.

As the Provisional Congress continued to meet, it provided that the term of the presidency be six years and that the president be ineligible for reelection. Though the citizens would have to wait a year for the opportunity to vote, their voting rights were provided for in the Confederacy's Constitution.

There was, however, dissent among the delegates. With an administration that had been chosen without the people's vote, and a Constitution for which there was no popular approval, several of the delegates felt that a great wrong had been done. But time was of the essence, and the new government had to be operational before Lincoln came into office. Though the new government did beat out Lincoln's inauguration, the general lack of satisfaction with its arrangements meant that the birth of the Confederacy was covered by a long shadow.[15]

As the secessionist states settled in and seized southern-based federal forts and arsenals during the winter of 1860–61, President Lincoln and the men around him sought ways to keep the Union together through peaceful means. They didn't have long to work though. Fort Sumter in Charleston Harbor— still a Union stronghold— needed provisions, and when Lincoln proposed to send in a ship supplied with food, South Carolina opened fire on the Union base.

The shock of the outbreak of hostilities at Sumter united states North and South in their opposing causes: Arkansas, North Carolina, Tennessee and Virginia seceded and lined up with the Confederacy, while the northern states banded together and prepared to defend their Union. War was inevitable.

Some thought the fighting would be brief, but when the opposing forces met that summer at Bull Run, it was obvious the armies were in for a siege. The North had on her side greater population, industrial resources including a more vast railroad network and wealth; the South had spirit, the easy ability to keep feeding the troops because of slave power and strong agricultural resources, and the fact that defending her territory, not taking new territory, was her aim.

## 1864: Civil War

The war dragged on for several years, and, as the time drew near for the 1864 election, the situation looked bleak for Lincoln. No incumbent president had been renominated for 24 years (since Van Buren had hoped to win a second term in 1840), and none had been reelected since Jackson in 1832. But more important, the war was going badly for the Union. Many thought another leader might be able to end this "irrepressible conflict."

No nation had ever before held an election while in the midst of a major war, but Lincoln was adamant that one take place, pointing out that a people couldn't have free government without an election.

In preparation for election day, there was a realignment of parties. The northern Democrats were split in two—War Democrats favored Lincoln's war; the others believed that the war should be ended quickly at any price. In the Republican Party, Lincoln led the mainstream Republicans, and those with more radical views, including Secretary of the Treasury Salmon P. Chase (who resigned from Lincoln's cabinet), and Horace Greeley, the influential editor of the *New York Tribune*, were strongly enough opposed to Lincoln's policies that they separated from the party for a time.

The mainstream Republicans opted to call themselves the National Union Party, intending to attract southern unionists and War Democrats who might not support the party if the name remained "Republican." As hoped, they were joined by non-Republicans, and when the group met in a convention in Baltimore, Lincoln was nominated on the first ballot. Lincoln knew his future looked dim, and when he received news of his nomination, he said: "I do not allow myself to suppose that either the convention or the League have concluded to decide that I am either the greatest or best man in America, but rather that they have concluded it is best not to swap horses while crossing the river . . ."[16] As running mate, Andrew Johnson of Tennessee, a prominent War Democrat, was chosen to try to pull major support from disenchanted Democrats. The convention was filled with excitement over running an incumbent rather than an unknown, and the platform planks calling for unconditional surrender of the South and abolition of slavery brought delegates to their feet for prolonged cheering.

The Republican nominating convention was scheduled for early June. The more radical Republicans, primarily made up of about 400 abolitionists and German-Americans, then scheduled their meeting for May 31 in Cleveland and by so doing, hoped to steal some of the Republican thunder. After considering Salmon P. Chase and Ulysses S. Grant, they finally settled on General John C. Fremont as their candidate for president. (Fremont had linked up with the Radicals because he was angry at Lincoln for not having given him an important military command.) General John Cochrane was chosen for the vice-presidential spot. The party platform called for abolishment of slavery and for Congress, not the president, to oversee reconstruction of the country. (The Radicals felt that Lincoln's plans for reconstruction were too slow and too conservative and that the southern blacks should be given their rights as quickly as possible. Lincoln felt that he would betray the trust of the people, and thereby doom all reconstruction plans, if he were to move much faster than public sentiment.)

In late August, the Democrats met in Chicago and, after proclaiming the war a failure, demanded an immediate cessation of hostilities. Their choice of candidate was General George B. McClellan, an egotistical military officer whom Lincoln had finally had to remove from active leadership during the Civil War for his overcautiousness.

The vice-presidential nomination went to George Pendleton, an Ohio congressman who had been maligning the Lincoln administration throughout the war. The party platform was for peace, with a firm declaration that the war was a failure, but, ultimately, McClellan refused to speak out on the futility of the war, feeling he couldn't face his men if he indicated that their fighting had been in vain. As a result, the Democrats began their campaign with a split identity. Campaign songbooks tried to straddle both sides by including songs both for and against the war.

For the most part, the public's attention was on the progress of the war, and they paid less attention than usual to any campaign doings. Lincoln, busy with the war, left the campaign to his managers. The campaign darts that were thrown were harsh and abusive—Lincoln was called everything from a liar and thief to a butcher and a buffoon. Some also referred to him as "Abraham Africanus the First," and "Abe the Widowmaker." (The latter was in reference to the fact that by the autumn of 1864 a half million young men had died.) Lincoln found all this very painful.

The Democrats also had another campaign tactic that they didn't hesitate to employ. In the Congressional elections of '62, the Democrats had been successful in campaigns where they stressed what life would be like once blacks were treated equally with whites. For this election, a campaign hoax perpetrated by an editor and a reporter for the *New York World* played, as intended, to the Democratic advantage. The two New York journalists coined a term, "miscegenation," (meaning the blending of the races) and anonymously wrote and distributed a pamphlet about *Miscegenation: The Theory of the Blending of the Races*. Cartoons around election time portrayed black men kissing rosy-cheeked white women or dancing with them at the "Miscegenation Ball" that would take place after Lincoln's inauguration.

Republicans threw their share of oratorical mud, calling the Democrats disloyal and accusing them of betraying their country. McClellan's military record was laughed at, and the Democratic peace platform was called the coward's solution to the war.

The South closely followed the campaign. The rebels knew that McClellan and the Democrats felt far less hostile toward them than the Republicans, and their desire was for a Democratic victory so that peace would be negotiated under McClellan rather than the possibility of the South being taken under Lincoln.

But only a few weeks after the start of the campaign, the military situation changed. On September 1, General Sherman captured Atlanta, a key area for gaining access to the lower South, and broke the strength of the Confederacy by cutting the Gulf states off from Richmond. Admiral David G. Farragut captured Mobile Bay, Grant made progress in Petersburg and General Philip Sheridan routed the Confederate Army from the valleys of Virginia.

The political picture had suddenly changed. The Democratic prospects that had looked so bright in late August quickly began to dim. Frustrated Union Republicans, who in midsummer had talked of a second convention to oust the "sure loser" Lincoln, made amends. The Radicals saw that the turn in the war meant they were doomed, and on September 21, Fremont withdrew his candidacy. Suddenly the Democrats were facing a united Republican Party whose leader was overseeing military victory.

On the eve of election day in Delaware, the Union men staged a torchlight procession to help kindle party enthusiasm and to welcome soldiers who had been sent home in time to vote.[17]

## Who Voted in 1864?

The result of the election in '64 was crucial to the outcome of the war; Lincoln had held firm that the North should have the opportunity to pick a new leader if it wanted one. What to do about the vote of soldiers became an important issue. At the time, most states had no provisions for soldiers voting by absentee ballots while in service.

Some regiments were sent home to vote. By request of the governor, the First,Third and Fourth Delaware Regiments were given a home leave at election time. Governor Cannon frankly stated, " . . . we cannot carry the state without them."[18] Two days before the election the troops arrived in Wilmington on a ten-day home leave; they

*At the time of the Civil War, few states had provisions for soldiers to vote by absentee ballots. If a sizable soldier vote were to be cast, arrangements needed to be made for the military to vote in the field. States sent tally lists, poll books and voting supplies to the captain of their state's regiments, and the military made provisions for conducting the election. Above, the men of the Army of the Potomac lined up to cast their ballots while a visiting politician chats with one of the soldiers. (*Harper's Weekly, Fall, 1864)

were entertained at City Hall, and then sent to their homes to stay until they cast their ballots.

But obviously this wasn't practical for all. Efforts were begun to let the soldiers vote in the field. Secretary of War E. M. Stanton received a letter from then-Lieutenant-General U. S. Grant dated September 27, 1864. Starting out with the fact that voting by the soldiers would be novel, he pointed out that the current war was "novel and exceptional," but considering that a large proportion of legal voters were in the field, or in hospitals, or otherwise away from home because of the war, he noted:

They have left their homes temporarily to sustain the cause of their country in the hour of its trial. In performing this sacred duty they should not be deprived of a most precious privilege. They have as much right to demand that their votes shall be counted in the choice of their rulers as those citizens who remain at home. Nay, more, for they have sacrificed more for their country.[19]

Grant went on to suggest that no politicking should be allowed, and that ideally, military personnel should have the tickets to distribute on request, but if necessary, then ordinary citizens might be brought in for ticket distribution.

Mail or messenger voting by soldiers was also permitted. The system developed was similar to the one used today when voters express preference by mail. Some used a proxy plan where soldiers signed an "instrument" similar to a power of attorney, appointing an elector in his home precinct to act as agent or proxy in casting his vote for him. In other cases, a soldier marked a ballot and sealed it in an inner envelope and enclosed it and his signed instrument in an outer envelope and mailed it all to his agent who carried the ballot envelope unopened to the polls.[20]

Newspapers were circulated freely throughout all regiments, and letters from home with clippings on local issues helped keep the soldiers informed.

States sent tally lists, poll books and complete voting supplies to the captain of their state's regiments, regardless of where they were based. The military made provisions for how the election should be conducted.

Like other elections of the day, this voting arrangement, too, was tainted with fraud. One Brigadier General M. R. Patrick, provost-marshall-general at City Point, Florida, was called out for being too cooperative with the election agents. In another instance involving a Pennsylvania regiment, state agents were arrested for distributing altered poll books. The alterations consisted of the improper spelling of names, and the omission of a name in the tally lists. All evidence was turned over to the proper authorities.[21]

A midwar election was important to all, particularly to those held prisoner. At Camp Lawton, a Confederate prison in Millen, Georgia, the prisoners couldn't get their tallies to the Union lines, but the men wanted to hold their own election all the same. From the diary of prisoner John Ransom, a 21-year-old brigade quartermaster from Michigan who had spent seven-and-one-half months at Andersonville, a prison camp where conditions were almost unbearable:

Nov. 6.—One year ago to-day captured. Presidential election at the North between Lincoln and McClellan. Some one fastened up a box, and all requested to vote, for the fun of the thing. Old prisoners haven't life enough to go and vote; new prisoners vote for present administration. I voted for McClellan with a hurrah, and another hurrah, and still another. Had this election occurred when we were at Andersonville, four-fifths would have voted for McClellan. We think ourselves shamefully treated in being left so long as prisoners of war . . . [22]

## The Early Days of Polling

Like today, the people of the 1860s wanted predictions of how the elections were going, and there is evidence that early polling took place. Straw votes (unofficial balloting to get a general idea of the election outcome) were taken in such places as on steamboats or on trains where a captive, cross section of people could vote. The newspapers reported on these straw votes and used them to make their predictions. Samplings could be as small as 50 or 60 people, but were still used to make projections.[23]

Another way to speculate on the election outcome involved the soldiers. As the troops moved through Washington, they cheered as they walked by various campaign banners strung along the street. Observers noted that the Lincoln and Johnson flag received a more positive reaction:

One regiment in particular, as it marched toward the Capitol, rent the air with cheers for Lincoln and Johnson, when they passed under the flag near Ninth street. But when they came in sight of the McClellan flag further on, the men began to groan heartily, and their commander wheeled them to the left, into C street, thus avoiding the necessity of marching under the banner of the Peace party.[24]

On November 8, Lincoln won decisively. He received 212 electoral votes to McClellan's 21 and carried every state except Kentucky, Delaware and New Jersey. His popular majority was substantial with 55% (2,206,938) of the vote to 45% (1,803,787). Though here and there intimidation led to trouble at the polls, overall the election was extraordinarily peaceful for one being held amidst a great war.

The North's domination of the South started even before the war had officially ended. Before counting the electoral college vote on February 8, Congress, where the Radical Republicans held sway, adopted the 22nd Joint Rule, whereby no electoral votes objected to in joint session should be counted except by concurrent agreement of both houses. This was to ensure the rejection of the electoral votes of Louisiana and Tennessee, newly reconstructed states that the Radicals were not yet prepared to accept on Lincoln's terms. (Elections had not been held in the other seceded states.)

## An Election Day Wager

Like any other election day, even a wartime election was a good opportunity for a wager. A story from Silver City, Nevada in 1864 tells of two fellows, L. D. Noyes and J. C. Benson, Union (the name by which Republicans were called in 1864) and Democrat, respectively, who met and after bantering a bit laid a wager. In writing, they agreed that if Mr. Lincoln were re-elected, Benson would saw an entire cord of wood in front of Chrysopolis Hall, in Silver City, in the presence of and to the satisfaction of a committee of 30 persons, half Democrats and half Union men. On the other hand, if General McClellan were elected, Mr. Noyes would be bound by the agreement to saw the wood.

When news came that Lincoln had won, and therefore, J. C. Benson had lost, a man was sent to obtain the wood. Several thousand people were expected to come to watch as Benson sawed "in sizes suited to making canes, and other useful articles."[25] The proceeds were to be donated to the Nevada Sanitary Fund and was not expected to be less than $5,000!

# *A Country Reunited*  *10*

It must have been with special interest and concern that southern blacks heard the news that they might one day participate in the electoral process. Even for those who had never thought of wishing for political rights, election day had always been notable because it was a plantation holiday—one of those rare occasions when only the necessary chores were done; slaves had the rest of the day to themselves.

What no one in the country could foresee was what was in store for the entire population once the voting system changed. Election days during Reconstruction were destined to be the darkest in our history. While voting transpired peacefully in a few parts of the South, at many of the polling places, hatred, coercion and bloodshed were the order of the day.

On the national level, the years between the wartime election in 1864 and the next election in 1868 were filled with uncertainty. Forty-two days into Lincoln's second term, the country had a new president, Andrew Johnson, a well-meaning southern Democrat and staunch Unionist who was unevenly equipped to help an ill-prepared country face the problems of postwar readjustment.

Had Lincoln lived, perhaps the rebuilding of the nation would have gone more smoothly. As it was, Andrew Johnson tried to follow the plan left for him, but did so with little regard for "playing politics," and the results were disastrous. After giving Johnson a year to get his plan underway, the Radical Republicans (who had only reluctantly supported the Lincoln–Johnson ticket in 1864 and had been vociferous in their criticism of Lincoln's moderate approach to reconstruction) rebelled, determined to see the South rebuilt the way they saw fit. Though Johnson's plan provided for prompt reacceptance of southern representation in Congress, the Radicals demurred. They wanted a guarantee of black suffrage in the South first. (And of course, if the South weren't represented, then the Democratic Party would be virtually impotent, leaving the Republicans to manage the country.) The Radical plan called for military occupation of the South to implement full black suffrage (for southern blacks only; northern states were to be left to decide this issue for themselves, and New Hampshire, Vermont, Massachusetts and New York were the only states that began the Civil War with constitutions that allowed blacks to vote), disfranchisement of most southern whites and the building up of Republican organizations in the southern states. Despite presidential veto, this Reconstruction plan was the one that was implemented, beginning with the passage of the Reconstruction Act of 1867.

On the eve of the election of 1868, a presidential impeachment trial was in progress. The Radicals were serious in their intention to dominate the government and saw

Johnson and his concerns about the constitutionality of their actions as an impediment to their progress. In March of 1867, Congress challenged the president's authority by passing the Tenure of Office Act, which provided that Johnson must seek Senate approval before removing any of his cabinet members from office. When Johnson decided to test the Act by removing an active Radical, Secretary of War Edwin Stanton, Congress started impeachment proceedings—a disgraceful moment in American history when little regard was shown for the Constitution or for the man accused. During a three-month trial that began in March of 1868, Johnson was tried on 11 counts—10 of which concerned his violation of the Tenure of Office Act; a final one accused him of having disgraced Congress and the presidency by having given some of his speeches in a loud voice. When the time came for the final ballot in the Senate, Johnson's fate hinged on only one vote. When that vote was cast against impeachment, the career of that senator, freshman Radical Edmund G. Ross from Kansas, was ruined, but Johnson, and the Constitution that Johnson had so ardently defended, were saved.

In the aftermath of this fevered excitement, the the Radical Republicans (calling themselves the National Union Republican Party) met in Chicago and nominated General Ulysses S. Grant, the only candidate they considered. An extraordinarily popular war hero, Grant had a clean record, hadn't said anything controversial and was a man who had voted only once—in 1856 when he cast his vote for Democrat James Buchanan. Speaker of the House Schuyler Colfax of Indiana was added to the ticket as vice president.

Grant's popularity was such that the Democrats were at a loss for a candidate, because they, too, had hoped to nominate him. When their national convention began in the newly built Tammany Hall in New York City on July 4, the convention deadlocked, and they opted to nominate the chairman of the convention, former New York Governor Horatio Seymour. On the 22nd ballot the nomination was finally his. General Francis P. Blair was chosen as running mate.

The two primary issues of the campaign were Reconstruction—how the country would be rebuilt and made whole after the Civil War—and "greenbackism"—the argument over whether or not paper money backed only by the credit of the U.S. government was right for the economy. Both parties were evasive on both counts.

Certainly, Grant was not interested in politics and was by no means a politician. He was content to let his campaign managers seek out voter support while he remained mute on the issues, maintaining his image of the strong silent soldier and allowing people to take him on faith and his campaign slogan, "Let Us Have Peace." His campaign was well-managed, and stump speakers traveled throughout the country for the Union Republicans. Tanner clubs (Grant had at one time been a tanner) were formed to "tan" the Democrats, and Union veterans were happy to participate in torchlight parades in honor of their leader. Always eager to besmirch the other candidate, the party also asserted that the Democrats' Horatio Seymour was a Copperhead (Confederate sympathizer) and had a streak of insanity.

Once Seymour accepted the nomination he became quite enthusiastic about having a platform from which to blast the Radical Republicans, and he was a tireless stump speaker on his own behalf. Seymour and the Democratic stump speakers criticized the Radicals' approach to Reconstruction, their solicitation of the black vote and made much of Grant's intemperate drinking (Grant had resigned from the military under pressure because of it).

In the election, 34 states participated (Florida chose electors through the legislature; Virginia, Mississippi and Texas, still under military rule, did not vote). Few southern whites were permitted to vote; both Johnson and the Congress agreed that southerners who had actively participated in the Rebellion should be disfranchised. But under the provisions of Reconstruction that went into effect in 1867, many southern blacks voted for the first time. Grant received 214 electoral votes to Seymour's 80. Amazingly, in the popular vote, Grant won by only a little more than 300,000 out of a total of 5,750,000. Since almost all black votes would have been for the party of Lincoln and therefore for Grant, this meant that without the 450,000 to 500,000 votes cast by freedmen in the South, Grant would have had a smaller popular vote than Seymour (though he still probably would have won in the electoral college because of his strength in the North).

Elated by the boost the black vote had given them, Republicans quickly realized it would be advantageous to gain this voting strength in both the North and the South. Despite the fact that the Republican Party platform had indicated that northern states would be left to decide on black suffrage for themselves, Congress quickly passed the 15th Amendment providing that the right to vote should not be denied or abridged on account of race, color or previous condition of servitude. Within a year, three-fourths of the states had ratified it.

## Black Suffrage in the South

Orders for the granting of black suffrage in the South were issued by Congress in June of 1866. Proportional reduction in southern representation was threatened if states didn't give blacks the vote—an action that would have had considerable impact on southern states. States that agreed to these terms would be admitted and regain Congressional representation. Only Tennessee accepted these terms; the other 10 states refused.

Congress then moved in with a plan to divide the South into five divisions, placing them under control of the military, which was charged with overseeing the establishment of state governments that would adhere to the following three provisions: 1. Blacks must be allowed to vote for delegates to the constitutional convention that each of the defeated southern states was required to hold; 2. The new constitutions must provide permanently for black suffrage; and 3. Newly organized states must ratify the proposed 14th Amendment (which provided that the black was a citizen and that no state could abridge the privilege or immunities of citizens or deprive any person of life, liberty or property without due process of law), in order to be readmitted to the Union.

Naively, some southerners reacted to the news of blacks getting the ballot with the feeling that the blacks' former subservience would mean that they would vote with their masters. Instead of decreasing the power of the landowner, some thought it would actually increase it. So cavalier were they that the southern Democrats (the Democratic Party, of course, being the party of choice for southern whites) made no effort to win over black voters. Political meetings were sometimes held separately for the two races, or sometimes they would meet together with seating for blacks in the rear. At barbecues and picnics, blacks ate separately or after the whites had finished.[1]

However, when it became clear that once given the chance, blacks planned to vote for the Party that had freed them, southern whites reacted with different forms of coercion. In general, there was a pattern. Verbal persuasion to vote Democratic was the first method used; if that failed, economic pressure was applied. The last resort was intimidation, which often led to physical force. (Blacks who agreed not to vote

*While this depiction of the "first" black vote is hardly representative of many election day scenes in the late 1860s, it does depict the craftsman (note tools in the voter's pocket), the well-dressed urbanite and the soldier, all of whom were now to be eligible to cast ballots in the South. (*Harper's Weekly, *November 16, 1867)*

or to vote Democratic as a result of intimidation or force were often offered "protection papers"—supposed passports to safety—by party leaders. One can only guess at how effective these papers were at holding off violence when the bearer was threatened again.)

Verbal persuasion took many forms. Some plantation owners appealed to former slaves by urging them not to "abandon those who have always cared for them, those who knew them intimately, and those with whom their destiny lay."[2]

On the other side when carpetbaggers—northerners who had moved to the South, generally for private gain—were urging blacks to vote Republican, they advised that if the whites were allowed to succeed at the polls, a return to slavery would result. Scare tactics were also used, and they threatened to cast spells that would fill the offending voter with "lizards, and scorpions and snakes, and bring diseases upon them."[3] In a Senate report, black Democrats of South Carolina testified to being threatened with murder; ostracism from their church; and verbal abuse for having voted Democratic.[4] Sometimes notices were circulated with the names of "bolters" (blacks who asserted political independence from the Radical Republicans), and warnings were issued not to allow them to vote or the accepting person would be prosecuted and sent to the penitentiary.[5] On the other hand, if the Radicals succeeded, they promised to have the whites' lands confiscated and "give everyone of you forty acres and a mule."[6]

But when words failed, in most areas, southern whites hesitated little before applying economic pressure. Though troops had been called in to supervise voting registration in Sparta, Louisiana, there was little they could do with a situation such as this—a local employer suddenly decided he didn't have work for blacks if they voted: "This morning I discharged 3 of my hands . . . I gave them from last Monday until Saturday night to decide as to whether or not they would vote. They being unwilling to give me a positive answer, I thereupon told them I would dispense with their services . . . I retain two who promised me last week without any parley that they would stay at the mill and attend to their work."[7]

Workers were usually docked for taking the day off to register or to vote, and merchants cut off credit to politically active blacks. Landlords threatened to evict from plantations "any negro who will not swear never again to vote the Radical ticket."[8]

When new contracts with his laborers were due, one employer in Alabama simply added a clause that forbade laborers to "*attend elections* or political meetings" without his consent.[9]

Economic coercion was often organized by state and local political groups (sometimes forcing employers to threaten or be ostracized or boycotted themselves), but there was a limit to its effectiveness. Although most blacks were dependent upon white landowners for their livelihood, the reverse was also true; employers, with plantations too large to manage alone, were often too dependent on workers to follow through with their threats.

Bribing was another form of economic coercion. A good example occurred in the early 1870s, when senators and representatives from Alabama secured an appropriation from Congress for bacon to provide relief for flooded areas of the state. It later developed that the bacon was not distributed in the spring when the appropriation came through, but held until election time. Blacks were told there would be a barbecue at Monroeville on election day and that all blacks who attended and voted the Republican ticket would receive bacon enough to last them a year. A deputy marshal who testified on the matter estimated that at least 500 illegal votes were cast there for the Republican ticket as a result of the bribe.[10]

Intimidation was the next step. Many blacks were afraid to vote because they had been told that if they ever voted Republican, then "their throats would be cut from ear to ear..."[11] One town went so far as to murder a black and leave on him a sign warning that others would meet with the same fate if they voted inappropriately. In rural Mississippi, the southern whites were desperate to carry an important local election and came up with a plan. For a week preceding the election, one of the whites bought black hair from the local barber who served blacks, and he got butchers to save waste blood from slaughter-pens. The night before the election, committees went out about a mile on every road and path leading to the town. They tracked up the ground and scattered hair and blood in each area, trying to leave evidence of furious fighting. The next day hundreds of blacks left their work in order to vote, but at the signs of what had evidently happened to others, they fled to their homes for protection. Not a single black vote was cast.[12]

In most of the Reconstruction states, boards of registrars consisted of two whites and one black, which they hoped would encourage blacks to register. Since thousands of whites were unable to qualify because of their part in the War, and still others refused to register, black registrants dominated in many areas. Of the 1,363,000 registered voters for the election of 1868, more than half 703,000—were black, giving blacks a majority of the electorate in Alabama, Florida, Louisiana, Mississippi and South Carolina.[13]

Despite the fact that many did register, other blacks declared that they wouldn't register; some expressed concern about the fact that their pay would be docked if they took the day to register, while others bowed to intimidation. Still others simply did not know what to do.

Realizing that ignorance might be one of the reasons blacks failed to participate, Benjamin Franklin Randolph, a black activist, toured the interior of South Carolina providing information to blacks as to how to register and what having the vote meant. Local whites made it difficult for him, however, and while canvassing these districts the following year, Randolph was murdered.[14]

## The First Election Day for Freedmen

In areas where it was calm on the presidential election day of 1868 when blacks first could vote, all ages, male and female, came by foot, in carts or in wagons to the polling places and camped out overnight. Usually, tables were set out with food, and often a political meeting resembling a great party took place with all the blacks sitting around large bonfires drinking, singing and playing music—in other words, partaking in the traditional election eve festivities that they had always watched from a distance. When the polls opened, they marched up and voted, almost always in groups. Generally, a leader, standing on a box, handed out ballots as voters filed past, and all were warned not to take any ticket other than the one given by the leader, usually a black preacher who could no more read the ballots distributed than could the recipients.[15] An observer of the election in Montgomery, Alabama, noticed that the freedmen standing in line seldom spoke, apparently deeming silence more appropriate to the solemnity of the occasion. Noticing one of his laborers in line, an employer in Montgomery, Alabama, discharged him on the spot; "the freedman smiled, looked down, said nothing, and voted."[16]

Fights were plentiful, and though most left the all-day picnic shortly after the closing of the polls, some stayed and partied into the night.

A Union officer in South Carolina reported that in his area (Greenville), a region inhabited by tenant farmers rather than plantation hands, things were better, the election passed off quietly: "Obedient to the instructions of their judicious managers, the freedmen voted quietly and went immediately home, without the reproach of a fight or a drunkard and without even a hurrah of triumph. Their little band of music turned out in the evening to serenade a favorite candidate; but a word from him sent them bedward with silent trumpets, and the night was remarkable for tranquillity. Even the youngsters who sometimes rowdied in the streets seemed to be sensible of the propriety of unusual peace, and vanished early. Judging from what I saw that day, I should have halcyon hopes for the political future of the Negro."[17]

This was overly optimistic. Chaos, lack of knowledge on the part of the newly enfranchised blacks, and the clash of wills between the Klan and its nemesis from the North—the carpetbaggers—made elections held in the South during Reconstruction ripe for abuse. Methods of violating the vote were numerous.

Inspecting votes was sometimes done to check what was going into the ballot box. A door of sorts would be made of rails, and all voters would be required to pass through it. Typically, white voters of either party were allowed to pass through without question, but blacks would be stopped and their ballots inspected before being allowed through. If a black had a Democratic ticket, it would be objected to and would not be accepted unless it was changed. Parts of the South had no effective registration laws, and it was also perfectly possible to cast additional votes under names of people who had died, moved or under names registered that day.[18]

Carpetbaggers were fond of helping the freedmen vote "early and often." In any area where a white plurality was feared, carpetbaggers carted blacks from one county to another, or from one state to another and let them vote over and over. In Florida, a pair of black brothers were instructed by the governor to start at the Georgia line and travel in toward the capital, stopping to vote at each of the polls they passed. (The counties were not yet divided into precincts, so voters could cast ballots anywhere in the state.) It was estimated that about 500 votes were secured by a handful of voters using this method.[19]

Other tricks included changing polling-places suddenly, and informing the blacks and not the whites; whites would walk miles to a registration place to find it closed.[20] The age-old maneuver of vote-buying was used as well as "voting the dead."

Obviously, angry white southerners weren't likely to take this without some form of retaliation. Coming into vogue at this time, was the "tissue ballot"—ballots printed on small, thin pieces of paper that could be hidden inside a regular ballot, meaning that one ballot might actually contain many votes for the "proper" party. With a little agitation of the ballot box, the "little jokers," as they were called, could be shaken free from each other and from the bigger ballot in which they were hidden. One southerner told of using the tissue ballot to trick his own clergyman into helping the Democrats: "I am free to say I used many tissue ballots. My old pastor (he was eighty and as true and simple a soul as ever lived) voted I don't know how many at one time, didn't know he was doing it, just took the folded ballot I handed him and dropped it in, didn't want to vote at all."[21]

Of course, there was always the danger that the ballots polled would exceed registration lists. In this case, according to law, the ballot box was to be taken into a private room, and a blindfolded elector would put his hand in the box and withdraw papers until ballots and lists tallied. Since a tissue ballot could be told by its feel, an elector could withdraw as sympathy dictated. (Some electors accepted money to guarantee the right outcome.) At one election, "the Republican ran his hand into the box and gave it a stir; straightway it became so full it couldn't be shut, ballots falling apart and multiplying themselves. The Republican laughed: 'I have heard of self-raising flour. These are self-raising ballots!' "[22]

In another instance, southerners brought the managers of a circus in on a scheme to trick the freedmen out of their registration certificates, which were necessary for voting. The white southerners made a deal with the circus management to accept registration certificates instead of charging admission. (The locals agreed to redeem the admission price on all certificates turned over to them.) The circus had tremendous crowds, but the blacks lost their opportunity to vote because of the hoax.

## The Ku Klux Klan and Election Day

No discussion of southern election days during Reconstruction would be complete without a discussion of the Ku Klux Klan. Originally formed in Tennessee in 1866 as a social club, the group soon became a terrorist arm for the Democratic Party. It generally began a reign of terror two to three weeks before an election. Allen Trelease's book, *White Terror*, describes it well: ". . . armed bands of disguised men rode through the countryside after dark, making the rounds of Negro cabins. Sometimes they fired shots into the houses as they rode by; at other places they called out the inmates and threatened them with the extreme penalty if they voted the Republican ticket."[23]

The Klan grew up in various parts of the South and the various groups were generally made up of the leading men of the town. Intimidation, beatings and murder were used to keep blacks from the polls. Generally clad in white sheets, masks and tall, pointed hats, the Klan usually rode at night, as further protection against being identified, and their night riding—more frequent in some counties than in others— tended to intensify on the nights just preceding an election. The incidents of terror occurred all over the South.

In Camilla, Georgia, 400 armed whites, led by the local sheriff, opened fire on a black election parade, and then scoured the countryside looking for those who had fled—eventually killing and wounding more than a score of blacks. When a mob destroyed a Republican newspaper in New Orleans, drove the editor out of the area and then invaded the plantations killing as many as 200 blacks, the commanding officer of the military unit in charge of reconstruction programs in the area refused to take action and urged blacks to stay away from the polls for self-protection. In some parts of the South, armed whites blocked blacks from going to vote or prevented polls from opening on election day. Unable to quell the violence, Georgia and Louisiana Republicans abandoned the presidential campaign of 1868.[24]

In Reconstruction Louisiana, every election between 1868 and 1876 was marked by violence and fraud. The Whit League, one of the Klan-style organizations in Louisiana that was openly dedicated to the restoration of white supremacy, targeted local Republican officeholders; in Red River Parish (county) in the early 1870s, six Republican officials were murdered.[25] A Radical Republican testified before Congress that on the day of the election the principal roads in the parish leading to the different places of voting were patrolled by armed men of these Klans "for the purpose of intercepting Republicans going to vote; and in many instances, plantations where freedmen were employed were guarded by armed men to prevent the freedmen from going to the polls."[26]

In 1868, the local New Orleans elections held in April had gone Republican, partly because blacks were imported by steamboat to vote in the elections. Fearing a recurrence in the presidential elections in November, local Democrats were intent on seeing that things went differently.

Saturday night was the most popular night for political gatherings and processions, and on Saturday, October 24, when both Republican and Democratic clubs were out in procession, the Republicans were jumped by a group hiding in the tree- lined center of the street. They fled, but several blacks were killed and the rest went home and armed themselves. Rioting continued for several days. Republican clubs were entered and destroyed, and black homes were broken into and voter registration certificates stolen. On October 27, U.S. troops began arriving from Mississippi, and by Wednesday the rioting had abated though isolated incidents of violence continued until election day. The death toll was estimated at seven whites and 14 blacks.[27]

Though there were few incidents of harassment of blacks on election day that year in New Orleans, the majority of Republicans failed to vote. In the city, Democratic votes cast numbered 23,897 to only 276 Republican. Violence and intimidation did not need to take place on election day in order to keep black voters from the polls.[28]

Perhaps nothing can convey the terror of those nights when the Ku Klux Klan patrolled the South as the testimony, given before Congress in 1871, of a black man in South Carolina who lived through it. Speaking slowly and haltingly, the man, whose name was Lewis, described being awakened by the Klan one night after an election. Knowing that the men meant ill toward him, Lewis stalled and didn't open his door until the Klansmen so intimidated his wife that she opened the door for them. When Lewis finally emerged from the house, he said a Klansman asked: " 'How did you vote?' I says, 'I voted the radical ticket.' 'You has, sir?' he says. I says, 'Yes, sir.' 'Well, by Christ,' says he 'Ain't you had no instruction?' "[29]

The verbal badgering continued and one of the men used a pistol to poke Lewis under the chin, after which Lewis testified:

"He says, 'Now Lewis, by Christ, you get down on your knees.' I says, 'It is hard to get down on my knees and take a whipping for nothing.' Then I dropped down. He says, 'By Christ, don't you get up until we get done with you.' They set to work on me and hit me 10 or 15 licks pretty keen, and I raised up. 'Get down,' he says; 'If you ever raise up again you'll go dead before we quit you.' Down I went again, and I staid [sic] down until they got done whipping me. Says he, 'Now, by Christ, you must promise you will vote the democratic ticket?' I says, 'I don't know how I will vote; it looks hard when a body thinks this way and that way to take a beating'; . . . 'You must promise to vote the democratic ticket, or you go dead before we leave you,' he says."[30]

Throughout the South, both whites and blacks were victims, and the Klan tended to aim for leaders—both elected officials and party leaders, not just those who went to the polls.

In Tennessee, one white county commissioner had received Klan threats, so he hid in the woods nightly for many nights. Finally in January, he stayed inside to avoid the cold, and he was discovered, taken from his house and beaten because he was a Radical.[31] In Alabama, a circuit judge wrote an impassioned letter to the governor in 1871 telling of damage to his plantation and threats received by fellow officeholders in an effort to get anti-Klan officeholders to resign.[32]

In many parts of the South by the 1870s, intimidation by the Klan had gone a long way toward effectively subduing the Republican vote. In Kemper County, Mississippi, a Radical Republican, brought in after the War whom all acknowledged to have been a good mayor of Meridian, was the cause of a three-day riot for threatening to end Klan dominance. He was eventually escorted out of the state (locals spared his life because of his otherwise good service as mayor).

Some Republicans remained in the area trying to lead the way to more equality for the races, but theirs was a tough fight. Throughout the 1870s, they were effectively threatened and kept from participating on an equal footing with Democrats. One particularly grisly set of incidents comes from Kemper County concerning Judge

William Chisolm (a man who earned the enmity of many by trying to break the Klan) and John P. Gilmer, the leading Republicans in the area, who were slated to be assassinated on election day in 1874. They escaped assassination that time by leaving the area by back roads. Only three or four Republican votes were cast at their local precinct, an area where, if the blacks voted Republican, they should have had a majority by more than 100.

In 1876, Judge Chisolm was nominated as a candidate for United States Congress. Campaigning was virtually impossible because of death threats. Eventually the crowds who harassed the judge, both on aborted attempts to campaign and at his house, were so threatening that the family had to take refuge in the local jail (a rather common practice of people seeking protection at this time). After a time, the mob broke into the jail and murdered Chisolm's son and critically wounded the judge as well as his daughter. Upon being shot, Judge Chisolm whispered to his wife: ". . . when I am gone, I want you to tell my children that their father never did an act in his life for which they need to blush or feel ashamed. I am innocent of the charge these men have preferred against me, and have been murdered because I am a republican and would live a free man!"[33]

Some efforts for improvement were made in the early 1870s with the passage of the Enforcement Acts, which made it easier to bring charges for fraud, bribery or intimidation of voters, followed by the Ku Klux Klan Act of April 1871, which designated certain crimes committed by individuals as offenses punishable under federal law, but there was still a long way to go.

## The 1868 Election in St. Louis

While disfranchised Confederate white men stood on the sidelines— politically impotent for the moment—and blacks in various communities throughout the South met with a variety of circumstances ranging from peaceable voting to quiet coercion or open violence over their right to cast the ballot, it is interesting to read how election day was conducted in an area unaffected by Reconstruction. The newspaper reports from St. Louis highlight items such as the conveniences brought about by preprinted poll books, the police telegraph and a luminous bulletin board. The stories of the atrocities taking place appear elsewhere in the paper, but St. Louis was obviously untouched by trouble.

Election day in November of 1868 is described as busy, but quiet and free of trouble. The weather was fair, and many were out early to cast their votes. Because of the preprinted poll-books, voting took place more quickly, and the police telegraph reported tallies much more rapidly than ever before.

Between 6:00 and 7:00 P.M. crowds began to gather in front of the newspaper office to learn the latest news. The publisher of the *Daily Missouri Republican* had arranged for a luminous bulletin board to display the news, and the crowd was delighted with the invention. A large white sheet was suspended across Chestnut Street in front of the newspaper's office, and, using a scientifically devised lantern with a prismatic lens, the returns were cast upon this sheet and could be read clearly from a distance. First, a large circle of light would appear on the sheet, and then as the glasses were inserted the letters and figures written on the glass would come into distinct view. "During the intermissions between the receipt of reports some beautiful dissolving views were exhibited on the sheet, to the delight and amusement of the crowd,"[34] reported the newspaper.

There was also a special telegraph wire from Main Street to the newspaper office, so that the correspondents did not have to wait for messengers to arrive with the news.

It was past midnight before the crowd in front of the *Republican* office dispersed, and, in fact, some lingered until the sheet on which the bulletin had been displayed was drawn in.

## 1872: The "Age of the Spoilsman"

From 1868 to 1872, President Ulysses S. Grant, seemingly unwittingly, oversaw some of the sorriest years the nation had yet experienced. Grant has been referred to as the "most harmful president the country ever had," and it was certainly true that he was in a job for which he had no ability and in which he unfailingly listened to bad advice. Corruption was rampant, and descriptions of the scandals that took place during his administration know no end. Misdeeds took place everywhere from the post office to the navy yards. While it appears that Grant's only indulgence for himself was that he and his wife were entertained lavishly by the wealthy (which he greatly enjoyed), his close advisors and relatives savored gains they could put in their pockets.

It has been called the Age of the Spoilsman, and it must have been. One disgruntled congressman from Ohio declared in 1873 that "the House of Representatives was like an auction room where more valuable considerations were disposed of under the hammer than in any other place on earth."[35] Between 1866 and 1872, the Union Pacific alone spent $400,000 on bribes.

The Republican Party met in Philadelphia and renominated Grant on the first ballot with Henry Wilson of Massachusetts as running mate. Some Republicans were disenchanted with the way things were going, and they formed a new group and called themselves Liberal Republicans. The Liberal Republicans considered nominating Charles Francis Adams (son of John Quincy) and Salmon P. Chase, both of whom would have been fine candidates, but through political maneuvering the candidate of choice turned out to be Horace Greeley, the long-time editor of *The New York Tribune*; Greeley had established a reputation for liberal stands on social reform but his erratic and eccentric personality was ill-suited for politics.

The Democratic Party basically folded its tents for the election of 1872. Desperate to defeat Grant, the Democrats met in Baltimore for only a few hours before deciding to accept both platform and candidate of the Liberal Republicans, despite the fact that politically the two parties were certainly not a "fit."

*These two illustrations appeared in the October 26, 1872 issue of* Harper's Weekly *in connection with the October elections. Perhaps the description that appeared at the time says it best: "... the above [illustration] exhibits a scene at the polls which was of frequent occurrence during the recent elections of Pennsylvania, Ohio, and Indiana. The right of challenge [to question whether or not a certain person is eligible to vote], when properly exercised, is one of the great safeguards of the purity of the ballot-box, though it may be abused, through partisan zeal, and made an obstruction to an honest vote.*

*The illustration below shows a party of Pennsylvania miners, who have made their appearance at the polls previous to descending into the mine. They have all their mining implements with them, and can ill afford to spare the time necessary to cast their votes before going to work. But they are men of sturdy character and conviction, who believe in doing their whole duty as freemen and patriots; and before descending to their labors they mean to do what they can to secure the triumph of the party which saved the country when it was threatened by rebellion, and will save it again from shameful surrender to the party which once plotted its destruction."* (Harper's Weekly *October 26, 1872*)

Grant, in keeping with his previous campaign and in the tradition of incumbents, remained aloof from any political activity and summered at his home in Long Branch, New Jersey. Republican campaign managers organized stump speakers, parades and rallies for the "man who whipped the South." The opposition launched personal attacks at Grant for his drunkenness, dictatorship and corruption, but the public didn't seem to listen—he was still their war hero.

Social reformer and editor Horace Greeley took to the stump for several weeks and spoke well and convincingly for what he believed. This was a surprise to the public for he had achieved notoriety through the merciless caricatures of Grant drawn by Thomas Nast in *Harper's Weekly*. Greeley was already viewed as an eccentric—he generally wore a long linen duster over wrinkled clothes and a white hat from which long silver locks emerged. He was an easy target for lampooning. Unfortunately, neither Greeley's nor the party's efforts were enough to get him taken seriously by the people.

Notable during the campaign of 1872 was the dilemma of the press. Up until this time, the newspapers had been totally partisan, but the seriousness of the corruption in Washington at this time caught some of the Republican editors by surprise. While they seemed to have given Grant until the end of his first term to come around, a few of the editors finally responded to the malfeasance of the era by moving their papers away from their partisan voices and into investigative journalism (preceding the muckraking that was to come in a few years). The Chicago *Tribune*, the Springfield *Republican*, the Cincinnati *Daily Commercial* and the Louisville *Courier-Journal* all helped carve out territory for Greeley's party, the Liberal Republicans, by attacking the patronage, graft and fraud of the administration they had formerly supported.

By the time Election Day 1872 dawned, most polls saw peaceful voting. A local newspaper gives a glimpse:

> The voting places were surrounded by crowds of men, sometimes several hundred at one place. There was the ordinary number of persons engaged in distributing the tickets of the contesting parties, and quite a number of spring wagons suitably labelled, engaged in bringing the candidates' friends to record their votes. Under the supervision of the officers of the law everything went off with the most unprecedented regularity and tranquillity. Although the weather was somewhat cloudy and chilly, it was not on the whole unfavorable, and appearances indicated that rather a heavy vote was being polled. Only a few arrests were made, and these were slight cases of disturbing the peace or violating the mayor's ordinance.[36]

Grant was reelected carrying every northern state and most of the carpetbag South. The popular vote was 3,596,745 for Grant to 2,843,446 for Greeley. Votes were thrown out in several southern states on technicalities.

The defeat was too much for Greeley, whose wife had just died and who feared he was going to lose the *Tribune*. He broke down under the strain and died in a sanitorium on November 29. At the electoral vote-counting in February, Greeley's electors split their votes between the vice presidential candidate and several favorite sons, but Grant won decisively with 286 of the 349 electoral votes.

## Women Suffragists Work for the Vote

Women in Wyoming Territory had been given the right to vote in 1869, and in Utah, women had gained suffrage rights in 1870, but women elsewhere were still agitating for the vote. A woman suffrage campaign had begun at Seneca Falls, New York in 1848, and Lucretia Mott, Susan B. Anthony and Elizabeth Cady Stanton were still traveling and working for women's rights. In 1872, Susan B. Anthony decided to take decisive action; she tried to vote in Rochester, New York. Thirteen days later she was arrested.

Elsewhere, women were making statements about their desire to vote. Election Day 1868 in New Jersey was a day chosen for a demonstration. At Union Hall election judges sat at a table on which sat a ballot box where voters were to deposit their ballots. Opposite them was a table where self-appointed women election judges sat at their own table with a ballot box. During the day men entered, sometimes accompanied by their wives. The men cast their ballots as usual; the women first attempted to deposit ballots in the regular box, and when they were refused they walked to the left and "voted" in the box designated for the women. Many then went to the homes of acquaintances where they took care of the children in order that others could come and vote.[37]

A few women decided to test whether or not the 14th Amendment (forbidding any state to abridge the privileges of citizens), protected their rights as well. In New York, Susan B. Anthony carried her case all the way to the federal courts; in 1873, the Supreme Court held that the right to vote was not a privilege necessarily accompanying United States citizenship.[38] The same issue was retested in Missouri in 1874 with the same result.[39]

## 1876: The Disputed Election

Throughout the latter part of the 19th century, elections were considered a lively spectacle and something that most people truly enjoyed. Participation was often boisterous and exuberant, and Americans loved a good election fight. In 1876 they were to get one like no other. Ironically, this election, featuring two reform candidates, was destined to be one of the most controversial in history, and the dispute it aroused lasted from November 8, 1876 to March 2, 1877 before being resolved.

Times had been tough since the Panic of 1873. Midterm elections had removed control of the House from the Republicans for the first time since 1865 and had greatly reduced their power in the Senate. Discoveries of wrongdoings continued, and the taint of corruption directly touched men throughout the Grant administration. Among those sullied by scandal were the secretary of war—who was found to be taking kickbacks on the sale of trading posts in the West—and Vice President Colfax, who was implicated in a major business scandal—the Credit Mobilier affair. Despite all this, Grant was still popular, and there was some feeling he should run again; however, the House passed a resolution 234–18 that a third term would be unwise at this time. Grant was glad to comply.

When the Republicans met in Cincinnati in mid-June, James G. Blaine of Maine was the popular favorite, but a recent scandal in which he had been involved had just been uncovered. Though Blaine led the first ballot, and Rutherford B. Hayes, governor of Ohio, had only 61 votes, Blaine didn't have enough to win, and party leaders decided to regroup and unite behind one candidate in order to defeat Blaine. On the 7th ballot, Hayes received 384 votes to Blaine's 351 and won the nomination. New York Congressman William A. Wheeler got the vice-presidential nomination.

The Democrats met in St. Louis in late June and had an obvious choice in Samuel Tilden of New York who had achieved fame for bringing down Boss Tweed while serving as district attorney. For a reform campaign, no candidate could have been better. To run with him, the Democrats selected Thomas A. Hendricks of Indiana.

Though both candidates were in agreement on the major issues such as hard money, withdrawal of federal troops from the South and civil service reform, nevertheless the campaign was extremely ugly. Tilden was accused of making millions as attorney for the robber barons, evading taxes, aiding Tammany Hall and planning to pay off Confederate debt if elected. He was called a thief, a liar, and a swindler and gained nicknames of Slippery Sammy and Soapy Sammy. Hayes was accused of stealing pay from dead soldiers in his Civil War regiment, cheating Ohio out of vast sums of money while governor and shooting his mother "in a fit of insanity."[40]

The Republican machine of Roscoe Conkling, party boss of New York, and national chairman Chandler tried to ignore Hayes during the campaign, feeling that a reform candidate meant that the Republicans had something to apologize for. They campaigned by reminding people of the Civil War and the dangers of the Democratic Party as the party of treason and rebellion. A riot in South Carolina in July in which several blacks were slain served to show the dire consequences if the southern- controlled Democrats came into power.[41]

There was every indication that local communities were expecting a difficult election. In Missouri, the U.S. Marshal wrote: "Desirous of having a free and untrammeled expression through the Ballot Box at the approaching Election—I have under the acts of Congress of the United States appointed a large number of Special Deputy Marshals . . ."[42]

In Delaware, the Republicans also had 100 additional deputy marshals appointed to guard the polls, and, said the Democrats, to intimidate voters. (The mayor was a Democrat, so he immediately appointed 200 extra city policemen with orders to arrest any deputy marshal interfering with the voting.) When the deputies arrested some voters, the mayor intervened and went with them to the marshal's headquarters, where he was able to get them released.[43]

Excited crowds gathered outside *The New York Times* office election night to watch for bulletins on the closest election in the nation's history. New tallies brought cheers from the appropriate group, and torchlight snake dances formed.[44]

As the evening ended, it appeared that Tilden had won. He received about a quarter of a million more popular votes than Hayes (4,284,020 to 4,036,572) and 184 undisputed electoral votes to Hayes's 165. Tilden was only one short of the votes needed for victory. Twenty electoral votes (seven from South Carolina, eight from Louisiana, four from Florida and one of Oregon's three) were in doubt. Tilden needed only one to win, Hayes needed all 20.

Hayes made a diary entry that night before going to bed, acknowledging his loss. But all that was soon to change.

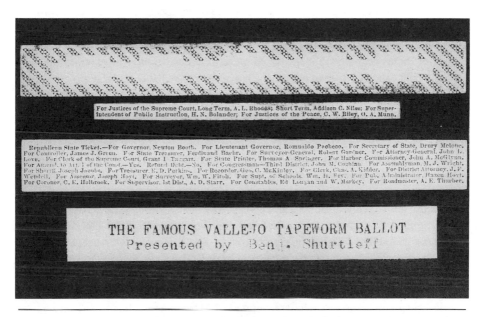

*Political parties were constantly trying to find legal methods for preventing voters from balloting for anyone other than candidates listed on the party ticket. Since "pasters" (a sticker with the name of an opposition candidate that could be pasted on the ballot) or writing in another candidate's name were the ways in which voters could alter a party ballot, the "tapeworm ballot" came into being as a way to discourage any alteration. The above ballot, used in California in 1871, featured type so small it could barely be read, and the use of stickers or pasters to alter the ballot was out of the question. The cross-hatched design on the back of the ballot prevented anyone from writing in a change of vote there. (Courtesy California State Library)*

Republican politicos soon began calculating. With 20 votes in doubt, maybe victory was still within their grasp. National committee members sent telegrams to party leaders in South Carolina, Florida and Louisiana telling them that the national outcome depended on holding their states. (Without this prod, they might have sent in definitive returns.) Agents well supplied with money were soon heading southward, and shortly the Republicans started announcing that Hayes had 185 electoral votes; Tilden, 184.

Grant sent additional federal troops to the three southern states to help preserve peace and order and to assure that the election boards were able to perform their duties.

Once looked into, the Oregon vote had clearly gone to Hayes. But in the South, fraud continued. The canvassing boards refused to count the returns (largely Democratic) from districts where blacks allegedly had been denied the right to vote, transforming Tilden's wins to Hayes's. Since both parties refused to accept the other's conclusions, both Louisiana and South Carolina sent to Washington two sets of returns—one for Hayes and the other for Tilden. Florida sent three—two for Tilden and one for Hayes.

Congress had to decide which votes to accept. Because of partisanship in Congress this couldn't be done to anyone's satisfaction, so the decision was made to form an Electoral Commission composed of five senators, five representatives, and five justices of the Supreme Court. These commission members would be selected so that seven of them were Republican, seven were Democratic, and there would be one independent to be the voice of neutrality. However, when the Illinois Democrats voted into the Senate the lone independent justice who had been counted on for the one unbiased vote, the picture changed. He resigned from the Court and was replaced by Justice Joseph Bradley, who was presumed to be more independent than the other justices but who still fell solidly in the conservative camp. Tilden was doomed.

Congress, meeting in joint session, began to count the electoral votes in alphabetical order. When the conflicting returns from Florida were announced, the Electoral Commission took over. It first had to decide whether to go behind the returns and conduct an investigation at the state level. The Republican majority rejected this approach, 8 to 7, arguing that with the inauguration less than a month away, there was no time for a full investigation. The commission merely voted—8 to 7, of course—to accept the returns from the Republican-controlled canvassing board. This procedure was repeated for Louisiana and South Carolina; the disputed Oregon vote went to Hayes.

In the meantime, Hayes had been cautiously making some deals through intermediaries. He promised an end to federal support of carpetbag rule; he offered one cabinet post and other patronage favors to the southern conservatives; and he said that he would press for federal aid for education and internal improvements in the South, including a government subsidy for the Texas and Pacific Railway. In return, he received promises of equal rights and fair treatment for southern blacks, and he was assured that the electoral count would proceed unobstructed. These negotiations became known as the Compromise of 1877.

The electoral count continued before the two houses on February 1, with a great crowd present in the House of Representatives. At 4:10 A.M. on Friday, March 2, the president of the Senate made the announcement that Hayes had received 185 electoral votes to Tilden's 184.

Hayes was inaugurated privately on Sunday March 4 and had his formal inauguration on the following Monday.

While Hayes went on to serve the country admirably, he was never able to shake the taint of a stolen election. "Rutherfraud Hayes, the Fraudulent President" and "Old 8 to 7" were some of the names he endured. And while ending Radical Reconstruction in the South concluded a poor chapter in our country's history, it also ended any thought for black civil rights. The black population was to wait a long time for any sort of justice.

## California's Election Day

While most of the country was very involved in the doings of 1876, California remained somewhat aloof. Not yet a pivotal state in national elections, the candidates had not considered California's concerns when drawing up their platforms, and, as a result, California's election day was a comparatively quiet one with little threat of violence.

The *St. Helena Star* ran an announcement that the local railroad would run a special excursion train from St. Helena to Napa. The train would run 19 miles with passengers for both parties and was scheduled so that members of each political party could hear the speaker of their choice in Napa before the return trip home. No violence was expected, and none occurred.

Pre-election coverage in the *St. Helena Star* was also dominated by what the newspaper found to be a far more important story: Evidently "at a gathering of about two hundred men a stranger suggested that it might be great 'sport' if he released some rats (which he claimed to have trapped in a box) in the crowd; the group of men gleefully agreed. But instead of the anticipated rats, an agitated skunk was turned loose. More than one hundred suits of clothing were reported destroyed in the resulting 'spraying.' With pistols drawn, the victims vainly searched for the jokester—who successfully 'lit out.' "[45]

As one might expect in the Gold Rush state, wagers on the election were part and parcel of the day. Though many newspapers ran notices warning that it was illegal to bet on the election, other papers notified their readers that wagers of as much as $10,000 were being offered.

The news of Hayes's electoral victory reached California about 2:00 A.M. on March 2, 1877, and as a result, there was one death because of the election. However, according to a local historian, the stabbing did not result from any particular difference of political opinion, but, instead, because a landscape gardener wanted to sleep while his boisterous rooming-house partner, a blacksmith, insisted on vociferously expounding his views on the electoral commission's vote. "Therefore, in order to sleep, Busby said 'Shut-up!' and stabbed his noisy fellow boarder."[46]

# Voting on the Wild Frontier     <u>11</u>

During the latter half of the 19th century, many areas of the United States were still considered "frontier," and as the influx of immigrants continued on the coasts, more and more people pushed on to new territory to establish better lives for themselves. They brought with them a continuing need for law and order and for an electoral system for choosing the government.

The areas being settled by these pioneers were, of course, the United States territories, which were organized under a specific form of government that had been designed immediately after the Revolutionary War by the Continental Congress and that was intended as a precursor to statehood. All the powers of the territorial government were vested in a governor, a secretary and a court of three judges, all of whom were appointed by Congress. A legislative body—consisting of a house of representatives chosen by the people of the territory and a five-member council chosen by Congress from nominees selected by the people—was to come into existence as soon as any territory had 5,000 free male inhabitants. The governor and legislature were to pass all laws and were to elect a delegate to the United States Congress who would be given the right to participate in all Congressional debates, but who would not have the right to vote. When the population reached a certain level (which differed as time went on), the territory had the right to hold a constitutional convention. The proposed state constitution needed to be ratified by the territorial inhabitants and could then be used to apply to the United States Congress for admission into the Union with all the status of full statehood.

Despite the very specific and careful provisions for the territorial government, the frontier was still the frontier, and though election day scenes were sometimes quite orderly, more often they were rowdy and boisterous.

Politically, this was an interesting period for several of the new western settlements. In Utah, the Mormons were wrestling with what role the church would play on election day; in Wyoming in 1869, women achieved voting rights; and in Colorado and Texas, election day activities lived up to the best of what one might dream of for a campaign on the frontier.

## Utah: The Church and the Vote

One part of the West unique in its political development was Utah. The Church of Jesus Christ of Latter-day Saints had been formed in Fayette, New York in 1830 during a period of religious revival. However, the Mormons, as they were commonly known, found themselves unwelcome in most communities. Non-Mormons were uncomfortable with their desire to remain separate and were puzzled by the Mormon belief that church officials could dictate the political beliefs of the entire group because they received divine guidance. Attempts to settle in Ohio, Missouri and Illinois proved futile, so the Mormons set out to establish their Kingdom of God on land that was then owned by Mexico.

They arrived in the Great Basin in 1847 and established a High Council, which assumed civil, economic and social authority, and drew up a plan for the governance of the people. Poll and property taxes came early to help pay for the cost of civilization.

The first election in the area was held on March 12, 1849 to choose officers and members of the General Assembly. A single roster of candidates was presented to the assembled convention for approval or disapproval. There was no campaigning or electioneering since only one slate was offered, and Brigham Young was elected first governor.

Because the people were in agreement that church leaders should make the decisions, almost all elections were unanimous in the early years. At that time, the Mormons did not see voting as an opportunity for individual expression, and elections were highly informal affairs. The citizens gathered at some point within the city, usually at "early candle light," to nominate and elect officers for the coming two years. The elected were usually put into office by acclamation and also were retained in office from year to year.[1]

The ecclesiastical government was satisfactory for a time, but by 1849 the gold diggers were stopping in on the way to California and there arose a need for a government that would work for Mormons and non-Mormons alike. Church officials foresaw the day when not all elections would go so smoothly. A marked ballot where the voter who cast it could be traced, instituted in 1853, was the solution. Utah law allowed clerks to write the name of the voter opposite the number of his ballot. In this way one illegal or improper vote could be extracted without destroying the validity of the entire vote. This, however, also gave the church the ability to scrutinize the votes to see who, if any, voted against its candidates.[2]

In the 1860s, the area's non-Mormon population increased markedly. Fort Douglas was permanently established to protect the overland mail route, and the general in charge encouraged non-Mormon immigrants to come in to mine in order to help counterbalance the Mormon population. But like other parts of the country, the party in power (the Mormons) was able to take action to prevent non-Mormons from voting in any numbers. In one case, the matter had to do with the location of the polls. With mostly non-Mormons working in the mines, the judges located the voting places in the mining counties some 20 to 50 miles from the mines. When asked for more convenient polling places, the judges refused.[3] Few miners were willing to forego a day or possibly two days' work in order to vote, thereby leaving control of the government to the Mormons.

Utah gave women the vote in 1870, trailing Wyoming by only a year. In 1870 every woman 21 and over, born or naturalized in the United States or who was the wife, widow or daughter of a naturalized citizen, who had resided in Utah Territory six months prior to an election was entitled to vote.

While this liberalism may seem unexpected, it really wasn't out of character for the Mormons. Within the church, women had always been permitted to vote equally with men on ecclesiastical matters, though their place was always below that of the men. However, the timing of giving the women the vote was dictated by two ongoing issues. First, the Mormons were likely hoping to discourage the introduction of antipolygamy legislation in the U.S. Congress (the Mormons' practice of polygamy had been the main impediment to Utah's achieving statehood) by placing Utah's political stance toward women way ahead of the rest of the country.

The second reason was to secure the women's votes for added strength because of the continued influx of outsiders. In Utah in 1870, the population was about 87,000, and giving the women the vote gave Mormons a decided advantage. Though most miners were unmarried or did not have wives residing in Utah, the population was very evenly divided between males and females, meaning that most of the women were Mormon. The new law came close to doubling the electorate, which meant that no influx of non-Mormons was likely to upset the Mormon majority.

To assure a proper turnout of women at the polls in Ogden and Salt Lake City, carriages were provided to transport them to the polls and special entrances were provided. Ladies who could drive drove others; otherwise, the men provided transportation. Several carriages made many trips back and forth. The *Salt Lake Herald* reported afterwards that all had gone well and that utmost respect was shown to the ladies. Said the paper: "It was a pleasure to see so many of the fair ones thus conveyed to the polls."[4]

As the non-Mormon group grew stronger and a newspaper developed to be their mouthpiece, the church methodology was criticized: ". . . Early in the day young girls not over fourteen years old went to the polls and deposited their votes. Soon after we heard of large numbers of women, who are not citizens of the United States, exercising the right of suffrage."[5] Still later, citizens from other precincts came in to Salt Lake City in order to vote. The local anti-Mormon paper in the area noted that the size of the vote alone, nearly 4,000, was sufficient evidence that outsiders had participated. Later the marked ballot also came under attack:

> To compel electors to number their ballots so that the ticket they vote may be known, is a violation of the first principles underlying the exercise of a free electoral franchise, offensive to the sense of justice and right professed by every American citizen.[6]

By 1878 the marked ballot was abolished, but statehood still had not been achieved. Congress continued to require the church to remove itself from political involvement, to encourage Mormon and non-Mormon economic interaction and to drop the practice of polygamy. Slowly, the church began to change its stand. By 1896, Utah had achieved statehood. Soon non-Mormons began to be elected to important political posts, and by the early part of the 20th century, the church was out of politics altogether.

## Wyoming Gives Women the Vote

Most people mistakenly believe that the first time American women cast ballots was in 1920 after the passage of the 19th Amendment, but this is not the case. Despite evidence of some women voting early in 19th century New Jersey, women in the Wyoming Territory in 1869 were the first to be explicitly given the right to vote—51 years before the nation as a whole gave women full suffrage. (Actually, many western states followed Wyoming's lead. By 1914, all states west of the Rockies, except New Mexico, had adopted full suffrage. Only one state east of the Rockies, Kansas, had done so.)

History often credits Wyoming newcomer Esther Hobart Morris with having had a tea for two legislative candidates where she asked for their pledge to support suffrage for women; there is no hard evidence that this "tea" made the difference,[7] but whatever occurred, legislator William H. Bright introduced a bill to allow women to vote, and it was quickly passed. (The 1870 census shows that there were six men for every woman over 21, making this a forward-thinking, but not a totally earth-shaking step for the Wyoming legislature to have taken.)

The first woman voter on that eventful election day in September 1870 is said to have been 75-year-old Eliza Swain. Evidently she walked to the polls as soon as they were open and cast her vote. Then as if she had done nothing at all extraordinary, she stopped at the grocer's for yeast and went home to bake bread.[8]

Contemporary reports have it that the presence of women gave a certain level of respectability to the day. As elsewhere on the frontier, election day often meant drunkenness, rowdyism and even bloodshed, but this kind of behavior did not take place that day. One historian noted, "It seemed more like Sunday than election day."[9] A newly arrived minister noted that impending quarrels were often silenced by the warning "Hist! Be quiet! A woman is coming!" He continues: "I saw ladies attended by their husbands, brothers or sweethearts, ride to the place of voting, and alight in the midst of a silent crowd, and pass through an open space to the polls, depositing their votes with no more exposure to insult or injury than they would expect on visiting a grocery store or meat market."[10]

Though Wyoming was a start, women in the United States still had a long way to go in gaining their right of suffrage.

*The above picture ran in* Harper's Weekly *on November 24, 1888, and depicts women voting in Cheyenne in 1870. Fifty-one years before the passage of the 19th Amendment providing for full women's suffrage throughout the United States, women in Wyoming Territory were given the vote. Many western states followed the lead taken by Wyoming in 1869, and by 1914 all states west of the Rockies (except New Mexico) had adopted full suffrage. Kansas was the only state east of the Rockies that had done so.* (Harper's Weekly, *November 24, 1888*)

## Arizona

Greed-driven politics predominated in prestatehood Arizona as politicians in the 1870s vied for control of the territorial government to benefit from economic development. A group of federal appointees became known as the "federal ring," and there were frequent accusations of election wrongdoings by "ring" politicians as well as by those who opposed them. After about 400 ineligible Indians of both sexes were taken to the polls to vote, the *Weekly Arizonan* wrote: "We believe in the right of women to vote . . . but it would appear more gallant on the part of [politicians who got them to the polls] had they first extended this right to the white ladies of Arizona City and compelled the squaws to remain for next season."[11]

## Coercion and Fraud in Colorado

Throughout history, local elections have always been the ones to cause excitement and bring out the people. Colorado elections were no exception. The national contest in 1904 between presidential contenders Theodore Roosevelt and Alton Parker couldn't hold a candle to what was going on locally in the gubernatorial election that pitted former Democratic governor Alva Adams against the incumbent Republican James Peabody. This election was to engender more rancor and bitterness than any election in the history of the state. The 1904 contest came on the heels of such tension over the legislature's 1902 selection of a U.S. senator that fear of violence in the state house required the constant presence of police, and state senators ate and slept at their desks or in the cloakrooms rather than leave.

In Pueblo, Colorado, enthusiasm abounded. Puebloans had had a native son in the governor's mansion for a term in 1886 and again in 1896, and now former Governor Alva Adams of Pueblo was running again with all of Pueblo behind him. Reporting about November 8, 1904, the local paper noted: "Never before have citizens of Pueblo been so interested in any election and never have they put forth such an effort to get out the entire vote as yesterday."[12] With the exception of a few straggling shoppers, stores were populated only by clerks, and the business section of town was all but shut down while members of both parties devoted the greater part of the day to working for the interests of their favorite candidates. Automobiles, cabs, carriages, hacks, single rigs and all kinds of vehicles—often decorated to represent political loyalties— were drafted into service and there was not a moment of the day that some of these rigs could not be seen carrying the voters to and from the polls.

Elsewhere in the state, other preparations for election day were taking place. In early November of 1904, Denver Chief of Police Michael Delaney spoke to several hundred gamblers, saloon keepers, ex-convicts and prostitutes in Kopper's Hall all but insisting that they sell their votes:

> "Well, we've got to win this election, boys. You want to do the best you can. We will see that you don't go to jail. You know what to do; do the same as you did before and do all you can. If we don't win this election the chances are we will get ditched. You know what you got before—protection."[13]

The chief promised to look the other way while "voters" went from precinct to precinct to vote the Democratic ticket.

That same week another political meeting was held in Hastings, the site of the Victor Fuel Company coal mine in Las Animas County. Here, Republican leaders were looking for votes for Peabody. The mine owner, Delos Chappell, told the miners and town citizens that if the Democrats won, the mine would have to be closed. Even if the Republicans won, but it was discovered that a miner had helped the Democrats, then he would be fired immediately.[14] Here, intimidation was the only hope. Peabody had helped mine owners put down strikes and was greatly disliked by laborers. Chappell took a carload of men to Hastings to make them register, but when questioned later in a joint assembly investigation, he testified: "I think perhaps I could be construed as advising them. I think my remarks were along the line that our interests were mutual in the election." [15]

Miners in Cripple Creek and elsewhere were warned similarly, and, on election day, most miners voted for the man they hated and feared, hoping it would save their jobs.

Meanwhile, in Denver the "repeaters" who had received voting instructions from the chief of police moved from precinct to precinct to vote under false names. Sometimes the women wore bathrobes, kimonos or evening dresses and simply reappeared to cast ballots again at polls where they had already voted.

With both sides contributing their share of fraudulent votes, the final tally was Alva Adams with 123,092 to 113,754 for the incumbent Governor Peabody. Adams was seated as governor, but on January 4, 1905, the Colorado legislature met to decide how to restore integrity to their government.

Because both parties had participated in fraudulent voting, it was decided that a compromise must be reached. By the agreed-upon terms, the assembly voted to unseat Adams on March 17, 1905. Peabody was installed as governor, but only after he had submitted a letter agreeing to serve only one day. At 5:00 P.M. on March 17 he evacuated the executive chambers and the vacancy was filled automatically by Lieutenant Governor Jesse F. McDonald of Leadville. This solution did not end Colorado's political tensions, but it eased them for awhile.

## A Texan Gets His Vote

The population of Texas was largely rural well into the 20th century, and the majority of votes were cast at precinct headquarters, which were usually post offices of major population centers. Until the early 1900s, voting was *viva voce* (by voice), replaced by secret balloting. Vote tallies were gathered by election officials at the precinct and county level and were forwarded to the secretary of state. Until recently, the reporting process took days, even weeks.[16]

Where there were frontiersmen, there was usually drinking, and, as always, the people came up with various ways to practice politics and have a good time. A story goes that in the mid-1800s at the local "groceries" (saloons), candidates used to put up barrels of liquor with their name on them. Voters were invited to express their preference by drinking from the keg of the candidate they favored. Local "pollsters" could then determine who the winner would be by comparing the amounts imbibed from each barrel. However, historian Richard Lingeman points out that the system wasn't foolproof, since an opponent's supporters would sometimes sabotage a candidate by drinking all his whiskey.[17]

But sometimes it took more than whiskey to get a man's vote. In West Texas, little had changed from the earliest frontier days to the 20th century. One 1904 tale of a sheriff's campaign comes from a fellow who traveled the countryside with the candidate, and offers a wonderful perspective on the electoral process:

> Campaigning had then advanced from the horseback stage to that of the two-horse buggy, which wasn't much of an improvement because of the fact that there were very few roads over which one could travel with much pleasure. As was customary in those sometimes forgotten days, that candidate carried along a box of cigars and a quart of PAUL JONES LIQUOR,[18]

the reminiscence begins.

On one occasion they traveled for 30 miles to visit a ranch in Pecos Country where two voters lived.

> When we got there one of the men was down with rheumatism, and we had to remain while the other voter went to town after a bottle of liniment. We did our own cooking, milked five pasture cows to get cream for our coffee, and had to pull the casing in a well and fix something about the windmill in order to get a drink of water.
>
> We were out just a week and campaigned with thirteen voters. My friend cinched every one of them, however. He did it not alone by talking but by performing some useful service on the different ranches. He helped one fellow vaccinate a lot of calves and at another place he ruined a five dollar pair of breeches dipping sheep.[19]

One fellow had a horse he thought was the finest animal in the world, so after visiting him once and admiring the mare, the would-be sheriff came back a second time with a photographer. They took a picture of the man's horse, and that clinched it—there were three voters in the family, and they all voted for the candidate with the photographer. Evidently, voters were scarce in West Texas in those days and every one of them counted.

# The Gilded Age _____ 12

During the period immediately following the Civil War, both the North and the South were struggling with change. The war had accelerated the growth and development of large-scale manufacturing, banking, and foreign commerce, and had ushered in the telegraph and the railroad, greatly changing the way Americans lived. While the South struggled to rebuild, the North forged ahead with growth and development, and the national figures who fascinated everyone were the new titans of business and industry—the Morgans who prospered at investment banking; Carnegie and his fortune built with steel; railroad builders like Vanderbilt, Stanford and Harriman; meat packers like Armour and Swift; and oil barons like John D. Rockefeller. The war had enabled many others to make fortunes, some respectably, others not so. But whatever the means—during the Gilded Age, money was king.

With little interest in humanitarian causes or human well-being and an emphasis on getting ahead at all costs, the time was ripe for fraud and corruption. So vast was the debauchery (Grant's unscrupulous administration provides an example) that it eventually bottomed out, and, by the turn of the century, reforms in many aspects of life—including election methodology—were well underway. Black voters, however, were not to benefit. Hayes's lifting of the military occupation of the South, one among many corrupt bargains made throughout this period, permitted blacks to be shunted aside and forgotten about for the time being.

Politically, the fact that the Republican Party had become a constant in politics was a very important development. A young, sectional party at the beginning of the Civil War, the Republicans soon proved to be a prominent force nationally.

## 1880: Spent Parties; Active Voters

In 1880, the political parties seemed sapped of their strength. It was as if they had not yet recovered from the energy expended on 1876 and couldn't face up to another contest so soon. The corruption of the last election was in keeping with the mood of the era, but it had taxed even the political masterminds of the time. As a result, the campaign of 1880 was uneventful and devoid of real issues. Only the Greenback–Labor Party, which ran General James B. Weaver of Iowa, bothered to come up with any serious proposals for addressing the concerns of the rapidly industrializing nation—issues such as the need for an eight-hour workday, a graduated income tax, regulation of interstate commerce and curtailment of the use of child labor.

When the Republican Party met in convention in Chicago on June 2, an immediate clash developed between the machine-controlled faction, the "Stalwarts," who favored a third term for Grant, and the more independent "Half- Breeds" who favored James G. Blaine, a very charismatic congressman from Maine. James A. Garfield, who nominated John Sherman of Ohio for the presidency, led the anti-Grant movement and successfully stemmed the Grant tide. When the balloting began, Grant led with 304 votes, but it wasn't enough. On the second day, Sherman telegraphed the convention instructing his supporters to vote for Garfield, and on the 36th ballot Garfield became the nominee.

Chester Arthur, an active member of Roscoe Conkling's New York machine, won the nomination for vice president. Because Arthur was a henchman of Conkling's and had been tainted by corruption, many Republicans were horrified at his nomination. Readers of the *Nation* wrote in asking if there was a way to vote for Garfield without also voting for Arthur. The editor replied that they could not but that it didn't really matter: "There is no place in which his powers of mischief will be so small as in the Vice Presidency . . . It is true General Garfield . . . may die during his term of office, but this is too unlikely a contingency to be worth making extraordinary provision for."[1]

The Democrats met in Cincinnati on June 22 and had much less trouble coming up with a nominee. Tilden, who was presumably in ill health, was out of the picture, and after a diverse vote on the first ballot, General Winfield S. Hancock of Pennsylvania was given the nod on the second ballot. He had no real competition, and his record as a soldier looked like the best thing there was to offer. William H. English, a wealthy Indiana banker, became the vice-presidential nominee.

In the campaign that followed, the Republicans stressed " Boatman Jim" Garfield's log-cabin birth, his boyhood job working on the Ohio canal (hence, the nickname), his contributions to the Civil War and his service in Congress. The party established Towpath Clubs and organized small delegations of people to travel to hear Garfield speak at his home in Ohio.

The Republicans railed on about the Democratic sins of the Civil War, and the Democrats denounced the Republicans for the election "Fraud of '76," and after those issues and the tariff were discussed, personal sniping dominated the campaign. The Democrats painted and chalked the number "329" on sidewalks, doors, fences and walls to remind Americans of what they insisted was Garfield's participation in the Credit Mobilier scandal in 1868. (A congressman who was a director of this bogus company had set aside a certain amount of stock for Garfield, hoping he would accept it as a bribe and help keep the scam going. Although Garfield never claimed the stock, he was eventually sent a dividend check for $329—the number used by Democrats to remind the electorate of Garfield's "involvement.") Later in the campaign, a damaging letter, supposedly written by Garfield, was also made public. In it, he spoke up for unlimited importation of Chinese workers, a stance that would have alienated the labor vote. However, Garfield's spelling prowess was well-known, and, when the letter was discovered to contain errors, the Democratic plot backfired.

Democratic candidate Hancock was so colorless that little could be said about him, but the Republicans finally came up with a pamphlet entitled "A Record of the

*The* Leslie's Illustrated *spread of November 8, 1884 depicts several scenes of that election day. Betting on the election often involved having the loser push the winner a certain distance (frequently across a bridge) in a wheelbarrow, as is shown in the top picture. The middle illustration shows a repeat voter being arrested for his wrongdoing. In the bottom left picture, a rider travels at top speed to bring in returns from the mountain districts, and in the bottom right, two young ladies aid an elderly voter in getting to the polls.* (Frank Leslie's Illustrated Newspaper, *November 8, 1884)*

Statesmanship and Political Achievements of General Winfield Scott Hancock . . . Compiled from the Records," and upon opening the pamphlet, the reader found seven blank pages.[2]

On election day, Democratic hopes were dashed. Garfield won decisively in the electoral college—214 to 155; however, the popular vote had been extremely close. He won 4,453,295 to Hancock's 4,444,082, a majority of fewer than 10,000 out of 9,000,000 votes. Voter turnout was exceptional with 78.4% of the eligible voters coming forth to cast their ballots.

Politics were to play a part in Garfield's sudden demise as well as his election. On July 2, 1881, Garfield and his sons left the White House for a trip to show the boys his alma mater, Williams College. At the Washington train station, a disappointed office seeker, Charles J. Guiteau, approached from behind, and as he shot he shouted "I am a Stalwart, and now Arthur is President." Many speculate that modern day medicine would have pulled Garfield through. As it was, he lingered for 79 painful days before succumbing to his wound. Chester Arthur then became president.

## The Blacks Lose the Vote in State Constitutions

Though the Democrats did not celebrate their own victory in 1880, they did rejoice that their dream for a "Solid South" had at last come true. President Hayes had withdrawn the last of the federal troops in 1877, thus there was no more hope for the Republicans in the South. All former slave states voted Democratic—the southern whites had resolved "to vote as they shot." They also saw to it that as few blacks as possible went to the polls.

A regional song about southern disfranchisement of the blacks went like this:

Sing a song of shotguns,
Pocket full of knives
Four-and-twenty black men,
Running for their lives, . . .
Isn't that a bully way
To make a solid South?[3]

By 1890, the South felt politically comfortable with looking to constitutional means to deprive blacks of the vote, and that year Mississippi drew up a constitution that several other southern states used as a model. It required payment of a $2 poll tax prior to election day with the stipulation that receipts must be shown at the polls to prove payment. It also provided that after 1892, everyone who wished to vote must be able to read the constitution, or understand what was read to him or be able to give a reasonable interpretation of passages that might be read to him. A potential voter also had to be willing to answer truthfully all questions concerning his right to vote.

These stipulations provided election officials with a great deal of latitude. Blacks, but usually not whites, would have to provide their poll tax receipt, and, in all likelihood, the matter would end there since many receipts would have been lost or misplaced. (A copy of the tax records kept at the polls would have readily provided election officials with the means to check on tax payment, but, of course, that would have defeated their ability to trip up the black person.)

Many Southern states followed Mississippi's lead with minor variations. Some states were concerned that some whites might get caught in the net designed to eliminate black voters, and so in states like South Carolina, another stipulation was added: No man who could vote in 1867 (immediately after the Civil War) or the descendants of such, nor any foreigner naturalized prior to ratification of South Carolina's latest constitution should be required to submit to any educational test.[5] Of course, this automatically qualified most whites and no blacks since no southern black would have had the vote in 1867.


## 1884: Political Mudslinging

At a time when Barnum and Bailey were touring the country with their circus and sideshow, the government was running a sideshow of its own. Most politicians were for sale at any price, and the industrial age was ushering in the domination of big business. As one old saw put it, "the Standard [Oil Company] has done everything with the Pennsylvania legislature except refine it."

Despite fears that Chester Arthur would be nothing more than a tool of Roscoe Conkling and the New York machine, President Arthur ran an honest, relatively effective administration. Ironically, his own lack of loyalty to machine politics in his effort to run a clean administration cost him a nomination of his own. When the Republicans met in Chicago on June 3, 1884, they turned, not to the incumbent, but to James G. Blaine, a man with extraordinary personal magnetism. The reaction to his nomination was overwhelming. Delegates rose from their seats with a roar, and there was much rejoicing. General John A. Logan of Illinois was taken on for vice president.

However, positive response to Blaine was not unanimous. Blaine was suspected of shady dealings in the sale of some railroad stocks and bonds. A reform group, which couldn't bear to support a candidate who "had wallowed in spoils like a rhinoceros in an African pool,"[6] split off to consider what to do. Initially calling themselves "Independent Republicans," they were more popularly known as "Mugwumps" (an Algonquin Indian word meaning "chief," but used several years previously to refer to independents who thought they were bigger than their party). Led by prominent men such as Carl Schurz, New York legislator Theodore Roosevelt, Harvard President Charles Eliot and Henry Cabot Lodge, they planned to await the nomination of a candidate by the Democrats and to then consider joining forces with them.

When the Democrats met in Chicago in July, they were looking for a reform candidate who could and did win over the Mugwumps. They turned to New York

Governor Grover Cleveland, who was known for his honesty and the fact that on numerous occasions he had stood up to Tammany Hall. Thomas A. Hendricks, an experienced politician from Indiana, took the second spot.

The campaign that followed was one of the dirtiest in history. Both parties managed to ignore the issues of the day such as labor unrest, farmers' problems, public-land policies, railroad regulation, growth of monopolies and even tariff reform. Mudslinging knew no bounds.

Blaine's earliest problem was the newspaper publication of the Mulligan Letters—letters that exposed some of Blaine's misdoings, one of which (to a Mr. Warren Fisher) ended with the close: "Kind regards to Mrs. Fisher. Burn this letter." The Democrats responded with campaign activities that included marchers chanting: "Blaine, Blaine, James G. Blaine, the Monumental Liar from the State of Maine," and "Burn this letter, burn this letter, kind regards to Mrs. Fisher," while holding lighted matches to sheets of paper.[7]

Cleveland's albatross came in the form of an illegitimate child whom the Republicans discovered in his past. In a July issue, the *Buffalo Evening Telegraph* published an account of one Maria Halpin, who had been on intimate terms with several men but, when a child was born, named Cleveland as the father. He didn't resist the charge, made some financial arrangements for the boy, and, when Halpin was no longer acting as a responsible mother, he arranged for the boy to be adopted into another family. When his advisors contacted Cleveland about what to do about the story, he replied, "Above all, tell the truth," winning over some whom he might have lost had he avoided the issue. The Republican cry that followed was "Ma, Ma, Where's my Pa?"

Throughout the campaign, Cleveland remained primarily in Albany, but took time for a couple of speeches and a great celebration in Buffalo, and, the Saturday before the election, he reviewed a parade of 40,000 in New York City.

November 4, 1884 brought the first Democratic victory in 28 years. The final electoral vote was 219 for Cleveland to 182 for Blaine, giving the Democrats a new ending for the Republican chant: "Ma, Ma, Where's my Pa? Gone to the White House. Ha! Ha! Ha!"

Nowhere was reaction to the news more jubilant than among the southern whites who celebrated the Democratic victory with parades, fireworks, cannon salutes and hymns of thanks.

## 1888: Cleveland Stands Tough; Will He Prevail?

As Cleveland took office, he faced a host of national problems— among them: a government being undermined by the "spoils system" of job distribution; labor unrest; a need for railway regulation; the growth of monopolies; public land-use questions; and difficulties over the tariff. Learning as he went along, Cleveland was quite effective in certain areas. He made strides with civil service reform so that government jobs could be dispensed on merit. He also unearthed and redressed other kinds of government abuse including the discovery of thousands of acres of government land being held by the railroads; land taken unfairly under Arthur's administration from the Indians was returned; and he vetoed a bill that would have made Civil War veterans eligible for all kinds of questionable disability payments.

Though it seems inconceivable today, one of Cleveland's major problems was a huge Treasury surplus. He was convinced that the lowering of tariffs was the beginning of the answer to bringing down this excess (the country needed more of the money back in circulation). Had he not taken an extremely strong stand on this toward the end of his administration, he likely would have been reelected quite easily, but the tariff issue was deadlocked in Congress, and businesses that benefited from the tariffs were more than happy to contribute to the "merchant prince" John Wanamaker's campaign fund designed to get Cleveland out of office.

The Democratic national convention was held June 5 in St. Louis, and Cleveland received the nomination. Elderly former Ohio Senator Allen G. Thurman was selected as his running mate. The Republicans met in Chicago on June 19 and after Blaine wired his refusal of the candidacy from Europe, the convention remained deadlocked with favorite son candidates for seven ballots until it adjourned for the weekend. By that time, Blaine had wired that his support would go to the scandal-free former Senator Benjamin Harrison, a Civil War brigadier general and the grandson of President William Henry Harrison. Harrison got the nomination with a wealthy New York banker, Levi Morton, on the ticket as V.P.

Harrison didn't travel but instead waged a "front porch" campaign. From July through October thousands of visitors traveled to his home in Indianapolis where they could hear Harrison speak. The speeches were widely quoted in newspapers throughout the country, and Republican managers turned much of the information into pamphlets and handbills.[8] Harrison also wasn't above playing off his grandfather's reputation as "Old Tippecanoe." There were writing tablets labeled "Tippecanoe" featuring William Henry Harrison and the Benjamin Harrison family, and Harrison used mock log cabins as his campaign headquarters.[9]

Cleveland felt it unseemly for a president to campaign, so he made only one public appearance—to read his letter of acceptance. His running mate, frail, 75-year-old Allen Thurman, did the best he could speaking on Cleveland's behalf, but he often digressed and once even collapsed before finishing his remarks.[10] However, Thurman was responsible for originating the memento for which this campaign became known. After his habitual pinch of snuff, Thurman always used a red hip-pocket handkerchief, and people at the Democratic convention were so pleased about his nomination that those who had them waved red bandannas. The Democrats loved the idea and had scores of bandannas in all colors and with various slogans made to be distributed. The flurries of bandannas at political rallies soon became so irritating to Republicans that they started passing out their own bandannas.

New York and Indiana were two key states in the election of 1888, and fraud and deal-making helped pull the Republican vote out in both. New York Republicans seemed to have bargained to vote in favor of a Democratic governor if the Democrats would support Harrison, and both sides upheld the deal. In Indiana, a Republican poll was taken in early September that showed the Democrats leading in that state. Republican national headquarters stepped in with plans to send "floaters" (those who would sell their votes) in by railroad, and in a letter Republican National Treasurer W. W. Dudley wrote to Indiana party lieutenants: "Divide the floaters into blocks of five. Put a trusted man with the necessary funds in charge of these five and make him responsible that none get away and that all vote our ticket."[11] Republican National Chairman Matthew Quay denied party involvement, and Dudley threatened libel suits against the newspapers that published the leaked letter, nevertheless stories abounded of floaters who were locked up the day before the election and then marched to the polls with Republican ballots in their hands and as much as $15 in their pockets—a great sum to have earned for a vote. (In the end, Indiana voted for Harrison, the Republican candidate, by the scant margin of 2,348.)

Intimidation was also key to this election. Industrialists warned employees of wage cuts and unemployment if Cleveland should win.

*In cities across the nation on election night, crowds gathered near newspaper offices to hear voting results as soon as possible. The above illustration shows New York City's Madison Square on Election Night 1888 where* The Herald *is spreading the news. This tradition began in the latter part of the 19th century as broader use of the telegraph permitted faster transmission of the voting tallies and ended during the early 1950s, when more and more people started staying home to watch the election results on their own television sets. (*Harper's Weekly, *May 20, 1888)*

The election was close, but by midnight it was clear that Harrison was the victor with 233 electoral votes to Cleveland's 168. Ironically, Cleveland won the popular election by almost 100,000 votes. Cleveland knew it was the tariff issue that had defeated him, and he said about it early on: "What is the use of being elected or re-elected unless you stand for something?"[12]

## A Method Of Uniform Secret Balloting Comes To The Fore

By the 1870s and 1880s, manipulation of the ballot box had made voting meaningless in many communities. Candidates sometimes had to pay excessive sums to get on the ballot; voters were bribed, intimidated and, often, the ballot box was controlled.

As soon as a system was devised to prevent abuse, someone would devise a method to get around it. A good example of this was a change in the way parties printed ballots. Customarily, each party printed its ballot on a different color of paper. This made it possible for the judges in charge of the ballot box to tell how each man had voted. When later laws required all ballots be printed on white paper of the same size, the political parties countered this by using paper with different textures. That way election officials could still control the vote when necessary, because they could tell "by feel" for whom the vote was cast.[13]

In 1872, Britain replaced oral voting with a method pioneered in the Australian colonies in the 1850s, and various state governments in the U.S. began to take a serious look at this new "secret" ballot. To many, it looked appealing, and the move to adopt the Australian ballot became one of the major reform issues of the 1880s and 1890s.

In 1888, Kentucky became the first state to pass an Australian ballot law. (This was ironic since Kentucky was the last state to abandon oral voting.)[14] Many other states quickly followed suit. By 1892 it had been adopted by 33 states.

The basic provisions were as follows (these are the provisions that still govern our voting today):

1. Ballots are to be printed and distributed at public expense.
2. The ballot must contain the names of all the candidates duly nominated by law, either by party convention or petition by voters. This is known as a blanket ballot.
3. Only election officers at the polling places can distribute these official ballots. No others are to be accepted.
4. Physical provisions are to be made at each polling place to ensure each voter secrecy in casting a vote.[15]

Voter reaction was overwhelmingly favorable. In an account from Nevada, a newspaper reporter notes the ease with which the day's voting has taken place and remarks on the convenience and public admiration of it. He adds:

> There was no "friendly" assistance given the voter by interested voters yesterday. Moral persuasion and other inducements may have been used beforehand;

but when the voter entered the polls, he entered alone and with no ballot "fixed" for him. When he received his ballot from the election officers he went alone into a booth with it, and made it out alone under no menacing scrutiny, and without fear of being punished for exercising his honest opinions. The Australian ballot is the safeguard of the elective franchise.[16]

By 1910 the acceptance of the Australian ballot throughout the United States was virtually complete, and that reform, underway in so many states, helped stimulate other kinds of reforms leading into the 20th century and the Progressive era.

## 1892: Cleveland's Comeback

To the improvement of the country but to the suffering of his political career, Harrison made the same political mistake Cleveland did. He would not waiver from his efforts at civil service reform, a factor that infuriated those who put him in office.

During Harrison's term, the "Billion-Dollar Congress" had, unbelievably, managed to deplete the entire Treasury surplus, bringing the country close to the brink of disaster. Many Civil War veterans had been won over to the Republican ticket with promises of very comfortable pensions, and— as one former soldier put it—all veterans "whose conditions for health are not practically perfect" were eligible for pensions.

Though party bosses hoped to be done with Harrison, he was renominated relatively easily at the Republican convention in Minneapolis on June 7, 1892. At the Democratic convention in Chicago on June 21, Cleveland was nominated on the first ballot, and Adlai Stevenson was chosen as vice president.

This election was unremarkable except for two occurrences. The first was the rise of the People's Party, which became better known as the Populist Party. It grew out of increasing farmer discontent with governmental neglect of their problems and drew its strength primarily from rural voters, but its platform attracted labor as well. Populists sought to breathe life into the flagging economy and demanded national paper currency along with free coinage of silver, hoping these monetary moves would stop the deflation that was harming the farmers. They also campaigned for a graduated income tax and other reform proposals. For their candidate, they chose James B. Weaver of Iowa, the former Greenback candidate of 1880 and, for vice president, James G. Field of Virginia.

The second noteworthy aspect of this election was that in Lockport, New York, voters cast ballots on the very first voting machine ever to be used in America. The machine, invented by Jacob H. Myers, was a massive device that operated along the same lines as the machines we see today. Earlier American machines, and British machines created as early as 1869, had involved the release of a ball by each voter, but the drawback to that system was that later the individual balls had to be counted. Myers's machine was constructed so that a key tripped a counter that kept track of the number of votes for each candidate or issue. Though the invention of the voting machine was an important step forward in speeding up the counting of the votes and creating a more honest election (the machines were more or less tamper-proof both for the voter, who was mechanically prevented from casting multiple votes, and for the officials in charge of the elections), they gained acceptance slowly.

The campaign activity in 1892 was mostly unremarkable. The political parties organized nationally and also relied on local politicians and groups like Tammany Hall to drum up voter support. Harrison's wife was very sick prior to the campaign and died in mid-October; because of her illness, Harrison did not campaign. Out of deference to Harrison, Cleveland, too, refused to make public appearances on his own behalf. Adlai E. Stevenson, Cleveland's running mate, was a skilled campaigner and traveled the country by rail, speaking for the Democrats.

The Populists, with all the spirit of any reform movement, ran a very active campaign. Chief among those who came forward to help bring out the Populist vote was Mary Ellen Lease of Kansas. She toured through the southern and western parts of the country with presidential candidate Weaver, imploring farmers to "raise less corn and more hell."

On November 8, Cleveland won with 277 electoral votes to Harrison's 145. His popular majority was a landslide; Cleveland's count exceeded Harrison's by almost 400,000 votes. To the surprise of many, the Populists polled more than 1,000,000 votes. Unfortunately, Cleveland's second administration was not as pleasant as the returns on that 1892 election day.

## 1896: Bryan, The Relentless Campaigner vs. McKinley On The Front Porch

In 1896 the voters were desperate for a candidate who could promise them relief. The Panic of 1893 had followed shortly after Cleveland's second election, and times were bad. Few had jobs because so many businesses—including banks, factories and railroads—had gone belly up. In the city, soup kitchens attempted to feed the unemployed, but in outlying areas, bands of tramps wandered the countryside in search of handouts. Federal troop interference in the Pullman strike of 1894 and the brutal treatment of Coxey's army of unemployed in their protest march on Washington fostered no confidence in the administration's ability to help the common man fight the poverty that had overtaken so many.

The monetary situation was the major issue debated at the political conventions that year. Many in both parties believed that the poor economy was the result of the government's recent effort to adhere to a gold standard (where all United States money was backed by gold the government possessed). Critics of the gold standard were known as "silverites" because they felt that if Congress would open the way for the unlimited coinage of silver, the economy would right itself. The Populist Party was already prosilver going into the campaign—seeing it as a way of helping the common man, but the other two parties hammered out whether to be "goldbugs" or "silverites" in their respective conventions.

When the Republicans met in St. Louis on June 16, 1896, they were ready to set a new course. Wealthy Cleveland, Ohio business leader Marcus A. Hanna had stepped into politics with a specific goal in mind: to make William McKinley president. McKinley was currently serving as governor of Ohio, and with Hanna as Republican national chairman, the nomination was all but assured. Garret A. Hobart, a corporate lawyer from New Jersey, was nominated for vice president. Hanna masterminded the party stance on the monetary issue and though McKinley was basically a "straddle bug," Hanna saw to it that the Republicans positioned themselves as goldbugs.

The Democrats met in Chicago on July 7 with the silver men in control. Besides William Jennings Bryan, there were two other contenders for the nomination, but when Bryan gave his "You shall not press down upon the brow of labor this crown of thorns, you shall not crucify mankind on a cross of gold," prosilver speech, he clinched the nomination. The crowd was on their feet for a one-hour demonstration, carrying Bryan around on their shoulders during part of the time. For vice president, the Democrats chose Arthur Sewall of Maine.

The Populist Party met in St. Louis later in July, and it endorsed Bryan but put forth a different vice presidential candidate, Thomas E. Watson of Georgia, hoping that the Democrats would value support of Bryan and therefore switch to the Populist vice-presidential nominee. When this didn't happen, it was too late to do anything else, so the "Popocrats," as they were called during this campaign, supported Bryan for president and in many states their own candidate for vice president.

Once underway, the campaign was lively. Americans everywhere took sides in the debate about silver vs. gold. Because of high voter interest, merchandising the candidates was easy. People were eager to get their hands on all kinds of mementoes ranging from handsomely crafted "goldbug" pins to simple "No Cross of Gold, No Crown of Thorns" celluloid pins as well as various ribbons, ashtrays, soaps, McKinley dolls and "free silver" children's whistles.

When it came to the candidates and their campaigns, William Jennings Bryan was magnetic. At 36, he was handsome with a beautiful voice and an engaging personality. Almost every schoolchild has heard of his tireless treks crisscrossing the country during the campaign—during the course of which he covered more than 18,000 miles by train and made more than 600 speeches to approximately 5,000,000 people.

Marcus Hanna raised more than $3 million for the Republican campaign (making it the first campaign in history where a significant amount of money was spent) to the $650,000 the Democrats were able to raise for Bryan. Businesses were pressured to give, not according to feelings of generosity, but by ability to pay.[17] Hanna spent it wisely by sending out pamphlets and leaflets by the millions in seven or eight languages, preparing boilerplate stories for local small-town newspapers and creating McKinley buttons and billboards for the "Advance Agent of Prosperity." They also had 1,400 speakers nationwide who were available to speak on behalf of the Republican Party.[18]

Hanna and McKinley assessed their opposition's strengths and knew immediately that for McKinley to campaign cross-country in Bryan's wake would be a losing proposition. Instead, they decided to place him at home for a "front porch" campaign, similar to Harrison's but more massive in scale, that would allow him to appear refined and presidential. Thousands came to Canton, Ohio by special trains from June to November of 1896, sometimes at reduced fares; sometimes paid for by campaign funds. Everything was carefully orchestrated. The remarks of the leader of the visiting delegation were obtained beforehand, sometimes edited, and McKinley would then frame his reply. Upon arrival at the station, the visitors were met by the Canton Home Guards, a picturesque mounted brigade that escorted them to the McKinley residence. (A member of the Home Guards would gallop ahead to alert the candidate, so that all would be ready.) Generally a band would play. One day alone it was estimated that McKinley spoke to some 30,000 people.[19] Some visitors wanted souvenirs and took wood from the fence and the porch and blades of grass from the yard. Before long, the lawn and fence were gone, and the porch was in a state of collapse. They also brought gifts—flowers, food, clothing, badges, canes and flags.[20]

While part of the campaigning was done through legitimate banging of the drum, there was also direct pressure on voters. Workers were threatened with loss of jobs or the closing of factories if Bryan were to win, and some buyers of manufactured goods placed orders contingent on McKinley's victory; in some cases, workers were told not to report to work on the Wednesday morning after the election if Bryan won.[21] Holders of western mortgages announced that at McKinley's election mortgages would be renewed for five years and interest rates reduced.[22]

In addition to excellent campaign organization, McKinley was helped by a revival of business and rising prices, which made it look like the need for the silverite cause was less dire. Almost 14,000,000 Americans went to the polls, more people than ever before. By late in the evening of November 3, it was clear that McKinley had won. He garnered 271 electoral votes to Bryan's 176. The popular vote was 7,102,246 to Bryan's 6,492,559.

One aside: In St. Louis, an attorney noted in his diary an amazing experience. While waiting for election news, people in one neighborhood started seeing newspapers with the news that Bryan had been elected. Yet when the public left one particular neighborhood, it seemed that the news changed. Later it was learned that the whole thing had been a business trick to sell special editions of the newspaper.[23] It was still the Gilded Age.

## Return Day

One problem that plagued all election day participants was that it took a long time for all the returns to come in to be counted and for the results to be known. While by the 19th century, towns and cities seemed to have successfully satisfied curiosity through the use of bulletin boards (usually located at the newspaper offices), where people could drop by and keep up with the latest news, in more rural communities that sort of gradual newsbreaking wasn't practical. For that reason (and for the fun of getting together), Sussex County, Delaware had maintained its tradition of Return Day. By 1882 it had become quite an affair. Set for the Thursday following the Tuesday election day, people started arriving early in the morning from all over the county and many even from Maryland, to hear the election results. Often clad in ludicrous costumes to add to the festivities, thousands of people arrived in town to celebrate. In the center of town on the courthouse square, which at one time had been a slave market, booths and stalls were constructed for the day and all kinds of edibles were for sale: Delaware biscuits, hot corn pone with black molasses poured over it, sweet potato biscuits, roast rabbit and opossum, clams, oysters, hominy and fried chicken. Always a large steer would be roasted in the open air and eaten. Hogsheads of beer, fresh cider and vast quantities of Sussex County apple jack were also consumed. Band concerts and cock fighting were some of the entertainments of the day.[24]

At noon in the public square, the sheriff presided over the Board of Canvassers who awaited the arrival of mounted election officials to each deliver their area's election returns. The results were then hastily recopied in large numbers on a large white sheet displayed in front of the courthouse so that the waiting crowd could see the results, which were also announced aloud.

Afterward, the winning party held a parade. In 1882, on the election of Governor Stockley, the Wilmington *Sunday Star* noted that amidst cheers and booming guns, Governor Elect Stockley arrived, riding on a brightly decorated ship, mounted on wheels. Six men on horseback rode in front while 120 men marched in the rear: "When the ship was drawn into the Square the people flocked from all sides to shake hands with the new Governor and at length he was lifted on brawny shoulders and carried into the Court House above the heads of the crowd, which cheered louder and louder."[25]

Late in the afternoon, special trains began to fill and those who had brought wagons to town also began to say their farewells. Gradually the throngs dispersed, not to come again for another two years. "The day was regarded as a holiday as much as any day fixed by law for the suspension of business. As late as the 1930s, a Sussex farmer would never have thought of missing a Return Day," wrote a historian of the time.[26]

## Other Local Traditions of the Day

With the increase in political rivalry, party members were always looking for ways of expressing political dominance, and the erecting of liberty poles—tall poles from which party banners could be flown—was one of them. A story from Georgetown, Colorado, a community nestled among Rocky Mountain peaks, tells of the Republicans placing two liberty poles near the post office in 1880 in order to swing a Garfield banner. Not to be outdone, the Democrats chose to stretch a cable across town from mountain peak to mountain peak. Between the two, at an elevation of 1,230 feet above the town, the Hancock and English flag (of the Democratic candidates) flapped. The length of the cable was one and three-fourths miles.[27]

Torchlight parades were still a part of election day, and the *Rocky Mountain News* tells of one that took place in Golden, Colorado in 1880 to aid in swelling General Hancock's majority in November. When it took place with over 175 torch bearers in line, the oldest inhabitant of the place was obliged to admit it was "the biggest thing in its way that Jefferson County ever witnessed . . ."[28]

Placing bets on elections was very much a part of the fun of an election day. In New York two common ways to pay off a wager were for the loser to use his nose to push an apple 50 paces along the street, or to trundle a wheelbarrow with the winner in it across one of New York's new suspension bridges.[29]

Wagers on election results were nationwide, as evidenced by this description of the 1888 New Hampshire celebration of the victory of Benjamin Harrison over Grover Cleveland:

The Republicans of Brentwood New Hampshire Tuesday evening gave vent to their enthusiasm over the recent national victory by a torchlight parade, illuminations, booming of cannons, guns, bonfires, etc. The Kingston, New Hampshire band and Nute Guards marched from Crawleys Falls to West Brentwood, where they escorted John F. Ayer on a wheelbarrow wheeled by Herbert Lyford of Fremont, New Hampshire to pay an election wager made a few weeks ago. The line of march extended to Flander's Hall, where an oyster supper was served. The jollification was highly satisfactory to those who participated and a host of spectators.[30]

By 1886 a new custom was beginning, and it was the early rustlings of a well-organized labor movement in politics. With labor candidate, Henry George, running for mayor of New York City, 30,000 union men gathered to march behind their union banners in a cold drenching storm on election eve. Among the regular trade organizations that marched were: the printers; the bakers; the plate-printers; the journeymen tailors; the United Umbrella-makers; the walking-stick dressers; the plumbers; the framers; the United Brassworkers; the Bartenders' Union; the Waiters' Union; the locksmiths; the shoemakers; the brewers; the carpenters and joiners; the chandelier-workers; the tobacco-workers; the furriers; the fruit-handlers; the brush-makers; and the tin and sheet-iron workers.

The marchers kept time by singing various chants. Among them: " 'Hi! Ho! the leeches—must—go!' 'George! George! Hen—ry—George!' 'George! George! Vote—for—George!' and 'Vote! vote! vote—for—George!' "[31]

## The First American Election in Hawaii

The first American election ever held in Hawaii took place long before the islands had been considered for statehood. The voters were American soldiers stationed there during the off-year election of 1898. "The American flag was hoisted over Iolani Palace for the first time on August 12, 1898, and on election day of the same year, soldiers of the 1st New York, the 10th Pennsylvania, and the 20th Kansas, U.S. Volunteers organized respectively voting precincts at Camp McKinley near Diamond Head, on the S.S. *Arizona* in the Harbor, and on the dock in Honolulu."[32] They were casting ballots *in absentia* for candidates for office in their own home states. To do so, the Kansans had to organize a voting precinct by having a mass meeting and selecting three judges and two clerks of election. A soldier who was there recollects that he and four other men had agreed to act as election officials (he remembers with some humor that in selecting the election officials the men chose enlisted men to be the judges while the officers had to do the "dirty work" of clerks.

The ballots were taken to Manila and after waiting some time for a transport were sent on to the secretary of state in Kansas. "In telling this story I have always asserted that the ballots arrived in Topeka early in January 1899 in time to prevent several candidates, who up to that time had expected to take office, from so doing. Whether this is an actual fact or just typical embellishments which occur in an old soldier's story of what occurred forty years before deponent knoweth not,"[33] wrote the former soldier.

## 1900: McKinley/Bryan Redux

The picture of the United States in 1900 was much rosier than it had been in 1896. The country was prosperous, and voters weren't prepared to agitate in the way that they had in the previous election.

The campaign was very similar to the one waged in 1896, though a new and important issue had been added—imperialism. Although McKinley expected to be occupied with domestic affairs during his administration, what he walked into was a country that was enflamed by "yellow journalism" reports in the New York press and was ready for war with Spain to give Cuba her independence and to preserve American trade and property there ($16 million had been lost by Americans in Cuba thus far). When the Spanish–American War was won relatively easily after only a few months of fighting in 1898, McKinley was as surprised as anyone to find the U.S. to be the possessor of the Philippines and Puerto Rico and to have the ability to give Cuba her independence. And while the victory won McKinley his share of fans, the anti-expansionists felt he was a tyrant.

The candidates for 1900 were a repeat of 1896. The Republicans met in Philadelphia in June and quickly nominated McKinley on the first ballot. In July the Democrats met in Kansas City and nominated Bryan for the presidential slot while selecting Illinois silverite Adlai E. Stevenson, who had been Cleveland's vice president for a term, as vice-presidential nominee.

The only drama of either convention concerned McKinley's running mate. Theodore Roosevelt was a leading contender, a fact that infuriated Marcus Hanna, who felt he was "unsafe"; however, Roosevelt, who was currently serving as governor of New York and who had made national headlines as a "Rough Rider" during the Spanish–American War, was being championed by political leaders Thomas Platt and Matt Quay, bosses of the New York and Philadelphia machines, because he wasn't as pliant as they wished him to be and they wanted to maneuver him into what was viewed as a politically impotent spot. However, the western delegates loved him, and periodically they would march up and down the convention aisles crying, "We want Teddy! We want Teddy!" Hanna urged McKinley to come out for someone else, but McKinley refused to interfere. Hanna said: "Don't any of you realize that there's only one life between that madman and the Presidency?"[34] Despite this, that "damned cowboy" (Hanna's words) got the nomination and proved to be a tireless campaigner. Hanna intended to keep McKinley at home again, and this time, he rarely even saw people. In contrast, Roosevelt traveled 21,000 miles, speaking in hundreds of towns to large crowds. He wasn't the electrifyingly eloquent speaker Bryan was, but he was a larger-than-life character who never failed to please.

Bryan again toured the country, and despite the economically prosperous times brought about by an expansion in the gold market through the discovery of new mines, he refused to let the silver issue die. When that failed to excite audiences, he moved on to the negatives of imperialism, but that, too, held little interest.

*Torchlight parades continued as an important part of election day into the 20th century as evidenced by this depiction of a parade that took place in 1902. (Scribner's, October 1902)*

Bryan had lost touch with the issues that were important this time, and the November results showed it. McKinley had 292 electoral votes to Bryan's 155. The silver states (Colorado, Idaho, Montana and Nevada) had remained loyal, but the West again went Republican. In the popular vote, McKinley carried 7,218,491 to Bryan's 6,356,734.

And, of course, what Marcus Hanna had most feared occurred a brief six months after the inauguration. McKinley's assassination in Buffalo, New York, put that "unsafe" candidate, that "Rough Rider," yes, that "damned cowboy" in the White House.

And with that transition an era passed. McKinley was the last Civil War veteran to be elected to the White House; he had helped the United States expand halfway around the world, and he had seen the last of the frontier as it was rapidly being replaced by steel mill stacks, urban growth and the power of big business. A man of the 19th century, by misfortune, had turned the reins of the country over to a "cowboy" who was ready to lead the nation into a new type of frontier—the 20th century.

# A New Political Beginning _____ 13

The early years of the 20th century are known as the "Progressive Era," and election day issues were very much a part of the gains made at the turn of the century.

But progress at the national level with Theodore Roosevelt leading the way was speeded because of the seeds of reform that had been planted during the last decade or two of the 19th century. The growth of the Populist Party, the labor movement, unrest over political corruption and the quick acceptance of the Australian ballot during the 1880s and 1890s all paved the way for a forward-thinking man like Roosevelt to move ahead in many areas.

## 1904: Roosevelt—"A Legend in His Own Time"

Roosevelt finished out William McKinley's term of office trying to maintain McKinley's policies as well as doing what he could to give the "little guy" a "Square Deal." Perhaps his greatest challenge during these years was the United Mine Workers strike involving 150,000 workers. When management refused to respond to worker complaints about low wages and poor working conditions, Roosevelt, concerned about the effect of a prolonged strike on the nation's coal supply, stepped in. He arranged for the Army to take over the coal mines and then appointed an impartial commission to investigate the dispute and to produce an agreement by which both sides would abide. When the commission recommended settlement in favor of labor, Roosevelt lost the campaign backing of many of his wealthy supporters.

Under his leadership, the country also took important steps toward trust-busting, set new regulations on industry and in early efforts toward land conservation, set aside some 15,000,000 acres of timberland for national use and to establish game preserves and more national parks. In addition, he laid the groundwork for some notable achievements by smoothing the way for the Panama Canal and by purchasing from the Wright brothers a $25,000 plane that eventually gave birth to the U.S. Army Air Forces.

As the 1904 election neared, Roosevelt was eager. He desperately wanted to legitimize his position by being elected president in his own right. As early as 1902, Republican state conventions in Kansas and Pennsylvania came out in favor of Roosevelt. Although some delegations still considered Roosevelt "unsafe," most were eager to support this larger-than-life figure, and at the Republican national convention in Chicago, Roosevelt was nominated for president on the first ballot. Indiana's Senator Charles W. Fairbanks was chosen as running mate.

For the last two elections, the Democrats had supported a prosilver platform with William Jennings Bryan, one of the most magnetic candidates ever to run for president, as their aspirant for the top office. But despite Bryan's charismatic appeal that generated such excitement on his cross-country speaking tours, he kept losing. As a result, the Democrats were ready for a change. Meeting in St. Louis in July, they turned to Judge Alton B. Parker, chief justice of the New York Court of Appeals, with the hope that he might attract New York's large electoral vote. His running mate was octogenarian and millionaire Henry G. Davis from West Virginia—they hoped he would donate money if nominated (he didn't).

The campaign itself was lackluster, remarkable only for kindling so little interest. Following the tradition that incumbents didn't take to the stump, Roosevelt remained at the White House, thus removing the most colorful candidate from campaign activity. And after years of practicing the impartiality necessary for a judgeship, Alton Parker failed to arouse voter interest. Intending to sponsor a front porch campaign, Democratic advisors soon realized that they needed to change their strategy. They scheduled Parker for speeches in his home state of New York as well as neighboring states, but his lack of oratorical skills and his noncommittal attitude put him at a distinct disadvantage. Parker added nothing to the ticket, and he quickly lost those who had rallied around Bryan.

Roosevelt was fast becoming a legend in his own time, and the electorate demonstrated just how popular he was. Roosevelt emerged with 336 electoral votes to Parker's 140. The popular vote was 7,628,461 to 5,084,223. His margin of victory was the greatest ever given a president.

The inaugural festivities were every bit as exciting as Roosevelt himself. More than 200,000 people visited Washington on March 4, and the president was escorted by a palette of colorful groups that were representative of the national and international news of that time: Roosevelt's "Rough Riders" from his military efforts in Cuba; a native battalion from Puerto Rico; Filipino scouts; and American Indian chiefs all participated in the inaugural parade.

Theodore Roosevelt likely would have been off to an even more fruitful four years had he not already made the single largest political blunder of his career. On election eve he announced that he would not be a candidate for president again, thereby diminishing his effectiveness for the next four years and eliminating the possibility of a run in 1908.

## Tammany Doings

In the early part of the 20th century, Tammany Hall was at its zenith. Led by a wise, savvy, but taciturn fellow by the name of Charles F. Murphy (and known to all as "Mr. Murphy"), the well-known political machine was functioning at its best. While there was still graft and wrongdoing in many wards, Murphy had a keen eye for good political leaders and brought along men like Al Smith and Robert Wagner who were to dominate the political scene for several decades. He also knew about taking care of his own, and with immigration totals at an all-time high (8.8 million in the decade prior to World War I), there were plenty of people the Tammany system helped who were willing to pay back with a vote. A father without work, a family fallen on hard times and in need of food or coal, a recent immigrant requiring assistance with naturalization papers or a street peddler wanting legal assistance were among those whom Tammany looked after in the districts where the system worked well.

In the Tammany system of that day—before the New Deal and before any sort of social welfare agencies existed—the precinct (election district) captain was the link between the people and the government. While elected officials were sometimes available at the clubhouse, residents knew and were known by the precinct captain, who was the one who saw that their needs were met. Writes Louis Eisenstein, a former precinct captain, in *A Stripe of Tammany's Tiger* (Robert Speller & Sons, New York, 1966): "One day a year, Election Day, I received my reward . . . It was for me, not my party's candidate, that my constituents cast their ballots. 'The average Joe Jones in my precinct votes for me, not you [candidates],' I would say."

## Foreigners Unwelcome

Despite huge numbers of immigrants brought in by the mining companies, immigrants had very little chance to vote in Colorado in the late 1800s and early 1900s. (This would have been typical of many states.) Large companies tried to mix work forces ethnically to prevent unionization and sometimes brought in new groups to supplant old. In 1903, Walsenberg, Colorado boasted residents of 32 different nationalities.

Many immigrants didn't even become citizens, perhaps intending to return home; perhaps because they feared officials or didn't see the purpose. Orientals were totally excluded after the Chinese Exclusion Act of 1882 denied them naturalization. Between 1908 and 1918, more than 30% of all naturalization applications filed in Colorado were denied, making it the 7th most stringent state in the nation.[1]

## 1908: Roosevelt Backs Taft

Having announced his noncandidacy on the eve of the 1904 election, Roosevelt considerably reduced the efficacy of his second term. Though he did get a few reform measures through Congress—the Hepburn Act, which extended the powers of the Interstate Commerce Commission over railroad rates; a Meat Inspection Act; and a

*In this illustration by D. B. Frost, which first appeared in* Collier's Weekly *in 1904, townspeople in a frontier community listen while one among them reads the election results from the newspaper. Though communication of news would have been rapid, vote tallying in most locations was still slow, meaning that official results were often not known until several days after an election.* (Collier's Weekly, *1904)*

Pure Food and Drug Act, many of Roosevelt's programs were stalled by a recalcitrant Congress, particularly after the Wall Street Panic of 1907.

Nevertheless, Roosevelt was able to handpick his successor for 1908, and the man he supported was Secretary of War William Howard Taft of Ohio. A former federal judge, Taft and Roosevelt were in agreement on many issues. Taft's work on the bench had supported what Roosevelt stood for; his decisions helped strengthen the virtually unused Sherman Antitrust Act, and, among other things, he was the first judge to rule unequivocally that laborers had a right to strike. He had also served as the first civilian governor of the Philippines.

Taft was a reluctant candidate and would have preferred a Supreme Court appointment, but with his wife and Roosevelt pushing, he agreed to accept if nominated. At the Republican convention in Chicago in June there was a 46-minute demonstration for Roosevelt to run again, but Roosevelt remained firm in his resolve to bow out, and Taft got the nomination with 702 votes. Congressman James S. Sherman was nominated for vice president.

Meeting in Denver in July, the Democrats brought national politics farther west than they had been before. With access to Rocky Mountain snow in July, Denverites had masses of the stuff brought in by rail and piled it in 10-foot mounds near the auditorium where the convention was to be held. The snow was under police guard, and while natives were to leave it untouched, out- of-state visitors, many wearing white suits and Panama hats, plunged their arms in the cool white piles, rolled snowballs, washed each other's faces with it and rolled small marble-sized balls in order to suck the coolness.[2]

Denver enjoyed a greater influx of business than it had ever seen and a more wonderful parade of people arriving at the train station than it had ever before witnessed. *The Denver Republican* had great fun with their description of the Tammany "tiger" from the "jungles of the Bowery," and the Tammanyites were described as the "men with the moulting bankrolls."[3]

Eager to wipe away the embarrassment of Parker's overwhelming defeat, the Democrats turned again to William Jennings Bryan. The demonstration that followed was even longer than the one that followed his Cross-of-Gold speech in 1896. John W. Kern of Indiana was chosen to run for vice president.

Until Franklin Delano Roosevelt altered the custom in 1932, candidates commonly did not attend the political conventions. Party leaders realized the benefit of creating a hoopla around the official nomination notification, and these occasions had essentially become the kick-offs to the campaigns. Taft was informed of his nomination on July 28 in the town where he grew up—Cincinnati, Ohio; Bryan was told in his hometown, Lincoln, Nebraska, on August 12. (Each party spent more than a month after their convention preparing to make it official.) Throngs of people attended both events and there were great demonstrations.

Although neither candidate planned to do much traveling (which would have been a tremendous change for Bryan), apathy among their constituents soon made it clear that taking to the stump would be necessary. Both Taft and Bryan as well as the William Randolph Hearst-financed Independence Party candidate, Thomas Hisgen, went on extended tours.

The only flame of campaign excitement was ignited by William Hearst and fanned by none other than President Theodore Roosevelt. When Hearst obtained letters from the Standard Oil Company indicating that Ohio Republican Senator Joseph Foraker and Governor C. N. Haskell of Oklahoma, treasurer of the Democratic National Committee, had had dealings with the great oil trust, the newspaper publisher released them, hoping to disgrace both major candidates. (With the country feeling unfriendly toward trusts, any sort of arrangement with one was viewed as suspect.) Roosevelt saw clearly what Hearst intended and sought to save Taft and the Republicans while permitting the letters to tarnish Bryan and his party. The president counseled Taft to shun contact with Republican Foraker, and then Roosevelt set out to publicize Democratic Committee treasurer Haskell's connection with Bryan. (Haskell resigned in the midst of the unpleasant wrangling between Bryan and Roosevelt, and Taft would later sponsor the Publicity Act, which opened to public scrutiny the lists of campaign contributions made in races for the House of Representatives, a first step toward campaign-fund disclosure.)

Taft ran on the platform that he would continue the work established under Roosevelt. Bryan realized that the silver issue was no longer viable as a main campaign theme, and this time he tried to focus on issues that would appeal to middle-class

Americans who were suffering because of the difficult-to-check strength of big business. But the former "Boy Orator of the Platte" was now a middle-aged political speaker whose ideas had been around a long time, and Bryan failed to generate much enthusiasm.

This was to be Bryan's last campaign for the presidency, and he was defeated soundly. In the electoral vote, Taft received 321 votes to Bryan's 162. In the popular vote, Taft garnered 7,675,320 to Bryan's 6,412,294.

Breaking with inauguration day tradition, Theodore Roosevelt did not accompany the new president, his hand-picked successor and future nemesis, back to the White House. Instead, he attended the swearing-in, which was held in the Senate Chamber because of inclement weather, and left directly for the train station to go home to Oyster Bay. Taft, Vice President Sherman, and their wives went on to review the inaugural parade despite the stormy weather.

## Election Reform

Though a grass roots movement on election reform had started in the late 1880s and '90s with many states adopting the Australian ballot and investigating other changes that made the election system more serviceable, it wasn't until the early years of the 20th century that many of these changes took hold. Reform met with great resistance from party regulars, and, because the changes generally started at the local level by ordinary citizens, it took many years for the reforms to become more widespread.

For a long time, state legislatures were reluctant to interfere with the conduct of primaries, viewing them as the private concerns of political parties, but problems with the system cropped up again and again, making legislators realize that it was a matter of public concern. Since the party bosses controlled the caucus and convention system, sometimes potential candidates found it impossible to be nominated in the first place. Progressive Republican Robert La Follette spent a good part of the 1890s simply trying to get nominated, while the party bosses in Wisconsin passed over him for more malleable candidates. In New Jersey, where these issues had been carefully scrutinized and which was relatively typical of what was happening in other parts of the country, some helpful legislation was finally passed: Only qualified voters of the appropriate area could participate in the area primaries; bribery of convention delegates as well as bribery of voters in primaries was punishable by law. Voting procedures similar to the system for general elections were established. Still, the fact that the party bosses controlled who was nominated was a problem. Eventually it was provided that local officeholders such as aldermen, freeholders and township committee members were voted for directly.

By 1907, the platforms of both major parties called for the direct primary for the nomination of candidates. As a result, by 1910 all candidates at the municipal or county level were chosen by direct primary (where nominees could get their name on the primary ballot by filing a petition with a specific number of signatures), while congressmen, electors and the governor (because people from more than one county voted for them) were still nominated by convention. By 1911, even congressmen, the governor and presidential electors representing specific parties were put in nomination through the direct primary. While it was still difficult to defeat the "organization" candidate, these measures were a step in the right direction.

And as a sign of things to come, a preferential primary was held so that New Jersey voters could express who they favored for senator, though it wasn't until 1913 that people were able to vote directly.

Fraudulent voting was still very much a problem. Because no good system was in place for voter identification, "repeaters" voted early and often. More than 1,000 illegal registrants were discovered in Atlantic County in 1910, and many more were suspected. Gangs of voters from as far away as Philadelphia were brought in by the Republican machine, and votes were sold for from one to two dollars. According to historian Richard McCormick, in some wards the "bought" voters were required to take carbon paper into the polling places and bring out a copy of their marked ballot. At one poll, challengers were given drugged water to put them out of commission; in other districts, they were physically intimidated and even arrested. One Democratic poll worker was kidnapped.[4]

Because of situations like these, the Progressive Era was a time when great attention was fixed on establishing voter registration. In New Jersey, voters in large communities had to appear in person, and the police were expected to verify addresses. In small communities, house-to-house canvassing was done. Unfortunately, it was still hard to cross-check registrants with legal residences, and fraud was still prevalent.

## Voting Machines Used—and Not Used

In New Jersey, ballot reform did not move along as quickly as in other states, and during the first 10 years of this century, New Jersey was still using separate party ballots. Voting machines were just coming into use, and they looked like the perfect answer. Two were used in Trenton as early as 1902, and the state had acquired 361 by 1905. As happened elsewhere in the country, the "mechanical monsters" were accepted initially, but by 1907 voters were up in arms about them. They complained that the machines made it hard to vote a split ticket, and write-ins were also difficult. Many voters were distressed because they could not feel assured that their ballot had actually been registered or because they feared the machine might err in recording totals. Some even maintained that the vote wasn't secret; that skilled watchers could tell what was being recorded from the clicks and other noises made by the levers. While the legislature considered an educational effort to make it work, they ultimately decided to let the voters decide. In 1908, voters in 321 of the 335 election districts voted to return to the paper ballot. By 1911, $182,500-worth of voting machines were gathering dust in the State House.[5]

In 1911, New Jersey introduced a secret ballot to replace the machines. It was specified that only one ballot was to be used, and it was to be available only at the polling place. Names were listed in alphabetical order under the office being sought, and each name was followed by a party designation. Voters signified choice by marking an X in the square opposite a candidate's name or by writing or pasting in a name in a blank space provided for each office. No longer could a voter make a single X to denote voting a straight ticket, and since voters had to check off each candidate whom they favored, it was more conducive to voting a split ticket.

To further curb fraudulent voting, a voter was now required to establish that he was registered before he could obtain a ballot, and he had to sign the poll book. His signature was then compared with that in the registry book. Only then was he permitted to vote. Each ballot had a numbered coupon that was detached before the paper was dropped in the box, but first the number had to be noted by the voter's name in the registration book.

## Absentee Voting

The early part of the 20th century was a significant time for the evolution of laws concerning absentee voting. Though "sending one's vote by proxy" had been around since the 1630s, it had been used and defined in various ways according to what suited the time. For example, in 1635 in Massachusetts, it was deemed unsafe for residents of frontier towns to leave the towns unguarded in order to come to a polling place to vote, so arrangements were made for one or two people to bring in the votes.[6] Original absentee voting did not even specify that voters had to be away—just that they were unavailable to come to the polls then.

The first full-scale civilian law providing for absentee voting was enacted in 1896 and provided for in-state voting at a poll other than the voter's own. Some laws provided that the voter could only cast a vote for those items that were the same on both ballots (e.g., governor); other states provided that votes for local candidates not listed on a ballot in another locale could be written in by hand. In 1901, Kansas developed laws to help army personnel and railroad workers who weren't at home to vote.

By 1913, absentee voting was beginning to spread and broaden. Six more states enacted civilian absentee balloting laws; arrangements to vote by mail and provisions for early voting were made.

As absentee ballots became more common, some states enacted very limited laws (Tennessee's law of 1915 was limited to rural mail carriers), others enacted broader laws—some of which restricted absentee voting to in-state voting; others permitted voting from out-of-state as well. In 1917, with the country entering World War I, many indirect-voting laws were put into effect, but only 12 of those were limited to providing for the soldiers. However, by 1918, states that had not moved to do so provided for soldiers to vote, and 24 of the 29 laws that were passed were soldier laws.[7] Though war provisions were dropped at the end of the war, interest in civilian absentee voting continued and shaped the absentee voting system we have today.

## 1912: A Bull Moose Splits the Republicans

In 1912 Americans were to witness an election day phenomenon that had not occurred since 1860. It was the first time since pre-Civil War days that more than two candidates had the possibility of carrying a significant percentage of the vote. This time it wasn't the country that was being torn apart—it was the Republican Party.

Although the current administration was marked by a series of "firsts" (Taft was the first golfer-president; the first to throw out a baseball to open the American League baseball season; the first to have an official presidential automobile necessitating that the White House stables be converted into a garage), and one "last" (Taft was the last president to keep a cow at the White House),[8] these failed to make him well-liked.

As Roosevelt's hand-picked successor, Taft had done a serviceable job as president, but his popularity plummeted early, largely because he was between the proverbial rock and hard place—Roosevelt's followers were still wishing that Teddy himself had run for another term, while the conservative wing of the Republican Party found Taft difficult to like simply because he had been chosen for the spot by the radical Roosevelt.

Taft also suffered because of unfortunate blunders he made with his voting constituency. One instance occurred in 1910 when he spoke before the National American Woman Suffrage Association convention and awkwardly tried to convey his fear that, if women were to be given the franchise by constitutional amendment, intelligent ones might choose not to vote and that the privilege might be abused by political bosses who would round up other members of the fairer sex to participate in ballot-stuffing. That sentiment alone would have irritated his audience, but when he seemed about to compare women to unintelligent Hottentots, hissing began to fill the air—a shocking way to treat a president in that era. By 1912, one million women had received full franchise in their individual states, meaning that Taft, the first president who had agreed to speak before the suffragists, had certainly not done himself any favor.

By the midterm elections, the voters were looking for alternatives, and, as a result, the Democrats gained control of the House. Roosevelt, angered by this turn of events and by many of the decisions made by his trusted friend, returned from a trip to Africa to try to rectify the situation. Such was this former Rough Rider's popularity that he was greeted by a Fifth Avenue parade unequaled until that held for Charles Lindbergh in 1927.

In 1910, Roosevelt started speech-making and campaigned for broader reforms including health insurance, direct primaries and more powerful labor unions. In 1912, he announced his candidacy, and, in the state primaries, Roosevelt won nine states to Taft's one (though Taft received most of the delegates in states that held conventions rather than primaries). But since Taft still controlled the national committee, Taft delegates were seated in cases of dispute. Taft was renominated on the first ballot with James S. Sherman as vice president.

At that, Roosevelt's supporters bolted the convention, and, calling themselves the Progressive Republicans, on August 5 they nominated Roosevelt as their presidential candidate with Governor Hiram Johnson as Vice President. Earlier, Roosevelt had declared to the press that he was as "fit as a Bull Moose" for the campaign, and the name stuck—he was the candidate of the Bull Moose party. A chant for the party became popular:

> I want to be a Bull Moose
> And with the Bull Moose stand
> With antlers on my forehead
> And a big stick in my hand.

The Democrats met in Baltimore in June and had a difficult time deciding upon a candidate. The various factions were so much at odds that it took an extended convention to finally break the deadlock. Finally, on July 2 on the 46th ballot, Woodrow Wilson, governor of New Jersey and the former president of Princeton University, received the nomination. Thomas Marshall of Indiana was selected as the vice presidential candidate.

Taft ran a sedentary campaign from the White House while Roosevelt campaigned for a "New Nationalism" featuring social reform and regulation of big business. Wilson, whom people came out to see because they were curious about a professor-politician, campaigned for a "New Freedom" where he promised to curb monopolies and special privilege for special interest groups. He seemed to realize that if he took the middle road between Roosevelt's radicalism and the more conservative Taft, he would likely make it to the presidency.

True to his nature, Roosevelt campaigned hard and was reluctantly slowed only by a would-be assassin's bullet. In Milwaukee in October, he was shot but the bullet was stopped by his metal spectacles case and a folded copy of a speech that was in a breast pocket. Though injured, he finished his speech and went to the hospital only at the end. In deference to the end of Roosevelt's campaign, the other candidates stopped campaigning as well.

On election day, for the first time in 20 years, victory went to the Democrats. Wilson won with 435 electoral votes to Roosevelt's 88 and Taft's 8. Combined, Roosevelt with 4,118,571 of the popular vote and Taft with 3,486,720 had more popular votes than Wilson (6,296,547), so Wilson won as a minority president with only 41.9% of the votes. Had there not been a split in the Republican Party, the Democrats likely would have experienced yet another defeat. Eugene V. Debs, the Socialist candidate, received 6% of the votes—the most any Socialist candidate ever received in a presidential contest.

## Arizona Gains the Vote

After a prolonged political battle, Arizona achieved statehood in 1912; it was the last territory contiguous to the United States to achieve this. The voting population consisted mainly of farmers, miners or cattlemen with Populist/Democratic leanings. (Some even said that in order to have Republicans available for all the offices at the state level, they sometimes had to pay candidates to run. Because so many elections were settled in the Democratic state primaries, it was important to vote there. The term, "Pinto Democrat," came to be used to describe voters who registered as Democrats in order to participate in that party's primary, but then invariably voted Republican in the general election.)[9]

Coming into the union at this time, the state entered with few barriers to the franchise. Women had had the right to vote since statehood (1912), and the only groups prevented from voting were the insane, convicts and those "under guardianship." Because of confusion about the citizenship status of Native Americans, no one could decide whether they should be given the vote. A few polling places were put on reservations, but evidently these were to accommodate government employees. (It was 1948 before the state legislature specifically gave Native Americans the right to vote in both state and federal elections in Arizona.)

But just because a state had entered the union did not mean that there was necessarily dancing in the street on the occasion of an election. In Arizona the election of 1912 was reported thus: "Election day was the quietest election ever held in Flagstaff. They just walked down and voted— that's all."[10] The first state elections had been held in December of 1911 as a prelude to statehood in February of 1912, so interest had obviously decreased.

By 1916 enthusiasm had increased, particularly among the Democrats. There was a "monster" Democratic parade that included four bands, 400 mounted cowboys, 100 others on horses, hundreds of automobiles, 1,500 members of organized labor and 10 floats with hundreds of school children, followed by a rally at the Columbian Theater with a senator from Oklahoma coming to speak.[11] In the view of the opposition newspaper, the only people in attendance were straight-ballot Democrats and candidates and children were interspersed in the theatre gathering "to add enthusiasm to the gathering."[12]

Polling places were announced in local newspapers and most carried sample ballots (some premarked as an aid to the voters). The larger towns had multiple polling places, but outside the towns, precincts tended to follow school boundaries with schools as the polling places.

Arizona wasted no time in participating in election shenanigans. In the 1916 gubernatorial election, witnesses testified that election board officials in one country had been drunk and had been seen altering ballots. Ballots from one precinct in Cochise County were also suspect that year as they disappeared and then reappeared.

## Personal Election Day Reminiscences

Bits and pieces from American lives on election day help shed light on important issues of the time as well as remind us of the significance of the day to Americans. In Indianapolis in 1907, a lady noted in a letter to a friend that the Methodist Church was up in arms over cocktails being served at a lawn party and was threatening to steer votes away from the Republicans as a result.[13]

In another part of the country a cowboy recalls in a newspaper interview how very important voting was to the men he worked with. They willingly gave up a day or two's pay to travel as much as 70 miles to cast their votes.[14]

In Cheyenne, Wyoming in the early 1900s, candidate-sponsored suppers followed by rallies were held on the eve of election day, and the next night citizens went to the opera house where they could see a play while they awaited the returns. As the news came in, bulletins were read from the stage.[15]

In St. Louis, if Edward V. P. Schneiderhahn's diaries are an accurate reflection of the times, the average citizen enjoyed following politics and took great interest in it. In 1900, his November entries show that after voting early, he returned to the polls to see how the voting was being conducted. His predictions for the casting of the electoral votes are recorded in his diary and he notes political conversations with others as well. Though final results were not known for several days because of the time it took to tabulate votes, Schneiderhahn tells that he always went downtown to watch the final votes come in anyway.[16]

Not even in far off Hawaii did America's election day pass unnoticed. Annexed in 1898 and established as a U.S. territory in 1900, Hawaii had been strongly influenced by the U.S. for many years and participated early in the American way of voting. Though many of the residents were not eligible to cast votes, a good number of Americans lived in Hawaii and worked for American companies. One woman recalled that on the eve of election day, it was traditional for American companies to sponsor an evening of merriment and speech-giving to help voters make up their minds. Though only Americans and native Hawaiians could vote, many immigrants (Chinese, Japanese, Puerto Ricans and Filipinos) attended the festivities anyway. She recalls crowds arriving at a room normally used for processing sugar cane. Infants generally came along with their mothers, though older children were usually left at home. Speakers from both the Democratic and Republican Parties were in attendance and were introduced in both English and Hawaiian. All listened attentively even when the words were foreign to them. A dance area was left in one end of the room, and both Hawaiian and Portuguese bands played so that people could dance after the end of every second or third speech. Water pails were passed, and everyone drank communally from the long-handled tin cups. Refreshments were served toward the end of the evening with final speakers and dancing rounding out the night.[17]

## Progress for Women

Following Wyoming's 1869 lead, the western states had been granting women suffrage and when the state of Washington gave women the right to vote in 1910, there was a resurgence of interest in suffrage rights. Several states gave women the vote shortly after, and, by 1912, women were ready for a renewed national effort to work for a constitutional amendment that would make voting possible for women nationwide.[18] Carrie Chapman Catt now headed a united group, the National American

Woman Suffrage Association, consisting of Susan Anthony's National Woman Suffrage Association and Lucy Stone's American Woman Suffrage Association, and her political know-how would eventually lead them to victory on a national level.

By 1916 the possibility of a major reform of women's rights had increased dramatically, because—for the first time—a major political party included a women's suffrage plank in its platform.

For two hours on the morning of June 14, 1916, at the opening of the Democratic Convention, 7,000 women from across the nation lined the St. Louis streets along the route the delegates would take on their way to the Coliseum. Dressed in white dresses with "suffrage" yellow sashes, the women carried bright yellow parasols and said not a word as the delegates passed by.

Suffrage for women had been a topic thought and talked about for several years, but certainly the "Golden Lane of Silence" on the opening day of the Democratic national convention helped pave the way for putting suffrage in the platform.

Demonstrators also offered up a tableau for the delegates. In a two-hour pose called "Up To Liberty," a St. Louisan stood under a golden canopy dressed as the Statue of Liberty. Her attendants were dressed in mourning clothes and silently held out their manacled hands toward the passing delegates.

As the votes in favor of adding the suffrage plank to the party platform began to come in at almost 8 to 1 for the suffragists, one yellow parasol began to wave and then more and more. One writer noted that it "looked as if a field of golden California poppies had suddenly sprung up."[19]

## 1916: Staying Out of War

As president, Wilson achieved many progressive reforms, and his positive legislative achievements during his first four years were almost unprecedented. He implemented farm credit, federal workmen's compensation, restriction of child labor and an eight-hour day for railroad workers. The tariff was reduced for the first time since 1861, and the banking and credit system was put under public control through the Federal Reserve Act.

But it was Wilson, the man whose 1912 campaign had been waged almost totally on domestic issues, who was on watch in 1914 when Austria-Hungary declared war on Serbia for presumably harboring the terrorist organization that had assassinated an Austrian archduke. Territorial, imperialistic and economic conflicts in Europe made this declaration akin to throwing a lighted match onto a pile of fireworks. Germany rushed to assist its ally, Austria, and within a matter of weeks Russia and all of Europe had taken sides, engaging in what became known as the Great War (World War I). Insisting on American neutrality, Wilson—and the entire country—lived uneasily on the sidelines, watching Germany wage battle against its European neighbors by foot, boat and submarine.

How to remain out of the war was foremost in the minds of Democrats when they met in St. Louis in June. Wilson and Thomas Marshall were renominated, and at the convention it was decided the campaign theme should capitalize on what Wilson had done so well for the last two-and-a-half years. "He kept us out of war" became the Democratic slogan.

At the Republican convention in Chicago in early June, party regulars passed over the willing Roosevelt and turned instead to Charles Evans Hughes, an associate justice of the Supreme Court and a former governor of New York who was well thought of for his progressive reforms. Former Roosevelt Vice President Charles Fairbanks was selected as running mate.

The Progressive Republicans held a separate meeting in Chicago and offered the nomination to Roosevelt, but he ultimately deferred to Hughes after meeting with the new Republican candidate.

With Congress in session throughout the summer, Wilson did not begin his campaign until fall. However, his overall popularity had been boosted in the spring when he was able to use diplomatic pressure to get the Germans to suspend their unrestricted submarine campaign. In May of 1915, German torpedoes sank an American tanker as well as the Cunard liner *Lusitania*, the latter resulting in the deaths of 1,100 civilians including 128 Americans. These tragedies showed many Americans that neutrality was a questionable stance; some thought Wilson should have declared war then, but this new agreement helped him save face.

In the fall, Wilson traveled a bit and gave speeches from the front porch of Shadow Lawn, his new home on the Jersey shore. The Democrats also used various campaign speakers to travel the country on Wilson's behalf and distributed leaflets and handbills by the millions.

The reunited Republican Party presented a formidable challenge for the incumbent, and although Hughes's campaign was a tricky one—walking a fine line between party hawks and those who didn't want the country to go to war—he was surprisingly popular. He was often accompanied by Mrs. Hughes, who set a precedent for the spousal support we see today.

Had Hughes not committed a campaign blunder on the West Coast, he almost surely would have won the election. While traveling in California, Hughes seemed to attempt to stay clear of an intraparty fight between California conservative Republicans and the Progressives. Although Hughes even stayed in the same hotel as Governor Hiram Johnson, then a candidate for the U.S. Senate and the leader of the Progressives, no one arranged for the two of them to meet. Hughes's reluctance to reach out to Progressives turned them against him, and soon the Progressive Republicans cast their votes for Wilson for president, and Hughes lost a crucial state.

Early returns on election night gave the victory to the Republicans. Every eastern state north of the Potomac (with the exception of New Hampshire and Maryland) went for Hughes. The *New York Times*, which had backed Wilson, went so far as to concede to Hughes, announcing in the paper as well as to many thousands of people watching the board on the Times Square Tower that Charles Evans Hughes was the victor. Several other papers followed suit.

As returns came in from the West, the picture changed. Though it was Thursday afternoon before results could be predicted, the final outcome was in Wilson's favor. Carrying the entire West as well as all of the South, Wilson had 277 of the electoral votes to Hughes's 254. The popular vote was 9,127,695 for Wilson to 8,533,507 for Hughes. It was now left to the peace candidate to lead the nation into what could no longer be ignored—a world war.

## How Election Results Were Obtained in 1916

Perhaps the biggest changes in the ways people spent election day in the early 1900s were attributable to the drastic improvements in media and communication. The following letter written after the 1916 election by the head of the *St. Louis Republic* to the U.S. ambassador in Russia well illustrates how the news was obtained by the media and how it went out to the people:

I hope Mr. Goltra's cablegram sent on Thursday night reached you promptly, as it bore the good news of the re-election of the President. We had three days and two nights of agonizing suspense here with regard to the results of the election. The first returns indicated that Hughes had won. The New York newspapers all broke their necks trying to announce his election first. We received a message over the Postal wire at 6:45 Tuesday night, before the polls were closed in St. Louis and in thousands of other precincts, declaring a Republican victory. Even the *New York Times*, which had supported Mr. Wilson, was among the first to throw up its hands. We all felt pretty much depressed.

We gave bulletin service on Olive Street with our lantern and screen and had an enormous crowd which filled the street as far as Sixth. They stuck courageously through the depressing reports that came during the early hours of the evening. When we closed for the night, about half past twelve, there was very little upon which to ground our hopes . . .

Wednesday morning our crowd came back and stayed all day listening to bulletins which were given to them through a megaphone. In the evening we used bulletins in the windows, giving them the latest returns, as we did on Thursday until ten o'clock in the evening, when the re-election of the President was announced.

The Star had printed an extra about seven o'clock Thursday evening saying Wilson had won. Our crowd bought copies of the paper, but waited silently. They seemed to realize that the Star was only guessing. Of course, we had as late returns as the Star, but we determined not to make announcement until we were positive that it would be substantiated.

About ten p.m. Thursday the flash came from the A.P. that Wilson had carried California, which was all he needed to insure his re-election. We then put up a bulletin in the window of our counting room saying "Wilson wins," and had Old Glory ready to wave from one of the third story windows. The crowd then let go of their pent up feelings and started a celebration which lasted for some hours. It was an inspiring occasion; I know you would have enjoyed being in the midst of it.[20]

Even in Arizona, which had only just achieved statehood, elections in the second decade of the century benefited from the latest advances. Phoenix and Tucson newspapers (two in each city) used stereopticons to project results on large screens outside their offices. Citizens were invited to follow the progress of the vote-counting nationwide. They utilized Associated Press, Western Union and Mountain States (telephone) lines to gather local and national results. Smaller towns were not able to gather the information so quickly; however, the larger towns would have undoubtedly relayed national news to the smaller communities when they picked up local voting information from the outlying areas.

## The Inevitable Occurs

On March 4, 1917 Woodrow Wilson was sworn in for his second term of office; he began his administration with the intention of continuing the international neutrality America had maintained for two-and-a-half years. But just 14 days after his inauguration, the Germans sank three more American ships. Wilson had little choice. Before a special session of both houses of Congress on April 2, 1917, Wilson asked for a declaration of war, and he received and signed it on Good Friday, April 6.

Before the end of the war, 25,000,000 American men would register to fight for their country, but the question that was asked in 1917 was whether or not the U.S. could gather and train a reliable army quickly enough to stem the German advance that threatened to overrun the Allied lines (Great Britain, France, Russia, Serbia, and Belgium were the Allies; Germany, Turkey, and Austria-Hungary were known as the Central Powers.) A token American force was sent to France in June as a morale booster; but the United States needed time to prepare, and more than a year passed before sufficient numbers of American troops were ready to fight.

Wilson was a strong and good war president, and he ably led the country as the government mustered what it needed to enter the war by assuming the decision-making role for much of industry, agriculture and labor; the war effort also had first call on the railroads and telegraph lines. By 1918 massive convoys of men and supplies were being sent to Europe. In initial battles against the newly fortified Allied lines, the Germans were impressed by the new power, but they remained undaunted and steamed on toward the last Allied line that they needed to break to reach Paris. It was there, on the Marne River in July, that the Germans were finally turned back, and the tide of the war began to turn. The Allies took firm control of the offensive and, with German resources exhausted, took only a few months to defeat the Central Powers. By November 11, 1918, an armistice was signed, and the Great War ended.

# The 1920s: A
# Decade of Change _____ 14

The Twenties was a decade where materialism was valued above idealism, and changes in morals and social concepts created upheaval. The routine flouting of Prohibition led to cynicism regarding law and order, and the example set by the Harding White House—long remembered for its scandals, not its leadership—were part of the feel of the decade.

The entire nature of society changed in just a few brief years as the population shifted away from its rural roots. By 1930, more than half the population lived in towns and cities, and the vastness of America shrank somewhat as the "gasoline buggy" of the 1890s became the inexpensive car of the 1920s (9,000,000 were on the road in 1920 and that number had tripled by 1930). Moving pictures, radio, national advertising and the syndication of newspaper articles reduced provincialism and provided the possibility of a commonality of background and knowledge for all Americans.

This era of social and cultural turbulence began with a major election day change. Even before any results were known in 1920, history was being made. Though women had already been given the vote in some states—mostly in the West—the 19th Amendment had been ratified in August of 1920 meaning that November 2, 1920 was the first time that all American women were eligible to vote.

WOMEN ARRIVE EARLY TO CAST FIRST BALLOTS, and WOMEN THRONG BOOTHS EARLY IN RECORD POLLING,[1] were typical front-page headlines. While it was not a perfect day—black women were sometimes barred from voting with various excuses given, and, in some areas, turnout of women voters was almost nonexistent, but in general it was a historic occasion. An editorial in the *St. Louis Times* the following day said:

> One of the great victories at the polls yesterday was won by womankind. The sex was on trial before the nation as surely as were the various candidates. The jury was the whole world, and today that panel must agree that American womanhood acquitted itself magnificently in the discharge of its great new responsibility.[2]

There are many election day stories and activities surrounding women and their first trips to the polls, but it's important to look first at America and the campaign in which they were voting.

## *1920: "Back to Normalcy"*

In 1920, Americans were not pleased with the way things were. They hadn't wanted to be involved in a world war, and they weren't prepared for the economic and social adjustment that was necessary in its aftermath. The cost of living was high, and unemployment was widespread. The country's reaction to all the changes brought on by the war was an intense desire to pull inward. Wilson's interest in establishing and participating in a League of Nations was unpopular. The United States walked away from the opportunity to move ahead as a world leader and instead settled down to wrestle with domestic matters.

Wilson, whose ill health made it obvious that he would follow precedent and not run for a third term, hoped the Democrats would keep the focus on his League of Nations and crusade for world peace, but the Democrats sensed that Americans were voting for issues closer to home. When they met in San Francisco in June, they nominated James M. Cox, governor of Ohio. Chosen for vice president was Wilson's Assistant Secretary of the Navy Franklin Delano Roosevelt. The platform endorsed the League and Cox worked hard for it, but he also campaigned on domestic progressivism.

In backroom maneuvering, the Republicans decided against three major contenders and selected, instead, "favorite son" Senator Warren G. Harding of Ohio. Chosen for his pleasing personality and his affable nature, Harding won the nomination on the 10th ballot with Calvin Coolidge, governor of Massachusetts, winning as vice presidential candidate. With a country yearning for prewar better times, Harding campaigned on a "back to normalcy" theme. While Harding superficially seemed to embody the values of small town America and times gone by, he actually was of quite a different character. In an era of prohibition and restrictiveness, he drank, smoked and gambled, and shortly after the nomination, the Republicans learned he had a mistress with whom he had a child. (Mother and child were packed off to Europe for the duration of the campaign.) Harding's disregard for propriety was symptomatic and a harbinger of the White House to come.

Harding proved to be poor at addressing any campaign issues, but he became known as a highly skilled handshaker. One of the senators who had championed Harding's nomination recommended that the party keep him at home for most of the campaign so that he could avoid answering questions. The Republicans did just that. With the exception of a few specially planned campaign speeches for which he had to travel, Harding was generally found receiving delegations informally on his front porch in Marion, Ohio—something he did very well.

Cox traveled tirelessly for the Democrats, covering 22,000 miles and speaking to more than two million people. He campaigned for Wilson's postwar peace project, the League of Nations, and he called for the country to move ahead with reform, but the electorate seemed to like the Republicans' soothing promises of "Americanism" and the vow of a return to better days.

As election day neared, Harding was left to cope with one unfortunate campaign incident. Pamphlets, leaflets and fliers suddenly appeared that traced Harding's family tree back to a black ancestor—a ploy to diminish support among racist whites. The author of the material remains unknown, and although the genealogical literature was widespread and word-of-mouth passed quickly, Harding remained unaffected by the rumor.

A campaign "first" of 1920 was the first large-scale attempt to poll the electorate. Aside from the polling done on steamboats and the like during the 19th century, up until now there had been no good way to gauge the mood of the country. Conducted by the weekly *Literary Digest*, millions of postcards were mailed out, and though the sampling was primarily middle-class, the results were quite accurate.

With less than half of eligible voters casting ballots, Harding won by a landslide, garnering 60.2% of the vote. In the electoral college, Harding won 404 votes to Cox's 127; the popular vote was 16,143,407 to Cox's 9,130,328. Socialist Party candidate Eugene Debs was in prison for the entire campaign, yet still managed to receive almost 1,000,000 votes.

During the course of Harding's administration, it became evident that a good number of his cronies in the administration were fattening their bank accounts at government expense. Not since the Grant administration had so much wrongdoing been uncovered. In August of 1923, Harding and his wife headed West to get out of the spotlight for a time, and Harding died while they were away.

While the country stood amazed as affairs such as the Teapot Dome and other government scandals came to light, Calvin Coolidge, a quiet man who had achieved respect for his work as governor of Massachusetts, now stepped in to straighten out the Harding administration.

## The Mechanics of Election Day

Growing interest in running honest elections coupled with the dramatic increase in the electorate now that women could vote presented interesting challenges for election officials in 1920. More people than ever before had to be accommodated at the polls at the same time that very tight procedures needed to be followed in order to decrease the amount of fraudulent voting.

There were 600 polling places in a city like St. Louis and 315,000 registered voters. In 81 of the polling places more than 500 were registered to vote; two locations faced the possibility of having 1,000 voters come. Poll hours were to run strictly from 6:00 A.M. to 7:00 P.M., and the polls were to close whether or not everyone waiting had voted. With that in mind, it was estimated that in a precinct with 500 voters, a vote must be cast every minute and a half, providing there were voters utilizing every moment of the day.

To spread the voting out somewhat throughout the day, several measures were taken. One was to provide other options for workers. Some states passed a law stipulating that employers were to give each employee four hours to vote without docking their pay. In addition, election officials recommended that housewives and those not employed during regular business hours go to the polls after 9:00 A.M. and before 3:00 P.M. so as to leave several hours at the beginning and the end of the day for the expected rush of employed men and women.

Some local election boards also foresaw that they needed to do what they could to speed up what had to be accomplished for each voter during the minute and a half or so allotted to him or her. For each registered voter, the election official had to look up the name of the person before furnishing the ballot, so some timesaving steps were taken. In Missouri, one solution involved mailing postcards to voters in precincts where voting was expected to be particularly heavy. The postcards told the number of the line in the poll books on which their names appeared. Each voter was expected to present voting officials with this information.

Once checked off on the registration list, the voter needed to mark the ballot. To help out, newspapers ran sample ballots to be marked at home so that the voter could take the sample ballot to the polls to copy in order to speed ballot preparation. St. Louis had not yet adopted the Australian ballot, so each voter received six separate party tickets stapled together. Voters were to tear off the party ticket that most closely matched his or her voting preference. If voting a straight ticket was desired, then the party ballot could be submitted unchanged. If, however, changes were made, then a line was to be drawn through any candidate the voter did not want, and the voter could write in the name of opposition candidates from the ballots of the other parties.[3]

## Getting the News

St. Louis was also typical in its progress in the newest forms of disseminating the election news. In 1920, there was great excitement over the fact that election returns would be transmitted in a new, faster method than before. A Mr. W. E. Woods, who had been a radio expert with the wireless station in the navy, had installed in his home the third most powerful wireless telephone system in the nation, and from there promised to send out election bulletins received from the *Post-Dispatch*. He could transmit to about 5,000 wireless telephone receiving stations within a 1,000-mile radius. One of the stations receiving Wood's transmissions was the home of L. A. Benson who had a wireless telegraph with a range of about 2,900 miles—so Benson planned to repeat the *Post-Dispatch* bulletins by wireless telegraph, thereby broadening and speeding the reach of the news.[4]

As had become the tradition, election bulletins were generally given at the newspaper building as well as other public buildings and schools. In St. Louis in 1920, just under 25 locations were available to people to hear the election returns as they came in. The newspaper announced that returns would be read through a new sound-multiplying machine, the Magnavox telemegaphone, and shown on a screen with a stereopticon. People who planned to hear the returns at a location other than the newspaper office would hear them through the sound-multiplying device, which would also be used to amplify phonograph records ("as great volume as the original sound") that would be played during the time when there was no news. Those who opted to hear returns at the *Post-Dispatch* were promised movies. Among them, a brand new first-run release, Mutt and Jeff in *The Politicians*, a Harold Lloyd comedy, a review of current events, a Charlie Chaplin comedy and a never-before-seen-by-the-public motion picture made by "X-ray process, showing movement of kneecap when knee is moved up and down, also the movement of wrist, jaw bone, elbow, etc."[5] First time ever shown in public!

## The Women go to the Polls

From the vantage point of 1920, women could look back on 20 or 30 years where the seeds planted at Seneca Falls in 1848 had begun to bear fruit. As early as 1869, Wyoming Territory provided women with the right to vote, and, during the 1890s, three western states (Colorado, Idaho, and Utah) granted women suffrage (though Utah was merely reinstating suffrage after a lapse of nine years). The suffrage movement fell into the doldrums for a decade, but the social movement that was giving women the time and opportunity for civic interests did not.

Family size was decreasing, and domestic tasks like laundry, baking and the sewing of clothes no longer needed to be done at home, freeing women's time more and more. Even child rearing was made slightly less demanding by the establishment of recreational facilities, day nurseries, playgrounds and kindergartens for children outside the home.

Partly out of enthusiasm and partly because women in many states already had state amendments giving them the vote, American women were more than ready to organize for their first election day. Preparations for voting began several years before 1920.

An active League of Women Voters existed in St. Louis, and, as early as May of 1916, the League was busy establishing citizenship schools where women paid to attend to learn about the workings of government. The first one consisted of three sessions a day for five days with evening classes for employed women. Four hundred fifty women attended. The concept of explaining the mechanics of government to the citizenry was new, establishing this as a "first" for its time.

The League also furnished many speakers to various groups, ranging from political clubs to church groups, and arranged for voting demonstrations in department stores, hotel lobbies and other public buildings. Voting drills—complete with a prototype of an election booth—were also held. Speakers for groups and at these demonstration sessions answered questions and worked with women on the technicalities of registering and marking a ballot.

That summer women activists rode milk trains and other conveyances into the various rural areas to drum up interest in suffrage.

For some of the early elections, they also sponsored candidate forums similar to the presidential debates that they generally sponsor today.

*In New York, a special handbook, The ABC of Voting*, was assembled and fliers on "What Every Woman Needs to Know about Voting" were distributed.

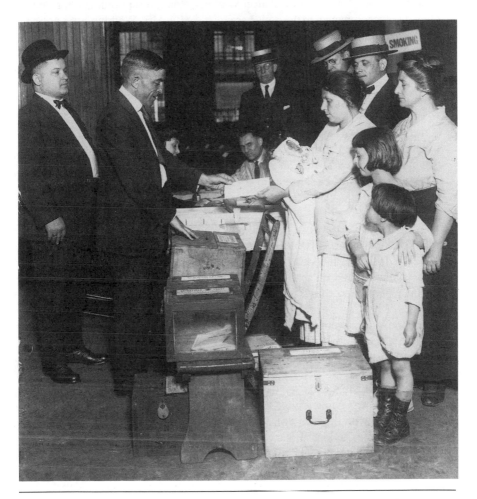

*The 19th Amendment giving women the right to vote was ratified in 1920. Though some states had permitted women to vote in local and state elections prior to this, 1920 was the first time American women were eligible to vote in a national election. Above, a woman registers to vote in the New York City primaries. (Courtesy The Bettmann Archive)*

While the presence of women was definitely felt, participation varied throughout the country. In New York, wire service stories reported that "every woman not suffering from Spanish influenza voted," but in some parts of the South not a single woman appeared to exercise her right.

Local newspapers tended to focus on the single individuals:

WIFE OF PROHIBITION CANDIDATE FOR PRESIDENT GETS LIFETIME THRILL

Cincinnati, OH, Nov. 3—Rev. Aaron Watkins, Prohibition candidate for President, was accompanied to the polls here by his wife. Mrs. Watkins, after voting for her husband, said it was the thrill of a life time to vote for him.[6]

There was also mention of the fact that vice presidential candidate Franklin Delano Roosevelt escorted his wife and mother to the polls in Poughkeepsie. Also noted were the unusual:

MRS. FOX WHO VOTED FOR GOVERNOR COX SEES JUDGES DROP BALLOT IN BOX

Officials of the Fourth Precinct polling place of the Eighteenth Ward sat up and blinked their eyes when an aged woman marched in and got these lines off:

"My name is Mrs. Fox, I came to vote for Cox, please be sure to put me ballot in the box."[7]

WOMAN ELECTION DISTRICT CAPTAIN PUTS IN PHONOGRAPH JAZZ MUSIC WHILE YOU VOTE RESIGNED TO MOVE THINGS FASTER

New York, Nov. 1—Music while you vote.

A woman captain of an election district has installed a phonograph in her polling place to jazz things up when the voting gets dull tomorrow.[8]

Other innovations were more practical. In White Plains, New York, a baby-checking service was organized in order to encourage women to vote.

The funny pages also took advantage of the special voting circumstance of that election day:

Weasel Jones's "Just Kids" comic strip introduced a doleful young man assuring us that his sister was going to vote this year: "So I ast her who she's gonna vote for. She said the one with the blue eyes." The comic strip ended with the kid beating his head against a pole, saying: "It's a good thing I kin Control myself."

"Somebody's Stenographer," another strip, portrayed one stenographer informing another that she would have to sign her ballot. The other retorts "Sign your ballot? Of course not. What do you want to sign it for?" Her companion answers: "Well if I don't, how will Bryan know I voted for him?" In another frame, a gentleman asks Miss O'Flage why she is laughing. She answers "Why–I asked Miss Katz who she was going to vote for an' she says either for referendum or Lodge—she hasn't quite made up her mind!"[9]

While voter turnout was light in many places, most women who wanted to vote did so without incident. An exception to this was in Savannah where a hastily passed state law kept black women from voting—they were refused ballots at the polls on November 3. Though they had registered since the suffrage amendment became effective, election judges ruled that they were not entitled to vote because of a state law that required that voters register six months prior to an election. (White women did not test this law as none of them came to the polls.)[10]

Overall, the conclusions were positive. A nonpartisan, who visited all the wards in St. Louis that day, believed that women throughout the city voted to the best of their ability and according to their conscience and ideals. "Not only in the more privileged sections was this true, but in the river districts and in those settled by foreigners. In 'Little Sicily' I found one woman much perturbed over the fact that she did not believe that the judge whom she had mark her ballot, had done it in the way she wished. I found a general desire among the women to have their ballots express what they really wanted them to."[11]

## Voting for a Female Candidate for Congress

In Muskogee, Oklahoma, voters who went to the polls had the opportunity to cast their ballots for a candidate whom they had read about in advertisements for a cafe.

The owner of the cafe was antisuffragist Alice M. Robertson, who won the election and became the second woman to hold a seat in the House of Representatives. Her tactics were simple. In preelection issues of the Muskogee newspapers, Miss Robertson ran classified advertisements whose headlines concerned the cafe and its food. In the body of the ad were heart-to-heart talks about the current political situation, telling people about why they should cast their ballots for the owner of the restaurant. Active in the campaign against woman's suffrage, Robertson served as vice chairman of the Antisuffrage Association of Oklahoma, but won her seat based on promises to work for legislation affecting the welfare of the Indian, women and children, farmers, soldiers and working people. Notes Miss Robertson of her victory: "A lot of my good friends thought I didn't have a chance, and they figured further that they could make money by betting against me. I warned them. But they would not take my warning. Now they are sorry for themselves and I am sorry for them, too."[12]

## 1924: A Compromise Candidate vs. Coolidge

Americans' lives were more settled by 1924, and businesspeople were prospering. Because of this, Americans were quick to forgive the incumbent administration, particularly since there was actually a new leader, Calvin Coolidge, who had not been tainted by the scandal of his predecessor. When Republicans met in Cleveland in June,

"Silent Cal" received the presidential nomination with General Charles G. Dawes of Illinois nominated as his running mate.

The Democrats were not so well aligned, and their convention provided for the American public what little excitement there was in the campaign of 1924. In what was to be the longest convention in history, spanning 17 days and requiring 103 ballots, the Democrats battled it out in New York during a heat wave. Tensions were high, speeches were endless and fighting (with words and with fists) was frequent. The eastern Democrats, anti-Prohibition and largely Catholic, favored New York Governor Alfred E. Smith. Against them were pitched the more rural, dry, anti-Catholic Protestants who wanted William G. McAdoo of California. Neither side would concede, and finally out of the weariness of the nine-day deadlock, the convention agreed on a compromise candidate, John W. Davis, an attorney, Wilson's solicitor-general and former ambassador to Great Britain. Governor Charles W. Bryan (brother of William Jennings Bryan) of Nebraska was nominated for vice president. The entire convention was carried on radio, doing the Democratic Party great harm in the coming campaign.

Liberal Democrats were dissatisfied and broke off to form the Progressive Party, with the farmer-labor movement as its base. They met in Cleveland in July and nominated Republican Senator Robert M. La Follette of Wisconsin and Burton K. Wheeler, a Democratic senator from Montana, as vice president.

With their slogan of "Keep Cool with Coolidge," Republicans felt that La Follette was the more viable candidate, and with a huge campaign fund, they set off to defeat him, fearing that his strength in the farm states might hurt them in the electoral college. Campaign managers portrayed Coolidge as the "poor man's candidate," stressing his interest in economy of government and his dislike of bureaucracy.

"Silent Cal," who got his nickname because of his preference for speaking only when he had something to contribute, was an odd candidate. He came across as unfriendly and lacking in social graces, but he was skilled at working with the press. During most of the campaign, he tried to hide out in Washington—leaving the campaign to his managers—but he was generally available for "photo opportunities" while executing his presidential duties. He would don an Indian war bonnet for appropriate occasions, pose with women in colonial garb for historical remembrances or wear chaps and a 10-gallon hat to meet with ranchers. Because times were so good, because Coolidge had remained untainted by Harding's disgraceful administration, and, certainly partly because Calvin never uttered a word that got him into trouble, he was an enormously popular candidate.

Wall Street lawyer John W. Davis's campaign fizzled quickly, and Robert La Follette was unable to achieve enough support nationwide to offer much of a threat.

Coolidge was elected by a plurality of 2.5 million popular votes over the combined total of his opponents. Coolidge ended with 382 electoral votes to John W. Davis's 136 and 15,718,211 popular votes to 8,385,283. Though La Follette ran second to Coolidge in several of the western states, much to everyone's surprise, he emerged with only 13 electoral votes and a popular vote of 4,831,289. With that election, the progressive movement of the 1920s passed into history.

By the mid-1920s there had been a couple of campaign improvements. Now that some candidates were making themselves more available for stumping, managers found that featuring their would-be officeholder in a parade in an automobile provided a wonderful "photo opportunity" as well as a way for people to see their candidate.

Whistle-stop campaigns were still very important. Harding added one innovation during his presidency that was used by other presidential campaigners. He had loudspeakers installed on the rear of the train so that more people could hear his speeches; he also had a speaker installed in the press car so that reporters needn't leave the train to hear him. This must have been a great relief to newsmen who sometimes got left behind when a candidate used a whistle-toot and a quick pull-out from the station to end his speech. The trains themselves were much more comfortable than before, and, typically, the press had its own car. The press car was a regular one stripped of seats and fitted with boards for typewriters. There was generally a darkroom for photo development and someone from Western Union was always along.

## Getting Out the Vote

While the percentage of Americans voting had peaked in 1896, voter apathy had begun to take hold in the early part of the 20th century. By the 1920s some communities were experimenting with ways to fight it.

With women becoming part of the electorate in 1920 vote tallies would automatically jump, and political activists were hopeful that interest in this new phenomenon would increase the percentage of voter turnout as well—and many hoped that a larger electorate would be harder for big-city machines to control. In addition, greater interest on the part of the people would force parties to search for the best people.

When the election of 1920 failed to stem the tide of voter apathy (only 49% of the total electorate, including men and women, voted that year), political parties, civic organizations and newspapers all over the United States joined in a drive to increase the proportion of eligible voters who participated in each election, and 1924 saw a burgeoning of a national network of Get-Out-the-Vote Clubs.

As part of this effort, several business organizations, including the United States Chamber of Commerce and the American Bankers Association, joined together to try to register a full businessmen's vote. The National League of Women Voters arranged for house-to-house canvassing and enlisted the services of a volunteer motor corps to drive voters to and from the polls. Citizenship forums and voter information booths were established in public locations, and telephoning was done to remind people to register and to vote. Newspapers, journals, the radio, the pulpit, the lecture platform and the theater were all used as places to talk to citizens about their rights and obligations as voters. More than 2,000,000 Boy Scouts also took part in this nationwide campaign.

In some communities, political groups had children write essays on "Why You Should Vote," and some wore placards reading "My Mother and Dad are going to Vote. Are Yours?"

In Grand Rapids, Michigan, election day became "tag day." School children and representatives of women's clubs were at the polls to put a tag on all voters as soon as they had performed the task of voting.

For a local election in Chicago, an information sheet on how to vote was sent to potential voters by the party machine. The front of the flier referred to the vote as a "Stockholders' Meeting for Citizens of Chicago," and asked "Are you interested in

Comfortable Rapid Transit?
Honest Police Administration?
Improvements and Extensions?
Clean Streets, Clean Alleys?
Adequate Fire Protection?
Good Railroad Terminals?
Orderly City Government?

A call to get out and vote was followed by a cartoon depicting an "honest but indifferent" citizen sleeping in a cradle with a man labeled "corrupt politics" rocking the cradle. The headline was "If you don't vote, the Hand That Rocks The Cradle Will." The voter's polling place and hours were given as well as complete instructions on how to vote—After a judge had initialed each ballot, the voter was to retire "at once and alone" into a vacant voting booth and mark an "X" in the square before the name of the candidate whom the voter favored.[13]

In 1928, similar measures were refined and employed throughout the country, and at 3:00 P.M. on election day, citizens in some communities heard the peal of church bells and the tooting of whistles all over town to remind people that there were only four more hours left to cast a vote.[14]

## '24: Results Come Quickly Via Radio

For the first time Americans across the nation were going to hear the results of the presidential election just as quickly as the ballots could be counted. Though the radio had helped broadcast the news in 1920, the election year 1924 saw a great increase in the number of locations where radio broadcasts could be received, meaning that even people in rural areas had a far better chance of being able to ride or drive to a location to hear the news soon after the election. In St. Louis, the number of locations where broadcasts could be heard jumped to about 150 locations throughout St. Louis County, with many other places broadcasting in the rest of the state.

Though some locations were by "member-invitation" only, most of the spots listed were where anyone could go as of 7:00 P.M. to hear the news broadcast projected throughout the room by loudspeaker.[15]

In St. Louis, those who came to the Twelfth Street Plaza where the newspaper building was located would find two screens, each 18 feet square, placed on the front of the building. One was to be used for moving pictures; the other for election returns. A public address system, which the newspaper promised would carry sound 1,000 feet up and down Twelfth Street, was to be used to announce the news.

Wednesday morning the newspaper reported on how exciting it was that many thousands of people could follow the election tide through one of the "latest devices of science"—the radio.

Those who gathered at the *Post-Dispatch* office "stood like sardines" in order to watch the new "telautograph stereopticon" write the results on the wall. The device used to project election results onto the one screen was a curiosity itself, and evidently people loved watching it. The telautograph screen is described as looking like a grasshopper's leg producing script on the canvas. It worked by transmitting news bulletins from the editorial department to a truck in the street where the machine was located. An operator in the truck copied the messages with a similar device operated in conjunction with a stereopticon machine, and this produced the writing on the screen with the shadow of the jointed metal pen plainly visible as it moved.[16]

Comparing the experience to watching the scoreboard news of an out-of-town baseball game, the newspaper reported that it was an orderly gathering. "Policemen had some difficulty in keeping Olive Street open for traffic, but in the main the gathering was well-behaved . . ."[17] Besides election returns some of the spectators found time to watch motion pictures that were shown from time to time on a screen beside that used for the stereopticon writing. These were comedies and animated strip cartoons and alternated with pictures of candidates and slides bearing typewritten bulletins.

## The Black Vote in the 1920s

Racial tension was part of the voting scene in Ocoee, Florida in the early 1920s. Election officials refused to permit July Perry, a black, to vote, on the grounds that he had not paid his poll tax. Perry left the poll, but returned armed with a shotgun, which was taken from him, and he was chased away. After dark, Perry again approached the polls, accompanied by other blacks, and at that point whites formed a posse and dispersed the blacks. With the posse following them, the blacks opened fire from the buildings to which they had fled and ended up at the Perry house, where two whites were killed in the backyard. The Perry house was then set on fire in order to dislodge the blacks. Perry apparently was captured and later taken by a mob and lynched. "It was stated that he was taken from an automobile in which he was being carried to the jail after having been treated at a hospital." Five blacks were burned and several others injured when the buildings were set fire, and several other whites were injured.[18]

This was just one among many racial incidents in the 1920s. The attitude toward blacks and the vote during the 1920s largely had to do with how much effect the vote was going to have on any given election, and even in Texas and the South, where black voting was fought the most strenuously, there were pockets where, because the black numbers were small and the votes would not make a big difference, no one bothered to stop them from voting. Elsewhere, it was a different story.

In some parts of the country, the black vote was viewed only as something to exploit. Enough blacks voting "right," could allow the calculating candidate to achieve victory. By the 1920s, the Democratic Party had begun to envision a way to take advantage of black voters. The Republican Party, the party of Lincoln, for the most part had failed to nurture its black supporters by acknowledging them and encouraging them to vote. For the first time, it occurred to the Democrats that they might profit from this. In 1924, the Democrats felt the black vote might swing some important states, and with their candidate John W. Davis, who successfully argued before the Supreme Court against the disfranchisement of blacks in Oklahoma, they felt the black vote worth pursuing, and special effort was made to woo those voters in certain states.

But in most of the South, the attitude continued to be that the 15th Amendment was something that was to be circumvented in the best way they knew how. Poll taxes, literacy and property qualifications, registration and residence requirements were all applied as legal means to exclude blacks from the polls. Requiring black voters to interpret the Constitution to the satisfaction of an election judge was also used.

States that had "grandfathered" (made eligible to vote only the descendants of those who could vote in 1867 when all the electorate was white) included North Carolina, Louisiana and Oklahoma, but in 1915, the Supreme Court ruled that "grandfathering" was unconstitutional and contrary to the 15th Amendment. It didn't much matter. Illiterate whites who qualified under the clause had already been added to the registration lists. However, an increasing number of blacks began to qualify under the literacy, property and tax clauses of their state constitutions, so the ruling did increase interest in finding new ways to restrict the vote.

One of these methods of restriction was the white primary. In the South where almost all viable candidates were Democrats, political contests were generally fought out in the primaries. Winners of the primary were generally assured of ultimate election. By restricting participation in the primary, those who were against blacks helping with decision-making essentially accomplished their purpose, and by 1930 eight states—Alabama, Arkansas, Georgia, Louisiana, Mississippi, South Carolina, Texas and Virginia—barred blacks from participating in the primary. (An increasing number of blacks managed to qualify under the literacy, property and tax clauses of the state constitutions and were thereby eligible to vote in regular elections, but their votes were negated by the fact that the true political battle had already taken place in the primary.) Only in Kentucky and West Virginia could blacks participate in the primaries if they qualified under the literacy, property and tax clauses.

The "whites only" primary technique was first tested in court in Texas where a legislative act held that: "In no event shall a Negro be eligible to participate in a Democratic Party primary election held in the State of Texas, and should a Negro vote in a Democratic White Primary Election such a ballot shall be void and election officials shall not count such."[19] Dr. L. A. Nixon, a black in El Paso, Texas attempted to vote in the Democratic primary of 1924. The judges of election declined to furnish the ballot to him or accept his vote. The case was carried to the United States Supreme Court, which decided in his favor in 1927.

In retaliation, the Texas legislature passed an act that provided that political parties in the state could prescribe qualifications of its members and could determine who shall be qualified to vote or otherwise participate in such political party. The Texas Democratic Committee then prescribed that "all White Democrats" and "none other" could participate in the Democratic primary.[20]

Dr. Nixon tried again to vote in the Democratic primary in 1928 and was again refused. That year, District and Circuit Courts upheld the election officials' right of refusal; and the Supreme Court in a 5–4 vote held that the election board couldn't discriminate even in a primary. But Texas was determined. When the Democratic Convention met in Austin, it passed a resolution stating that "all white citizens of the State, who are qualified to vote under the constitution and laws of Texas shall be eligible for membership in the party and as such eligible for participation in the primaries." The State Executive Committee ratified it.

Shortly thereafter, R. R. Grovery, a black of Harris County, Texas was denied the privilege of voting in the Democratic primary by Albert Townsend, the county clerk. *Grovery* vs. *Townsend* reached the Supreme Court and, in 1935, the Court held by unanimous vote that while a state could not abridge the right to vote on the ground of race or color, a political party was a voluntary organization that could decide the basis of its membership. It was therefore decided that blacks could be legally barred from voting in the primaries. Since the South had a one-party system at the time, that had the effect of denying suffrage on the basis of race and color. After this ruling, the Democratic Party in 1936 was generally successful in preventing blacks from participating in its primary.

Apathy and a feeling of despair on the part of blacks in the latter part of the 19th century certainly contributed to the continuing existence of restrictive suffrage, and the early part of the 20th century saw a build-up of organizations that were ready to fight for the cause of black suffrage. In 1906 in Ithaca, New York at Cornell University, the Alpha Phi Alpha Fraternity of Negro College Men was born, and the National Association for the Advancement of Colored People also worked to stimulate blacks to register and vote. The group launched several citizenship schools in black churches in Atlanta for the purpose of informing black citizens about their citizenship rights, registration and voting. During the 1930s, a well-planned program was launched with "A Voteless People is a Hopeless People."[21]

Unfortunately, despite a clear legal basis for black voting that hardly any court, no matter how racist, could deny, the fight for black suffrage in the early 20th century

South was a lost cause. Local officials, as the Texas example illustrates, would go to almost any length to keep voting all-white, and almost no governmental agencies stepped in to enforce even the most explicit laws.


## *1928: A Catholic for President?*

Though the stock market was booming and the president's popularity was still high, Calvin Coolidge had difficulties with Congress over economic issues and farm prices, among other things, during his second term. Because of this as well as Coolidge's own emotional fatigue, the campaign of 1928 featured two new faces for people to meet.

"I do not choose to run for President in nineteen twenty-eight," read the cards Calvin Coolidge handed to reporters that year, and with that, Herbert Hoover, then secretary of commerce, decided to run for the Republican nomination. Hoover, nicknamed the "Great Engineer," was known for his excellent engineering skills used in private industry, his administrative abilities as demonstrated when he served as the government's food administrator during World War I and his humanitarian impulses connected with charitable postwar efforts to help fight starvation in Europe. Hoover gained the Republican nomination with the vice presidential nomination going to Senate floor leader Charles Curtis of Kansas.

Nominated by Franklin Delano Roosevelt, the "Happy Warrior" Alfred E. Smith, four-time governor of New York, received the Democratic nomination in Houston. Senator Joseph G. Robinson of Arkansas was picked for vice president. Robinson, a Protestant Prohibitionist, was seen as a good complement to Smith, a Catholic from an urban area who favored repeal of Prohibition.

Smith's candidacy brought up many controversial issues that the nation couldn't ignore. Foremost was his Catholicism. Among the rumors that circulated were that if Smith were elected the Pope would move to the United States to live. Even more far-fetched was a story that went along with a photograph of Smith at the entrance of the new Holland Tunnel, which runs under the Hudson River. In the rural South, this picture was circulated with the rumor that the tunnel was to be extended under the Atlantic to the basement of the Vatican if Smith were to win.[22]

For the first time, radio was used as an important means of vote-getting, making a different kind of personal appeal important in the candidates. "Thousands of people throughout the nation for the first time in its history are in complete contact with the activities of the presidential campaign, and leaders on both sides freely predict that radio may elect the next President of the United States"[23] stated an article on the radio page of the St. Louis *Globe Democrat.*

While Smith with his quick wit, good personality and his trademark brown derby was a big crowd-pleaser, his extemporaneous style and New York accent came off less well on the radio. On the other hand, Hoover's radio addresses were dry and often boring.

But Hoover was a symbol of prosperity, and that was hard to fight against. Dinner pails were full, and the stock market was booming to make everyone richer. No one wanted to vote against what for many was a good life.

In the end it was a country *vs.* city victory, a vote for maintaining the prosperity the Republicans had built *vs.* the acceptance of the unknown with Smith's Tammany connections, his controversial stand on Prohibition and his different religion. Hoover took 58% of the vote to Smith's 41%, with 444 electoral votes going to Hoover and just 87 to Smith. Smith took a dozen of the largest cities, but just couldn't pull any more, though he made a good showing in the popular vote. Hoover had 21,391,993 to 15,016,169 for Smith.

But of course, what appeared to be Hoover's lucky night was actually the beginning of his most difficult trial. The stock market crash of '29 was to pitch the country into a Depression like no other the country had experienced. Hoover was unable to see his way clear to manage the way out of it, and, by 1932 countless factories and businesses were closing, many banks had failed and family farms were facing foreclosure. Hoover kept expecting the country to right itself, so he kept promising that "prosperity was just around the corner."

# The Election Days of a Four-Term President ___ 15

By the next presidential election year, nearly one out of every three voters was unemployed. Thousands roamed aimlessly across the countryside in search of a day's work; others set up households in "Hoovervilles," shantytowns where shelter was made of packing crates and whatever people could scavenge. Along the Mississippi, the Hoovervilles were so well established that there were subdivisions—Hoover Heights, Happyland, and Merryland were the names of no-rent colonies where several hundred people lived, raising some of their own food and going out each day to seek work enough to feed themselves for one more day. In the cities, breadlines grew in length, and 25,000 unemployed paraded in Chicago. On the street corners, unemployed men offered apples for sale. Others simply asked, "Brother, can you spare a dime?"

In the late summer and early fall of 1932, times were so bad that mothers wrote impassioned letters to *The Nation* hoping that someone would donate clothes for their babies. One woman in North Carolina had found a doctor who agreed to help her with a normal birth for only $40, but her older children lacked enough clothing for school. And she wrote: "My husband left this morning without food or money to go to another State to look for work." Thousands of people, young, old, and middle-aged were living on the edge of starvation.[1]

Hoover kept thinking the worst had passed, but in 1932 the glorious American dream of four years earlier had become an American nightmare.

## 1932: Campaigning During the Great Depression

Considering the condition of the country in 1932, it is a wonder that when the Republicans met in June they renominated Herbert Hoover, but there was some feeling that to switch candidates at that time would be to admit responsibility for the past four years. Promising a return to prosperity, the party moved ahead with plans to back the incumbent. (Vice President Charles Curtis was also renominated.)

When the Democrats met in Chicago, two-term governor of New York Franklin Delano Roosevelt was the frontrunner over Al Smith and Speaker of the House John

Nance Garner. Ultimately, a deal was cut with Garner's people, and they agreed to release Garner's votes in return for the second berth on the ticket. Breaking with the tradition of a candidate not appearing at the convention, Roosevelt flew to Chicago to accept the nomination in person, in part to dispel any rumors concerning his physical abilities since his bout with polio had left him in a wheelchair.

Roosevelt went on to lead a vigorous campaign, giving 27 major addresses from coast to coast and spreading the word about his promise of a "New Deal" for all Americans. Throughout the campaign, radio, newspaper and newsreel people honored an unwritten agreement never to show Roosevelt's leg braces, or aides lifting him into place at a banquet table or a podium. (This continued throughout his years in office.)[2] At the time of the election, most voters had no idea of his disability.

Roosevelt's campaign team also undertook an aggressive letter- writing and long-distance telephoning campaign. Every Democratic county chairman was expected to report back to Roosevelt's campaign manager, "Big" Jim Farley, on his district, and the candidate himself wrote thousands of letters, telephoned men and women in key positions and sent them autographed photographs and phonograph records of his voice appealing for their support. If a county chairman's son planned to marry or his daughter had a child, the chairman was sure to receive a congratulatory message from Roosevelt.[3] It was organized politics at its best.

By 1932 the radio had become an important factor in campaigning, and since their speeches now reached millions listening to their sets at home, the candidates faced new campaign challenges. Crowd reaction at public engagements would bring along the fence sitter less often, so candidates had to learn to use the medium effectively. While Hoover came across as dry and boring, Roosevelt's pleasing voice revealed a warm personality, and he used humor well.

Registration totals were up almost 5,000,000 from 1928, and radio was largely credited with the increased voter interest.

## Election Eve Interest

Hoover's last campaign stop was made in Elko, Nevada on his way to Palo Alto where he would vote. While there, he spoke to residents as well as to a radio audience. Once the train stopped, the president's car was converted into a temporary broadcast studio as radio engineers, working with men from the local power plant, strung wires in through the ventilators of the lounge. Then, under klieg lights and in front of microphones, Hoover prepared to speak. Though about 1,000 people had come to see him when his train pulled in, his only visible audience was a group of about 20 of his immediate party bunched at the other end of the railroad car. An Associated Press reporter describes the setting: "Outside, unable to see the dramatic scene because of the drawn shades, was a cross-section of the frontier. A Chinero leaned against the step of the last car of the train. About 50 men who appeared to be miners and cattlemen loafed around the frame station. Several Indians in store clothes mingled with them.

Across the tracks, the town's one movie house blazed brightly despite the fact that the town's two banks had closed last week."[4]

Shortly after Hoover's train passed through, a watchman was stabbed and shot after questioning two men near the train tracks. The men, one black and one white, were carrying dynamite, evidently to set off near the tracks, and one of them fired at the watchman. Firing back, watchman Charles E. Fish said that the men ran off, dropping a sack that was later discovered to contain about a dozen sticks of dynamite.

## Election Day Trouble

EMPLOYEES WARNED TO VOTE FOR HOOVER ran the headline on an Associated Press story datelined late October in Birmingham, Alabama and also published in the November 1, 1932 issue of the *St. Louis Daily Globe Democrat*. In Anniston, Alabama, the American Net and Twine Company gave its employees notice to support the Republican ticket under threat of "indefinitely closing its plant," according to the Democratic campaign manager for North Alabama, who said he believed it is "the first

*Election Night 1932 in Times Square is depicted in this painting by Don Freeman. A Democratic landslide is announced on the moving-bulletin sign that ringed the Times Tower. Additional information is also projected on the side of the building. For New Yorkers of that time Times Square was the best place to be to learn up-to-the-minute election news. (Courtesy of Lydia Freeman)*

time in the South an employer has so openly attempted by threat and intimidation to coerce its employees to support any particular party."

And in New Orleans, a judge had to order that a black's name be placed on the registration list. When John St. Charles presented himself for registration July 30, 1932 and filled out the application, "The clerk asked him to interpret that part of the Constitution pertaining to 'writs of *certiorari*.' He said he gave a reasonable explanation, but that he was told it was not sufficient and he was ordered to return at a later date."[5]

One hundred years previously, physical fighting was as much a part of election day as was voting. With unemployment high (and liquor restricted but still available on the black market), election day, like voting days of the past, was a time of coming together. This time, millions of people had little else to do. Violence was often the result, as a few examples show:

In St. Clairsville, Ohio, there were reports on a vote riot on Election Day 1932. Twenty-five people were injured, two seriously, when a fight broke out shortly after midnight in front of the Belmont County Workhouse. People were quibbling over the election returns being broadcast from the courthouse, and windows were broken and several automobiles overturned. Several hundred people gathered to witness the fray, but after about a half hour police, armed with nightsticks, were able to bring order. Officers attributed the disturbance to bad feeling over the election outcome and to liquor that "flowed freely during the night."[6]

In Boston, four men were sharing a Prohibition-forbidden bottle of spirits to celebrate Hoover's upcoming victory. One Malcomc McFarland was arrested and later fined $50 for keeping and exposing liquor. The man testified that all of them were Hoover followers and, in pleading his case, McFarland said: "I never sold liquor, and the gallon I bought was to celebrate the coming victory of President Hoover."[7]

In Fall River, Massachusetts, voters had trouble of a different sort when 15 voters and a policeman were hurled into the basement of a polling place when a portion of the floor collapsed. Though shaken, no one was seriously hurt, but as a result, several went home without voting.[8]

On election day, nearly 40,000,000 Americans went to the polls to vote their pocketbooks. All economic groups were being hurt by the Depression, and they were tired of Hoover and what seemed to be his empty promises of relief. Franklin Delano Roosevelt won 7,000,000 more votes than Hoover—taking 57.4% of the votes to Hoover's 39.7% (22,809,638 to 15,758,901). Roosevelt received 472 electoral votes to Hoover's 59. Such was party momentum that the Democrats also took both houses of Congress by large majorities.

## 1936: Campaigning Via Radio

There was no doubt that the country in 1936 was in better condition than it had been in 1932, but it had by no means returned to the prosperity of the mid-1920s. Millions were still unemployed, and lavish government spending had not yet restored the country to its former prosperity; it was on these conditions that the Republicans pinned their hopes.

When the Republicans met in Cleveland in June, they had difficulty selecting a candidate and finally settled on Alfred M. Landon, governor of Kansas, whose farm state background might bring in the Western farmers and whose business background and conservative bent might attract businessmen. Colonel Frank Knox, publisher of the *Chicago Daily News*, was selected for vice president.

The Democrats met in Philadelphia in late June and both Roosevelt and Garner were renominated. When Roosevelt delivered his acceptance speech, 100,000 people attended and the whole country listened by radio.

The campaign that year focused on the New Deal and on the soon-to-be-implemented Social Security Act. Democrats vociferously defended both; Republicans tried to shoot holes in both plans.

The power of radio created a unique phenomenon in 1936. In the past, candidates who failed to win over the press were doomed from the start as they had no other way of reaching the mass electorate—personal appearances could never reach enough people. Roosevelt was plagued with unfavorable newspaper publicity denouncing the New Deal and misconstruing many of his programs. Historians estimate that almost two-thirds of the press was against him. But for the first time, a candidate could take his case directly to the people, and he did so most effectively. Even in cities where he had no newspaper friendly to him, Roosevelt often won the town.

Poll-taking was becoming increasingly important, and the *Literary Digest*, riding on the success of the last four campaigns, came out with a prediction heavily in favor of Landon. Dr. George Gallup and *Fortune* magazine were coming up with their own form of "sampling," but none proved more accurate than Chairman Jim Farley, who relied on reporting from precinct captains from the local level on up. According to Farley, the election would go to Roosevelt by a landslide, with only Maine and Vermont voting for Landon.


## Around The Country In 1936

On Election Day 1936, it rained and snowed throughout the Midwest, but long lines of voters waited outside the polling places as early as 6:00 A.M.

It was hard to be up earlier than residents in New Ashford, Massachusetts. There, the community had a 20-year record of being the first community in America to report its citizens' choice for president. Tradition had it that all 48 registered voters of New Ashford rose at 4:00 A.M., had their breakfast and then hurried down to the little white schoolhouse that also served as the town hall. According to state law, the polls could open at 5:30 A.M., and the town could announce the total as soon as every vote was in. Unfortunately, this year they were beaten. Voters in Millsfield, New Hampshire took advantage of the New Hampshire law that permitted a 12:01 A.M. poll opening, and when the town received all seven of the ballots to be cast (five for Landon; two for Roosevelt), it reported in—several hours before New Ashford was even awake.[9]

Election day in Kentucky was accompanied by feuding, with one dead and another critically wounded. In Uvalde, Texas, Vice President Garner tried to coach Mrs. Garner on her voting, and was reprimanded with "I'll do my own voting." Candidate Alfred Landon and his family took a train to his home town of Independence, Kansas where they voted, and then took the train back to the governor's mansion in Topeka. In Hyde Park, New York, there was a registration foul-up, and the president's son, Franklin, was required to take a literacy test before voting. About noon the rest of the family appeared to cast their ballots, and townsfolk waited to see the president arrive to vote.[10]

Citizens in major cities throughout the United States were primarily casting their votes by machine by this time, but the 30,000 machines in use recorded (and instantly tabulated) only one-seventh of the total vote. Throughout most of the nation, written ballots had to be counted by hand, and election workers sat in schoolhouses, general stores, police stations, barber shops and firehouses and worked for hours counting up the vote.

Like today, the news media looked for the human interest story. Print and broadcast personnel were in New Ashford, assuming that it would again be the first community to cast ballots. The oldest and the youngest voters, as well as the first and the last were interviewed. Reporters dogged the steps of Roosevelt and Landon as they went to their polling places.

But more important, media competition spurred great progress in the reporting of the vote. While remote areas still presented many challenges, changes were made wherever possible in order to speed returns. In Kentucky, locked ballot boxes were brought by horseback to the county seats; some counties were without telegraph or reliable telephone lines, so results were taken by newspapermen who drove them to Williamsport, West Virginia.

To help gather the election news in New York City, 8,000 police participated. Officers carried the district totals to the nearest precinct stations where the tally was telephoned to headquarters. These totals were kept track of by a city news manager for the New York City News association, and he had to choreograph the calls carefully as 45,000 calls were expected over a period of three hours.[11]

Broadcasters used men who were lightning-quick with numbers to keep running totals as the figures came in, so that their news reports would be accurate and up-to-the-minute.

These innovations not only helped publicize the results in a few hours, but they also helped, to some degree, to keep the election honest. Officials could no longer take time to tamper with the ballot, since totals were due in at specific times. What's more, the big news services eliminated the duplication that always resulted when numerous uncoordinated newspapers, plus telephone and telegraph companies assembled the votes.

Of course, press totals were not official, and since the government had no way to collect the returns speedily, the official totals were not recorded until several weeks later, at which point the election news was history.

*In this drawing, Don Freeman demonstrated the way the Tammany "boys" worked to get out the vote on New York's Lower East Side on election day. While one Tammanyite escorts an elderly woman to the poll, another sees that a bearded voter gets into the booth. A trio of Tammany workers wait outside.*

*In addition to schools and public buildings, barber shops, garages, flower stores and bars are just a few of the kinds of establishments used as polling places. In the days of machine politics, "connections" likely helped dictate the location, but even today the only basic qualifications for a polling place are location within a certain precinct and public access. (Courtesy of Lydia Freeman)*

That year witnessed a great presidential victory, the greatest since Monroe's in 1820. What's more, pollsters should have listened to Farley. His prediction was right on the nose. Roosevelt took 523 electoral votes to Landon's 8, and had 60.8% of the popular vote, which was 27,752,869 to 16,674,665. Farley and Roosevelt also loved to joke. The old adage, "As Maine goes, so goes the nation," now became, "As Maine goes, so goes Vermont."

## 1940: "Out Stealing Third"

"There comes a time in the affairs of men, when they must prepare to defend not their homes alone but the tenets of faith and humanity on which their churches, their governments, and their very civilization are founded . . . This generation has a rendezvous with destiny." So ran Franklin Roosevelt's 1939 annual message, and it was the coming war that dominated the hearts and minds of the voters in 1940.

Politically, some were disturbed by the precedent-setting possibility of a president running for a third term. Always before, presidents had eliminated themselves from candidacy before this became a possibility, and in the late 1930s, it appeared that Roosevelt would also do so. But as 1940 began and the Nazis invaded Norway, Denmark, Holland, Belgium and, by June, France, the picture changed. Few began to view the third-term issue as more crucial than the availability of a man who had proven himself well able to lead the nation.

Roosevelt did not announce his availability for quite some time and was evidently undecided himself. In 1939 he had even given the "go-ahead" to several other Democrats interested in running in 1940. By May of 1940—when the Nazis overran the low countries—Roosevelt seemed to have made up his mind, but he held back, hoping he could be "drafted" to run. The "Draft Roosevelt" movement, begun by political managers several months before the nominating conventions, gained enough strength that other possible candidates were eliminated, and the nomination was accomplished.

The Republicans saw Roosevelt as a difficult force to beat, and though they had available able men like Senator Robert Taft and New York's Thomas Dewey, they made a nontraditional choice, selecting a dynamic personality, Wendell L. Willkie, an Indiana-born lawyer and businessman who had never held public office. Though he lacked experience, he was intelligent and articulate, and the public, tired of the party's Old Guard, was ready to support an outsider. His grass roots support—with people founding Willkie Clubs, circulating Willkie petitions, sponsoring Willkie appearances and bombarding delegates to the convention with letters and telegrams—all made it look as if he might have the necessary support. For vice president, Charles L. McNary, Senate minority leader, got the nod.

Republicans moved into action with strong grass roots campaigns, and nationwide, Willkie Club members (often middle-class housewives) mailed out literature, telephoned voters and performed chores usually done by professionals. Willkie campaigned against the New Deal and traveled 34,000 miles by rail. He described the possibility of a third term by claiming that Roosevelt was "out stealing third." The Democrats countered with "Better a third-termer than a third-rater."[12]

But the major issue, of course, was the war. Would the United States enter or not? Both candidates promised to stay out, but both favored helping Britain as much as possible without actually going to war.

In the end, there was an unprecedented turnout of voters on November 5. Roosevelt carried 38 states and took 449 electoral votes to Willkie's 82. In the popular vote, Roosevelt had 27,307,819 to Willkie's 22,321,018.

Again, Roosevelt had managed to defy the press through his fireside chats. Losing the endorsements of influential newspapers like the *New York Times*, the *Cleveland Plain Dealer*, and the Scripps-Howard chain, Roosevelt was still able to carry every city of more than 400,000 (except Cincinnati), sometimes without a single friendly newspaper.

Like many other Americans on November 5, 1940, Sheila Graham and her lover F. Scott Fitzgerald, sat by the radio in her California apartment. "[We sat] pencils and pads in hand, listening avidly to the Presidential election returns for Franklin D. Roosevelt and Wendell Willkie. And how delighted we were that Willkie had lost his voice to laryngitis in the days preceding the voting. As two strong Democrats we were rooting for an FDR third term."[13] Though the names are famous, their election day activities in 1940 were the same as those of any other American.

## *The Nation's Oldest Voter*

One hundred nineteen-year-old Mark Thrash of Chickamauga, Georgia, was generally believed to be the oldest American to vote in 1940 (he drew the honor in '36 as well), and he was interviewed on radio and for the newspapers. Wearing a white apron, he explained that he always wore it: "I was a slave for 43 years, and the man I belonged to had so many slaves that he wanted to distinguish between the rest of them and me. That's why I always wear an apron." When the father of 29 was asked in the radio interview about his vote, he answered: "I think that's personal and prefer not to answer."[14]

## *The Black Vote*

Franklin Roosevelt created, in the early '40s, a Committee on Fair Employment Practice, the first time in the history of the nation that there had been specific executive action to secure nondiscriminatory employment practices. In this climate, the black vote was increasing in its importance. A November 2, 1940 article in *The Pittsburgh Courier*, a black weekly newspaper of the time, put it best. Under a headline, THE NEGRO VOTE, ran the following: "Never before in the history of American politics has the expression 'The Negro Vote' offered the significance it now offers in the election of next Tuesday. . . . never before has its power loomed so portentous as today."[15]

Because the black vote had gone Democratic in '32 and '36, the Republicans finally realized that blacks, as a group, could no longer be taken for granted as Republican voters. At last, there was some interest in what might interest the black voter. The article continues:

> The Negro voter wants a chance to participate in the commerce, the industry and the entire economic life of the country like any other group of citizens. We want a chance on the railroads to be other than porters and red caps; we want a chance in the factories, to learn and work in skilled lines; we want a chance with the steamship companies; we want a chance in the steel mills, in the mines, in the factories of all kinds. We want a place in the armed defenses of this country.[16]

And in 1939, blacks won an important Supreme Court victory, which declared, in *Lane* vs. *Wilson*, that the provisions in an Oklahoma statute that permitted only people who were registered between April 30 and May 11, 1916, or those who had voted in the election of 1914 to vote and that all others were perpetually disfranchised to be invalid. The statute had permitted white people on the registration lists in 1914 to vote, but blacks had been kept off the lists, so it effectively disfranchised the majority. In *Lane* vs. *Wilson* the Supreme Court declared this provision invalid, thus reinstating an important right for blacks.

## *1944: A Wartime Election*

Less than a year after Election Day 1940, the Nazis sank a U.S. destroyer, and, on December 7, 1941, Japan made a direct attack on the United States, striking American outposts in Hawaii, Guam, Midway, Wake Island and the Philippines. These acts catalyzed the U.S.—it was time to enter the war.

Three years later, when Election Day 1944 loomed, the United States was in the midst of a war. The possibility of not holding an election was rumored to be under consideration by the president, but when Roosevelt was asked by reporters about the likelihood of the election's being cancelled, he noted that having read the Constitution precluded that possibility.

Of course, the risk was that America would appear weakened by the political battle, but Eric A. Johnston, president of the Chamber of Commerce of the United States, answered that charge well in a radio broadcast: "The Americans like to do everything hard. We play hard, we work hard—and we take our politics hard. [After the election] we will be on the job just as hard as we have been all the while. The final result will be universally accepted. The decision of the majority will not be questioned. Once more we will be in appearance, as we have consistently been in fact, the United States of America."[17]

The Republicans had three strong contenders, John Bricker of Ohio, Harold Stassen of Minnesota, and most notably Thomas Dewey of New York. Ultimately, the convention settled on Thomas Dewey with Bricker as the vice presidential nominee.

The Democrats were less unified than in other years. Anti-Roosevelt forces were stronger than before, though overall, the fourth term was less an issue than a third had been. But most felt Roosevelt was the only choice. As the Republicans had decided to remain with Lincoln in 1864 in the midst of the Civil War, so, too, did the Democrats decide that it would be unwise to "change horses in mid-stream." At the convention in Chicago in July, Roosevelt agreed somewhat reluctantly to accept the nomination: "All that is within me," he wrote, "cries out to go back to my home on the Hudson River . . . But as a good soldier . . . I will accept and serve."[18]

In 1940 Roosevelt's running mate, Henry Wallace, whom many Democrats opposed, was narrowly nominated, and by '44, the party outvoted Roosevelt and replaced Wallace with Missouri Senator Harry Truman—party leaders didn't like Wallace's liberal views, and they were seriously concerned that Roosevelt wouldn't live out the term.

Stories about Roosevelt's failing health circulated during this campaign, but the press remained true to an unspoken pact with their president: Throughout his political life, Roosevelt had made an effort to be on his feet, sometimes aided by a person, a cane or a crutch, when being photographed, and the press had never revealed that the president was primarily wheelchair-bound. However, the trying years of the presidency had taken an obvious toll on the man, and serious concern about Roosevelt's health pervaded the campaign. Finally the president's doctor had to issue a statement attesting to the fact that there was nothing organically wrong with him.

Other than the "health" issue, the campaign itself was quite dull. Because of the war, Roosevelt did little campaigning and waited to begin until after September. Another problem was that Dewey, a liberal Republican, basically agreed with the social legislation of the New Deal, so he didn't attack it nor, out of patriotism, did he speak out against Roosevelt's war efforts. (The Republicans did try one war slogan: "End the war quicker with Dewey and Bricker.") Dewey emphasized that it was time for young men instead of "tired old men," but the Democrats merely rebutted with a list of names and ages of the people older than Roosevelt who were leading America to military victory. While Dewey was a smooth campaigner, some viewed him as being stiff. As with all candidates, appearance was important, and while Roosevelt's craggy, tired face was one to which the public had grown accustomed, Dewey looked different. Some people vowed not to vote for him because he had a mustache.

Roosevelt was expending most of his energy on the war effort, but when he did address the public through his cozy fireside chats or on the occasional campaign visit, his comfortable manner and wry humor were always pleasing. Although Dewey accused Roosevelt of spending taxpayers' money on personal indulgences, Roosevelt had his audience in the palm of his hand when he rebutted one charge concerning his little Scottie dog, Fala. In answer to a story that the president had sent a destroyer back to an Aleutian island to find Fala at a cost of several million dollars, Roosevelt assured everyone that this offended Fala's Scotch blood and that he hadn't been the same dog since. The public loved it—and him.

A few weeks after the nominations in 1944, the political action committee of the Congress of Industrial Organizations, under the chairmanship of Sidney Hillman, began its effort to bring out the vote. Pamphlets, which urged citizens to go to the polls and argued in favor of Roosevelt's re-election, were distributed in great numbers nationwide, particularly in the large urban areas and in areas where war industry had sprung up and the normal population was greatly enlarged. As the registration numbers were totaled, they showed how effective Hillman's group had been. Including ballots from the armed services, 50,000,000 were expected to vote.[19] And perhaps almost as important as these efforts on this wartime election day was President Roosevelt's election eve radio broadcast where he expressed hope that Americans "50,000,000 strong" would go to the polls to "face the future as a militant and a united people."[20]

These hopes were answered; early balloting indicated a heavy turnout. From Pennsylvania, where they stood 40-to-60- feet deep waiting to vote, to Los Angeles, where war plant workers came off the graveyard shift and went directly to the polls, voter turnout was strong.[21]

Of course, the welfare of the soldiers was of paramount importance to Americans in 1944, and the Red Cross took advantage of people being out to urge voters to give blood. Appealing to voters who "may have a little spare time after casting their ballots today," the New York Red Cross Chapter called on voters to stop by the blood donor center on East 37th Street to give a pint of blood and noted that unless a substantial number of voters appeared, then the center might not be able to meet the daily quota of whole blood and plasma to be sent to the armed forces overseas.[22]

For the first time in more than 150 years, Return Day—one of the oldest traditional observances in Sussex County, Delaware, where people from throughout the surrounding area came in on Thursday following an election Tuesday to hear the results—was not held in the early '40s because of the war and lack of transportation.[23]

Despite the gravity of the times, there was still time for the unusual. The following Associated Press story appeared with a dateline of Chicago:

Chicago, AP—James Jankowski is a Democrat, and wants everyone to know it. He arrived this morning at the 82nd Precinct polling place leading a donkey. Its ears were bedecked with American flags and its side boasted a picture of President Roosevelt.

On Long Island, a voter chose to remind people of the original Americans. On November 8, 1944, a headline in *The New York Times* ran:

SIOUX CHIEFTAIN VOTES
CRAZY BULL, IN TRIBAL REGALIA, CASTS BALLOT ON LONG ISLAND
In Centereach, Long Island, Chief Crazy Bull, a full-blooded Sioux chieftain, arrived at the firehouse to cast his vote. Clad in full tribal regalia, including a buffalo hair headpiece, he voted under his adopted Christian name of William Jacobs.

The article reported that the chieftain was presently a teacher, had served in World War I and was the current national archery champion. When asked how he voted, he replied, "Just quote me as being neutral, and hoping the best man wins."

In Missouri, the gamblers were having a tough time because the odds were so skewed. According to the *St. Louis Post-Dispatch* the Missouri Betting Commissioner finally stated: "It's beginning to look like propaganda when I put them [the odds] out." On the president, bettors had to put up $4 to win $1; odds on Governor Dewey were three and a half to one.[24]

Franklin Roosevelt spent Election Day 1944 in much the same way as he had spent them in the past. After registering his profession as "tree- grower" and struggling with a voting machine that didn't work properly, he went home to Hyde Park to await the results that would come in that evening. A radio had been provided by NBC, and

Roosevelt, as usual, would tabulate the results himself as they came in while he dined on his traditional election night supper of scrambled eggs—what he considered his "lucky dish." That evening at about 11:15 a bass drum could be heard coming up toward the Roosevelt home from the town, and as the torchlight parade approached to help mark a fourth victory, the president was wheeled out onto the front porch where he reminisced about other election days during his boyhood when he used to climb a big tree in front of the house so that he could see the election night torchlight parade as it wound through the village.[25] Little would he have guessed how significant those torchlight parades would one day become to him.

## The Soldier Vote

Estimates were that more than 2.5-million military votes were being sent in from overseas, and tabulating all these absentee ballots was expected to test the election system.[26] While many soldiers had been able to vote in other elections, it had previously been handled on a state-by-state basis. Then in 1942 Congress enacted legislation that provided for the absentee vote of all American soldiers.

What still varied by state was the deadline by which ballots had to be submitted. Five states stopped accepting ballots the day before election day; 35 took them throughout election day; and eight others were willing to accept them even later, with Rhode Island and North Dakota extending the deadline to December 5. In three of the states, the elections were expected to be so close that the soldier vote would be decisive, leaving the electoral votes in doubt until all tabulations could be done.

Army and Navy voting officers were credited with helping to bring about the large vote by making state war ballot applications available to enlisted men and officers. Reported *The New York Times* on November 8, 1944: "On many a ship and in camps on both sides of the world the voting officers handed out at roll-call printed application cards to members of their units who might otherwise not have troubled to write for a State form."

A soldier who took the federal ballot, instead of sending home for a local one, had to forgo the opportunity to vote for local candidates, but he could mark for president, vice president, U.S. senator and his or her representative. In outposts, a map of the United States was provided that delineated the various congressional districts in order to avoid any confusion.

In one location in France, huge placards noted each state's voting requirements. These were of particular interest to black soldiers as several states, Virginia, Tennessee and Mississippi, had poll taxes but they had waived them for soldiers; Georgia exempted soldiers from taxes owed and to be owing, while Alabama and Arkansas still required a tax. (One soldier noted that in most of the poll tax states, they couldn't have voted anyway, even if they had paid the tax.)[27] Black soldiers were angry about the Texas requirement: Each application for a ballot had to carry with it the tax receipt or, if lost, an affidavit of where it had been lost.[28]

Nevertheless, the soldiers were enthusiastic about balloting. "I don't intend to miss my vote just because I'm far from home," said Pvt. Calvin R. Yorbrough of Louisberg, North Carolina.[29]

Or as one corporal, Roger M. Olsen of the United States Army, wrote in a letter to his wife:

> As I marked the little X's I could hear the thundering guns and big shells whistling through the air toward the enemy. Each little mark seemed to strengthen the chain of freedom which the enemy, a few miles away, had tried to break. It was indeed an honor to vote today.[30]

Because of the soldier vote, the general procedure by local election boards varied from other years. Usually, the civilian vote was tallied as soon as the polls closed, but in 1944, election officials had to tally the bundles of soldier votes for their polling district. Next, the two groups of votes were added together before being sent in. In cases of dispute over some of the pencil-marked ballots, all reporting was delayed, thus delaying the Associated Press's reports. (Later on, the soldier vote was broken out as a separate figure.)

Tabulation was watched carefully to see if there was such a thing as a "military vote," or if they voted about the same as at home. Absentee military votes, though voted weeks and months earlier in many cases, were often counted last. In cases where the combatants died since having voted, the votes were counted as valid.[31]

Pollsters predicted a close election, but as in other years, they were wrong about Roosevelt. On November 7, Roosevelt carried 36 states with 432 electoral votes to Dewey's 99 and won about 3,500,000 more popular votes than Dewey (Roosevelt had 25,606,585 votes to 22,014,745 for Dewey).

## Americans Await the News in Various Ways and Places

Tammany Hall had long been the scene of huge election night crowds as the boys gathered to discuss the results, but in 1944, the Tammany Tiger had lost its teeth. Only about 50 appeared at Tammany Hall in its seven fifth-floor rooms at 331 Madison Avenue at 43rd Street to hear election returns. While some Tammany candidates made an excellent showing, the air "took on something of the atmosphere of a funeral parlor," as not a single important candidate bothered to show up.[32] Tammany's power was at low ebb.

In homes across the U.S. in 1944, radio sets were the chief means by which Americans heard the election news. Listeners accustomed to hearing Fibber McGee and Molly, Bob Hope and Johnny Mercer on Tuesday nights heard them intermittently on election night as many radio stations cancelled regular programming, replacing it with regular news reports, commentaries and live broadcasts. Some newspapers published election score-sheets so that listeners could tabulate returns right along with the experts.[33]

Times Square, where the *New York Times* traditionally kept crowds up-to-date on the election news throughout election night, had long been a traditional spot for New York area residents to come to hear the election news. Of late, the news had been provided by a moving electric bulletin sign on the Times Tower and by a system of beacons, but the sign had been dark since wartime blackout restrictions had been enforced. As election night 1944 neared, and the news that the lights would flash again spread, excitement grew. In preparation, police planned for more than 1,000 officers to help control the crowd, and stores boarded their windows more heavily than usual to prevent the glass from breaking in case the crowds pressed too hard against it.

That night a crowd estimated at from 250,000 to 500,000 people gathered to hear the news. Even before the theatre break, the square was densely packed. The crowd was particularly notable for the absence of young males. Only sailors on leave and soldiers on furlough provided a touch of masculine youth to the festivities.

The crowd burst into a brief but full-throated roar when the bulletin board flashed at midnight the message announcing the Roosevelt victory. A second great wave of

*In the 1944 election between Franklin Roosevelt and Thomas Dewey, CBS News tabulates the state-by-state results for its radio newscasters to broadcast. (Courtesy of CBS)*

sound echoed in the square as a steady beam darted northward from the *New York Times* tower to signal the President's re-election.[34]

As the crowd moved toward the subway it took 30 to 35 minutes to negotiate a single block. Because the men and boys were "far from Times Square, engaging in grimmer noise making,"[35] there was little horn-blowing, little clanging of bells. The mood of the people was far more grave than previously.


## The World Awaits the News

People the world over listened to the election results. Soldiers, of course, listened with great personal interest. An Army News Service set up a 30-man staff to work around the clock until the returns were in to get the results to the men and women fighting in the Pacific, on the Western front and in Italy. Using two of the most powerful radio transmitters in the country, the Office of War Information was also responsible for sending out information by radio and by cable to Army newspapers and radios in London, Rome, Paris, Alaska, Australia, Cairo and China. Returns were broadcast in English, French and German. News bulletins regarding the national elections were sent out all night, and state results were sent out later using the facilities of the regular wire services.[36]

In Italy, the American Red Cross Officers' Club planned to stay open all night rather than close as usual at 10:30 P.M., providing free coffee to those who came in to listen to the returns on the radio.[37]

A special communication system had been set up to handle General Douglas MacArthur's communications on the fighting on Leyte, and as soon as the signal was established, the first word from the announcer on the island was: "Have you anything on the election yet?" When told it was still too early, the announcer replied, "Just break in when you have anything."[38]

Moreover, with the war against Germany mostly won but treaties left to be worked out and the war in the Pacific still to be settled, people in countries around the globe worried and awaited the 1944 election results. In every major Russian city, loudspeakers blared the news to street crowds; Germany's news agency issued bulletins all night.

A *New York Times* reporter wrote that interest in the election was lively among British troops at the front and that the general feeling was that FDR had been a friend of Britain and a great wartime leader of the United States. *Times* reporter James MacDonald wrote that when a heavily decorated British soldier, slogging toward the front line with rifle slung over his shoulder, was asked what he thought about the presidential election, he said: "All I know is this. I've seen FDR on the cinema screen and I likes him."[39]

Even countries that weren't directly involved in the war followed the news. In Panama, there was great interest in the outcome of the election and both the press and the people were said to have followed the campaign closely. One of their newspapers noted that if Latin Americans could vote, Roosevelt would win by the greatest landslide ever.[40]

And in Rio de Janiero, the newspapers must have held a mock election, as an article describes the newspapers closing their polls on the election and declared President Roosevelt the winner by acclamation. It noted that election dinner parties were scheduled to be held in private homes, hotels, and casinos and that there people would listen to the election returns from the United States. The *Globo* editorialized: "It is not necessary on the eve of the elections to insist on the universal sympathy that President Roosevelt holds. It is too bad Brazilians are not allowed to go to the polls in a foreign land."

## An Honest Election

In New York where honest elections were sometimes a rarity, there was great interest in the 1940s as a result of a three-phase inquiry into illegal registration and the creation of an Election Frauds Bureau. Throughout New York State, 4,000 to 5,000 names of registered voters were placed on official challenge lists. In the city, five agencies planned to work together to watch polls and prevent illegal voting. About 3,200,000 persons were expected to vote at the city's 3,700 polling places. The police were to be on duty all day in 1944, seeing that ballots were honestly counted and results reported. The *Times* noted: "Two uniformed men have been assigned to each polling place, one inside, the other outside. The outside men have instructions to place themselves at the end of any line of waiting voters when poll-closing time arrives. Anyone in line is entitled to vote if he is otherwise qualified."[41]

In addition, 3,500 special deputy assistant attorneys general were sworn in for the day in order to see that those entitled to vote did so and illegals didn't. Mayor La Guardia was expected to continue his custom of touring the polling places during the day when not busy with meetings in order to keep an eye on the voting "every minute of the day."[42]

Only three months into his fourth term, Franklin Roosevelt died of a cerebral hemorrhage. When word spread round the world that "the President" had died, no one had to ask which president; they all knew.

Into these very large shoes, and at a very important time, stepped Harry S. Truman of Missouri. To reporters, Truman said: "I feel as though the moon and all the stars and all the planets have fallen upon me. Please, boys, give me your prayers. I need them very much."[43]

Less than a month after Roosevelt's death, the war in Europe ended, but the war with Japan continued. In August of 1945, only four months into his new job, Truman—the man who had been number two on the election day ticket—made the fateful decision to drop the world's first atom bombs on Hiroshima and then on Nagasaki. The war in the Pacific drew to a quick close.

# The Postwar Years _____ 16

With World War II over, Americans were turning inward. They wanted their boys back, and they wanted time to establish a home and family. During the next decade, politics and election day interest shifted to matters of concern on the home front.

Throughout history, Americans have tended to be enamored of military heroes and to feel that strong leadership on the battlefield prepares an officer for able leadership

*Voices that broadcast election results to Americans via radio in 1948 were soon to become well known through the medium of television. Here, Edward R. Murrow, Charles Collingwood and Eric Sevareid keep radio listeners up-to-date on the 1948 election contest between Harry Truman and Thomas Dewey. (Courtesy of CBS)*

of the country. In the late 1940s and '50s, the people were intent on persuading General Eisenhower that he was the one to head the nation.

Civil unrest was beginning as blacks started agitating for equal rights. Their gains were small during this time, but the momentum was building.

This era was also a period of changing tradition. The communications boom was underway. Radio was well established; television was in its infancy. The lure of these two mediums began to change the way Americans spent election night.


## 1948: The Common Man's Choice

At home it was hard for the president to do the right thing fast enough. The people wanted quick disarmament, but Truman feared lowering American armed strength too far. There was also fear of a postwar economic depression that could bring bankruptcies and chaos. Finally Truman lifted price controls, but prices soared and, by 1946, severe inflation had set in.

The Republicans capitalized on this with their campaign slogan, "Had enough?" The midterm elections in 1946 had seen Republican gains, and now, they felt, it was time for them to regain the presidency.

Meeting in Philadelphia in June, Thomas E. Dewey quickly became the favorite after Eisenhower turned down the Republican "Draft Eisenhower" movement. Earl Warren, governor of California, was selected for vice president.

The Democrats were not pleased at the prospect of running Truman. But Eisenhower turned the Democrats down, too, as did Justice Douglas, so ultimately, the party turned to the only man left who wanted the job—Harry Truman. Senator Alben W. Barkley of Kentucky, who had served as the convention's temporary chairman, was selected as running mate. Meeting in July in Philadelphia, there were soon defections. Henry Wallace led a group of Progressives off the convention floor, and they then nominated him for president. A States' Rights party was formed in defiance of Truman's civil rights policies (these policies were the first attempt in recent history that a major political party had undertaken to improve the lot of black Americans). These "Dixiecrats" nominated South Carolina Governor J. Strom Thurmond for president and Governor Fielding Wright of Mississippi as vice president.

But Truman was ready for a fight. Tired of listening to the Republicans boast about all the legislative measures they would take if elected, Truman called a special session of Congress to begin on July 26, on what is Turnip Day in Missouri. During those sessions he asked Congress to pass all the legislation the Republicans claimed they favored: to check inflation, to secure better housing, give aid to education, assure a national minimum wage and expand social security and civil rights, among other things. Congress refused to act on most of the measures, and Truman, labeling them the "Do Nothing" Congress, took that story to the people.

From Labor Day to election day, Truman ran a vigorous whistle-stop campaign, and people loved it. He traveled 31,000 miles and spoke to some 6,000,000 people, many of whom urged him on with "Give 'em hell, Harry!" Although Truman was portrayed as being rough edged, he was very popular among the townspeople whom he visited on his campaign swings.

Truman's lack of popularity with party regulars left the Democratic coffers relatively empty, and his backers turned misfortune into a fund-raising tool. Radio listeners sometimes found that the end of Truman's speeches were cut off as the station returned to other programming. If Truman hadn't finished a speech in the time paid for, fund-raisers allowed the networks to cut him off to dramatize their financial plight. Money usually rolled in and votes increased when it happened.

Despite all of Truman's efforts, the outlook still appeared bright for the Republicans. The country was unsettled, there were strikes, Russian threats and soaring prices, and it was easy for the opposition to blame it all on the Truman administration. The congressional elections of 1946 had been dominated by Republicans, and now all that remained was to get a Republican in the White House.

Dewey ran an efficient, well-managed campaign and seemed cool and calm, a good contrast to Truman's fighter image. He was also well-spoken and used radio to his advantage. However, the campaign did not always go smoothly for the dapper Dewey. When Republicans boasted of his efficiency, Truman reminded them of Herbert Hoover, another Republican who had been an efficiency expert. Dewey spent most of his time criticizing the administration and rarely discussed plans for what he would do differently, and Truman chided the Republicans for their "We're against it" attitude.

As October faded into November, the press and pollsters still felt it was the year of the Republican. The *New York Times* predicted a Dewey victory, and *Life* featured Dewey, "The Next President," on the cover. By election day, Dewey already had his mind on who his cabinet appointees would be. As results rolled in, Truman's early lead did not seem enough to cause concern. The *Chicago Tribune*, put to bed before the final results of November 2's voting were known, appeared early on the morning of the third with the now-famous front page headline, DEWEY DEFEATS TRUMAN. Of course, all that was to change, but not until almost noon on Wednesday did Dewey finally concede defeat. The electoral returns were 303 for Truman and 189 for Dewey, 39 for Thurmond. In the popular vote, Truman received 24,105,812 votes to Dewey's 21,970,065. Only 51.2% of the voters cast ballots, and Dewey blamed it on "overconfidence."

This election once again pointed out the negatives of the electoral college, because up until a few hours after the close of the polls, it seemed that Dewey would have a majority of the electoral votes though he would run second in the popular vote, or that the election might go to the House for lack of an electoral decision. This produced nothing more than debates in Congress.

The 1948 election also showed the stubborn independence of the voters and their refusal to follow the forecasts of pollsters, newspaper opinion and the political pundits. One Gerald W. Johnson wrote:

*The news media were out in full force for the Republican convention in Philadelphia in June of 1948. Like others before him and many to follow, one nonnewsman, the fellow in the sailor hat, obviously found the news people and apparatus themselves worthy of note. (Courtesy of CBS)*

Mr. Truman stands there [on the inaugural reviewing stand] not in his own right, but as representing you and me and Joe Doakes down the street, and Martha, his wife, and the kids playing baseball in a vacant lot. He represents a Negro and a Jew and an American-born Japanese. In reality, it is a Minnesota farmer taking the salute, a New York girl filing clerk, in whose honor the bombers darken the sky over Washington . . .

. . . for his election is due to the fact that the common man took matters in his own hands . . . He is conspicuously the common man's choice . . .[1]

## 1952: A Military Hero Answers the Call of Politics

In 1948, Dwight D. Eisenhower had turned down both parties when they offered him an opportunity for the nomination. At the time he had written to a New Hampshire newspaper that politics ". . . is a profession; a serious, complicated, and in this true sense, a noble one . . . nothing in the international or domestic situation especially qualifies for the most important office in the world a man whose adult years have been spent in the country's military forces."[2] But these statements seemed to make him all the more popular, and by January 1952 he let it be announced that he was a Republican. Shortly after, though he was still serving as commander of the NATO forces in Europe, he let his name be entered in the New Hampshire primary. With this start, he was able to build enough momentum to win the nomination at the Republican convention in July over party-regular favorite, Senator Robert A. Taft, senator from Ohio. Senator Richard M. Nixon of California was selected as running mate.

In the spring of 1952, President Truman announced that he would not run for re-election and noted that he hoped Adlai E. Stevenson, governor of Illinois, would be the Democratic nominee. Though Stevenson was not eager, his eloquence in giving the welcoming speech at the Chicago-based convention made him a leading contender. He was nominated on the third ballot and was the first genuinely drafted presidential candidate since Garfield in 1880. John Sparkman, senator from Alabama, became the vice presidential nominee.

*Voters wait their turn at polling booths in a drugstore in Omaha, Nebraska to cast ballots in the state's primary on April 1, 1952. (Courtesy The Bettmann Archive)*

Television coverage of the conventions was unsettling to the public who had imagined conventions to be deliberate, thoughtful and orderly. With the glare of the television camera upon them, the conventions were at their worst with paid performers and "show-off" delegates who used any opportunity to gain an appearance on television. Radio had revealed some aspects of this, but never so glaringly as the view Americans got in '52.

The issues of 1952 were the Korean War—which had hit a two-year stalemate—the fact that incidents of bribery had been uncovered among Truman appointees and that Communists were said to be infiltrating the government (claimed the Republicans). Both candidates used radio and television effectively and campaigned hard, but it was a strange campaign. Stevenson hadn't been a part of the Truman administration, so Republicans couldn't blast him for the administration's mistakes, and Eisenhower (Ike) was a war hero, so Stevenson was reluctant to attack him directly.

Genial Ike eventually traveled 33,000 miles, mostly by airplane, and the people found him friendly and accessible. (Because Eisenhower disliked negative attacks on issues, the Republicans sent out "hatchet men" like Richard Nixon, Thomas Dewey and Senator Joseph McCarthy to campaign hard against the Democrats with antiwar, antibribery, anti-Communist messages.) In contrast, Stevenson was witty and urbane, but Americans didn't seem to warm to him. The Republicans dubbed him an "egg-head" because of the shape of his bald, rounded skull as well as his intelligence. The moniker further distanced Stevenson from the people.

The Democrats campaigned on the economic health of the country, illustrated by this 1952 campaign song:

> The farmer's farmin' every day,
> Makin' money and that ain't hay!
> Don't let 'em take it away.[3]

The Republicans hit hard on the bribery issue and counseled that the American public should "Throw the rascals out!," and they lectured on "Truman's War." When Eisenhower promised to end it, the public was elated. The people seemed to identify more with the fatherly Ike who, of course, was also a national hero and better known.

The scandal of the campaign was provided by vice presidential candidate Richard Nixon when it was revealed that wealthy Californians had set up a secret "slush fund" (supposedly for miscellaneous campaign expenses) for Nixon when he was in the Senate. Though Eisenhower hoped he would resign, Nixon chanced that by baring his soul on television he might be able to remain on the ticket. In a television appearance on September 23, Nixon revealed his own personal financial situation, called for all candidates to do the same, and in the "come clean" spirit of the speech, he had the family dog, Checkers, appear on television with him. Nixon announced that Checkers, too, had been a campaign gift, and one the Nixon family planned to keep. The speech attracted the largest television audience up to that time, and it won over the public. Ike kept Nixon as his running mate.

Mass communication gave a national forum to serious and not-so-serious third-party candidates. In 1952, third parties varied from the Progressive, with their presidential candidate a lawyer who had recently spent five months in jail for contempt of court during the perjury trial of a labor leader. For vice president they ran Mrs. Charlotta Bass, 62-year-old former publisher of a California black newspaper. In addition to the Progressives, there were the Socialists, the Prohibitionists, the Greenbacks, and the Church of God, among others. A Washington Peace Party selected Mrs. Ellen Linea Jensen, a 50-year-old Miami grandmother and astrologist who claimed to "be in close communion with George Washington,"[4] and a vice presidential candidate whom Mrs. Jensen didn't feel free to reveal. She promised to stamp out Communism within "nine minutes" of her inauguration. In addition, there was the American Vegetarian Party, which ran on the platform that women should be "childbearing instead of fur-bearing."[5]

In a voter drive sparked by the American Heritage Foundation, more than 20,000 businesses worked together to appeal to Americans for a record voter turnout. American Heritage hoped for a vote of 63,000,000, which—allowing for population growth—would still be less percentage-wise than the record vote of 1940. (In 1880, 78.4% of the eligible voters cast ballots; in 1940, 53.4% voted.)[6] "Don't be a Lanovoc [Lazy Non-Voting Citizen]," pleaded radio announcers day and night, and dog-food containers, cornflakes boxes and toothpaste wrappings carried the slogan, "Vote As You Please, But VOTE!"[7] Movie shorts, newspaper and magazine ads, and billboards also pounded away at the same theme.

Millsfield, New Hampshire was to retain its position as the first community to register its votes for the election. Wrote *Time* magazine: "The seven voters of Millsfield, NH (pop. 16) stayed up late on election eve and marked their ballots just as soon as the clock struck midnight. Everybody had gathered in the parlor of Mrs. Genevieve N. Annis' 125-year-old house well ahead of time, and the votes were cast, in the light of kerosene lamps, amid a fine, conspiratorial atmosphere. Mrs. Annis, the town clerk, collected and counted them quickly, recorded one absentee ballot, and at 12:02 o'clock, proudly reported the nation's first election returns (eight votes for Eisenhower).[8]

For this election, much of America was eager to vote, and a surprising number got to their polling places before dawn. Lines began to form outside schools, garages, country stores and basement voting places, and the queues continued all day.

In most towns and cities a ride to the polls could be had through a simple phone call (except in Minnesota, which barred transportation of voters as a corrupt practice). Some communities provided free taxi rides, and in Rochester, New York, an ambulance was used. Throughout the country, volunteers offered to babysit in order that mothers might get to the polls. Orange City, Iowa blew its fire siren every hour on the hour to remind the apathetic that it was election day. In St. Louis, people turned their porch lights on at dusk to remind people to stop at the polls.

The weather was good almost everywhere. One woman in Tarentum, Pennsylvania went to the polls six hours after giving birth to a baby, and when a woman in Miami was told that her "I Like Ike" skirt constituted electioneering, she took it off and stood calmly in her slip until it was her turn to vote.[9]

In most places lines were long, but people waited patiently to have their say. In Seattle, an old man waited in line for three hours, and when he reached the head of the line, he was told he hadn't registered. The man began to cry, saying: "This is my last time." The crowd yelled, "Let him vote!" Officials consented to do so; he voted, and he left saying: "I thank you all."[10]

On November 4, Ike won by a landslide. In the electoral college he had 442 to Stevenson's 89 votes, and took 55.1% of the popular vote to Stevenson's 44.4% (33,936,234 to 27,314,992). The vote was particularly interesting in light of the times. In a period of unprecedented prosperity, with 62.6 million men and women working, the voters repudiated the party in power, and voted for what they seemed to feel was long-term good.

## Voting from Korea

With national legislation put in place for the soldier vote during World War II, the soldiers in Korea knew that voting would be their right no matter where they were on election day. For many of the young men, it would be their first vote. Wrote *The New York Times* reporter with the Eighth Army in Korea: "Much of the talk here right now is about candidates and speculation on who will win. A newcomer from the United States is a popular man in these parts; he has the latest word on how the election is going."[11]

An officer estimated that about 30% of the soldiers would actually cast a ballot, a substantial figure when one considers that a ballot has to be requested and affidavits signed before one's vote can be cast. "One hapless fellow, a civilian radio reporter, displayed a ballot he received only two days ago, Oct. 31, from the Board of Elections in New York," reported *The New York Times* on November 3, 1952. It instructed him to mark the ballot and have it returned to New York on or before October 31. The ballot had been mailed to the radio reporter from New York October 20. When last observed the determined recipient was busy cutting out postmarks to send along as supporting evidence for his tardy ballot."[12]

Various arrangements were made for getting the results to the men. Army radios began pouring out returns as soon as the polls closed, and field telephones and small portable combat radio sets gave the vote counts; men relayed the news down the line.[13]

Soldiers in at least one division were able to simply pick up the telephone for election results, just as he might "ask for mortar fire on an enemy position." He was then plugged into a special switchboard where a staff person was on duty to give returns—rather than to dump shells on the enemy. The article noted "Of course, the shell-dumping department will remain open and the enemy can expect no respite in spite of the election excitement."[14]

## Candidates Await the News

In the '50s, radio and television were turning election night for the candidates into a media experience, and a new tradition was beginning. Candidates wait in a hotel suite and watch the returns come in on television as party regulars and workers hear the news in the ballroom below. Good news leads to dancing and partying; bad news means a more somber affair.

In '52, Eisenhower was upstairs in New York's Commodore Hotel. A party was going on in the ballroom. The crowd had been gaining optimism from about 8:00 P.M. on. At 10:47 victory was proclaimed. "Thereafter, almost continuously, pandemonium reigned in the grand ballroom and on all floors from the third to the sixth, allotted to the Eisenhower headquarters."[15] As the good news became known, Ike went down to thank his supporters. "Shouting, foot-stamping and applause filled the hall as General Eisenhower made his way to the rostrum. He entered the ballroom at 2:02 A.M., read the text of his reply to Governor Stevenson and then thanked the audience for its support,"[16] reported *The New York Times*.

## 1956: "We Like Ike" (Still)

Eisenhower's administration was a popular one. The Korean War had ended by the new election and the public liked Ike as he focussed his efforts on working toward peace. The press had access to him (though all film taken was screened by a public relations person), and the presidential image was polished by actor Robert Montgomery who was put on staff for just that reason. Though the midterm elections put the Democrats in control of Congress, Ike did well with a Democratic Congress, and his popularity rose even more when the "Big Four" (France, England, the Soviet Union, and the United States) met in Geneva in 1955 and some of the tensions of the Cold War were reduced.

Eisenhower's heart attack later in 1955 sent the Republicans reeling. Without him they would lack a strong candidate, and a favorable medical report, which assured that he would be able to run again, providing that he limited his activities, was not issued until six months later. However, a June attack of ileitis, necessitating an emergency operation, made the country jumpy and his health was definitely a campaign issue.

The speed of travel and communication meant that campaigns didn't need to be as drawn out as before, and in '56 both conventions were held in August—unusually late. Adlai Stevenson again got the Democratic nomination, and, breaking with tradition, Stevenson left the choice of a running mate entirely up to the delegates, and while young John F. Kennedy did well, Senator Estes Kefauver finally got the nomination.

The Republicans met in San Francisco in late August and, once they knew that Ike was healthy enough to run, all else fell in place nicely. Most of the convention business had been prearranged and was a formality. Nixon was again the vice presidential nominee.

Partly because of his health and partly out of confidence, Eisenhower did not campaign a great deal. He ran on the success of his administration and on peace, prosperity and unity. It was the year of the "We Like Ike" campaign.

Since Democrats were doing well in Congress, Stevenson hoped to employ a coattails strategy in reverse. By working with the local and state organizations, he hoped to capitalize on party popularity and win in that way. Stevenson visited 32 states and traveled more than 37,000 miles in the campaign, often referring to Eisenhower as the "part-time President."

Like two ordinary citizens of any small town, the Eisenhowers voted in Gettysburg, Pennsylvania before the president was whisked back to Washington to deal with a brewing international crisis in Egypt. *Time* magazine reported: "At 11:15 A.M. on a clear, blue Pennsylvania Election Day, the new couple from the farm over on Route 10 stepped into the one-room white clapboard Cumberland Township election house outside Gettysburg."[17] Identifying their professions as "housewife" and "President of the United States," they voted under the light of four naked electric light bulbs in a room heated with only a small oil stove. They dropped their ballots in a worn wooden ballot box as other citizens had for countless elections.

In record numbers, other Americans trooped to the polls. Despite the real fear of the Cold War and (by this time) the disgust with McCarthyism, Americans were basically a contented people that election day, with comfortable homes, shiny cars and television sets. They weren't likely to vote against that smiling man in the White House, and Ike won by a landslide. It was the biggest victory since Franklin Roosevelt won over Landon in 1936. Ike received 57.4% of the popular vote and garnered 457 electoral votes to Stevenson's 73. In the popular vote, Eisenhower had 35,590,472 to 26,022,752. Ironically, the Democrats maintained control of Congress.

## Civil Rights Becomes a Major Issue

In the '50s, serious campaigning for civil rights and social justice for blacks began. Martin Luther King was not yet well-known, but he and others were beginning to make the plight of black Americans known.

Television images of numerous events stick in people's minds. These were the days of the Montgomery bus boycott because the public buses segregated the races, of *Brown* vs. *Board of Education*, which stipulated that schools couldn't be segregated, and the Mississippi National Guard had to escort a black university student into school. By 1960 token integration had been accomplished everywhere but Mississippi, Alabama and South Carolina.

Of course, blacks' right to vote was guaranteed by the 15th Amendment, but it was persistently denied anyway. Looking back to 1948, it is apparent why new and strong legislation was still needed.

That year *The Chicago Defender*, a black newspaper, reported that more blacks than ever before went to the polls, but in many places violence flared, and election day was a day of beatings, arson, and threats. A sampling of events around the nation in 1948:

- In Florida a gang of thugs beat two black ex-GI's whom they suspected of participating in the election.

- In South Carolina, troublemakers fired on the barn of a black farmer.

- In Mississippi, a voting slowdown in identification hindered blacks at the polls: "While lines of whites moved rapidly, blacks said they stood in line for hours trying to convince polling place officials of their identity."[18] In smaller communities the old poll tax ruse was used—even though poll tax on federal elections was illegal.

- In several small southern communities, members of the Ku Klux Klan, in full bed-sheet regalia, staged election eve demonstrations in an effort to keep blacks from the polls.

- In other places in the South, whites armed with shot guns loitered near the polls hoping to frighten off blacks who were seeking to vote. However, they made no move to prevent blacks from casting their ballots.

In some communities, poll watchers employed by the NAACP notified election officials of irregularities, but, obviously, the problems persisted.

By contrast, in the North the black vote was desperately sought by both major parties and the Progressives. In few elections has the balance of power been so important.

The *Defender* editorialized: "For every cracked skull, and for every broken bone as a result of election and pre-election violence, thousands of blacks asserted themselves at the polls. They will do it again and again. And no other presidential candidates can go to the White House without taking full account of this."[19]

By 1952, the blacks again voted in record numbers—many for the first time, but efforts were still being made to keep them from the polls. In practically every southern state there were scattered efforts to bar individuals from the voting places, and hundreds were disfranchised by a court ruling in Alabama. A last-minute decision by the Alabama Supreme Court ruled that citizens who had failed to pay their poll taxes by Feb. 1, 1952 were ineligible to vote November 4.[20]

Despite a recent court ruling in Louisiana that all citizens must be allowed to participate in all elections, black residents complained that they had not been issued registration certificates. Certificates were issued to only five of 150 blacks who registered in St. Bernard Parish.

There were additional isolated incidents: An election registrar in Currituck, North Carolina was removed and replaced by the board of elections of that eastern shore county because she refused to register black citizens for the 1950 elections and the 1952 primary elections.

*Though various groups tried to register black voters during the 1950s, their efforts were often thwarted. Here, both black and white would-be voters in Charleston, South Carolina wait in line to register for the presidential election of 1952. Though two extra days were added to the registration period, many—some of whom had waited in line as long as six hours—were turned away at the end of the last day and were unable to vote that November.* (The Chicago Defender, *October 4, 1952*)

In Winston-Salem, North Carolina, a black woman was termed unqualified to register by West Highlands Precinct Registrar R. H. Chambers. She was asked to copy a page of the Constitution of the United States and became excited and left. The woman, Miss Mattie Boney, a servant, was the first black to attempt to register in West Highlands.[21]

In some areas, however, things were getting better: "There was no molestation at the polls in Mississippi as 4,000 blacks in Jackson voted in the Nov. 4 election. They voted about 60% for Governor Stevenson and 40% for General Eisenhower. However, in voting in this election, there was little regard for party loyalty."[22]

In Memphis it was reported: "So far as it is known, there has been no opposition to blacks either registering or voting in Tennessee. More voted in last August's primary than was ever before known in the history of the state."[23]

And in Houston: "Negroes voted in greater numbers Tuesday than ever before since they broke the primary in 1944. Around some of the polls the line formed for as much as a block and never really disappeared until the polls were closed at 7:00 P.M.

"Of great interest was the fact that Negroes were voting in mixed precincts in great numbers. It was almost impossible to pass a precinct where you did not see some blacks sprinkled in the line, waiting to vote, even in precincts that would be thought to be white entirely.

. . . "There was no opposition to blacks voting and no clashes or incidents anywhere, despite the large number that turned out."[24]

But in Mississippi, a state legislator was still urging for the passage of a state literacy amendment for voters. Anyone not registered prior to January 1, 1952 (more likely to be black) would be required to make out a sworn application for registration in his own handwriting unless he was physically disabled. In addition, he was to be required to give a "reasonable understanding of the ties and obligations of citizenship under a constitutional form of government" to the county registrar. Claiming it was not discriminatory, the legislator defended his amendment with the fact that Alabama, Georgia, Louisiana, North Carolina, South Carolina, Massachusetts, New Hampshire, Oklahoma and Oregon already had read-and-write clauses. With a largely illiterate black population, it would become more and more likely that the amendment would discriminate.[25]

By 1956 it was more than time for something to be done. Eisenhower proposed legislation in '56 to help protect black voting rights. That action helped bring many blacks back into the Republican Party for the fall elections. Southern Senators were angry, but he gained bipartisan support, and a compromise bill finally passed both chambers by overwhelming majorities. On September 9, 1957, Ike had the satisfaction of signing the first Civil Rights Act since the Grant administration. It created the Commission on Civil Rights, which had the power to subpoena witnesses in its investigations of violations of right of citizens to vote based on color, race, religion, or national origin. It was an Act that was badly needed.

## Voting Machines Still Difficult

While voting machines were becoming more common, there was still need for newspaper articles explaining how to use them. In New York a heavy vote in '52 meant that some upstate communities without enough voting machines were expected to use paper ballots. Those voters using machines were reassured that they could change their minds up until lifting the handle and that they would vote in complete privacy: "After entering the booth and swinging the handle to close the curtain separating him from others in the polling place, the voter, unless he requires help because of an infirmity, is strictly on his own. The levers must be left down before the voter swings open the curtain, which automatically registers the vote and returns all levers to their original positions."[26]

## Times Square Passed By

When it came to election eve in the fifties, Times Square's heyday was over, as were the glory days for election night street parties outside newspaper offices from Boston to San Francisco. Yet, like the aging showgirl who squeezes into a too-tight new costume still hoping the crowds will come, so, too, did Times Square come up with some new "attractions" for '52.

To start with, a new electric election indicator 85 feet high was placed on the north side of Times Tower. (It looked like a huge thermometer.) The intent was to enable moving crowds to get the basic results in the simplest terms with the tall, brightly lighted indicator showing how many electoral votes were won by Eisenhower and Stevenson. At the foot of the indicator was a large neon sign with the words "electoral votes" and at the top a similar sign bearing the word "elected"—numbers ran along the side. (A total of 266 electoral votes were necessary for victory.) The candidates' names were in the center in lights. There was also a new device to reflect how the contestants fared in key states. In addition, the *Times* was to have its regular headline service where bulletins could be displayed on the electric sign running around Times Tower, and WQXR and WQXR-FM planned to broadcast *Times* bulletins. In addition to all these items, a beacon was to be used. If the beacon swept north, Eisenhower was leading; if the beacon swept south, Stevenson was leading. If there was a steady beam to the north it meant Eisenhower had won; a steady beam to the South meant Stevenson won.[27]

But that year marked the slow death of a time-honored tradition. In 1952, Times Square had the smallest election night turnout in its long existence. There was no shouting, no horns, no bells.[28]

Between 9:00 and 10:00 P.M. no more than 10,000 people were in the square and these were packed thickest on the sidewalks from 43rd to 45th Streets, watching the new election bulletin board on the north wall of Times Tower. At the peak, the police estimated, fewer than 25,000 were in the square. Even when the theatres emptied, the crowd did not overflow the curbs to cover the pavement as in pretelevision days. Though no solid line of police horses stood at the curb to restrain them, bulletin watchers held to the curbs with only gentle reminders from patrolmen. Up to eight years ago police never estimated presidential election night crowds at less than 250,000.[29]

Shopkeepers had boarded up their windows to protect their plate glass, but it wasn't necessary, nor were ambulances or the radio cars and Civil Defense equipment. There was brief shouting when a lead for Ike showed up but it was nothing compared with the deafening roars of old Times Square crowds.

A last burst of shouting echoed in the square at 12:40 A.M. today when the line of lights on the east side of the new election board suddenly streaked to the top, to show that General Eisenhower had more than 266 electoral votes, and had won in a sweep.

At the same moment the line of lights on Governor Stevenson's side of the board, which had not moved for hours, symbolically went out. The moving letters in the running sign that girdles the Tower broke out with "Eisenhower Elected," with the news bracketed between golden stars.

Then the searchlight high in the Tower, which had been brooming the starless sky to the north all night, to show Eisenhower in the lead, held steady to show that he had won. The crowd cheered again, and slowly came apart to drift toward the subways.[30]

Times Square was part of an election day experience whose time had passed. The *Times* had hoped people would still follow the election by watching for the glow of the searchlights, but instead, Americans of the 1950s had begun to drift home to follow the election returns by the glow of their television sets.

# Election Day Today 17

To note a turning point in a process that has evolved slowly over the years is a very difficult task, but if one were to mark the beginning of "modern" election day, it would probably begin with the campaign of 1960 for it was then that the electronic media began to seriously influence elections. Vice presidential candidate Richard Nixon's "Checkers" speech in 1952 and the fact that Eisenhower kept an actor on staff as a media advisor certainly were harbingers of what was to come, but it was the 1960 Kennedy–Nixon television debates, and the meaninglessness of Nixon's good performance because of his bad appearance, that really presaged a new era. Today's audience is often thought fit to understand only what will fit in a "sound bite" (a 15–20 second statement from the candidate, easily usable by radio and television); and recent campaigns have been orchestrated to give the news media (and therefore, the public) only that "bite" of news.

Who is behind political campaigns is also changing. In the last 40 years, government social services have eroded the power of the political bosses since they can no longer build their strength through helping immigrants and the poor, and so the role of political boss is now played by a hired hand— the media advisor who is in charge of coordinating everything from television advertising to campaign appearances and where and when the candidate will talk to the press. On the plus side this has largely freed politics from the bosses who sometimes collected from the poor to line their own pockets, but gone, too, is a sense of honed political "history" since today's media advisors are around only as long as the campaign bills are being paid. Other than the candidate (who may be here today and gone tomorrow), there is no one to oversee the management of a winning party or the rebuilding of a losing one. As a result, Americans have dropped the strong party allegiances they once had.

Of course, long before these changes, many other changes were taking place, which has led to drastic alterations in the way election day is celebrated. Up until this century, America's population was largely rural. Election day was a time of coming together, a social occasion as well as an opportunity to share political views and cast one's vote. Today the majority of the population lives in urban areas, and they socialize daily at work as well as during leisure pursuits on the weekend. There's no need for election day social festivities in the way that there was less than a century ago.

Today we are no longer a land of immigrants; most citizens are American-born, and fewer carry with them the memories of oppression. We assume the American way of life is our right, and with this assumption we have lost some of the American spirit, if you will, the feeling shared by our forefathers that a vote was something so important that it was worth fighting for. Today cynicism and apathy abound. But it is less than three decades since three civil rights workers were killed trying to help blacks register to vote in Mississippi, and one can't help but think that there is still election day spirit in Americans, just waiting to be kindled.

Though all of these election day changes were brewing before this, the campaigns of 1960 and after are when they began to take shape.

## 1960: Televised Debates Used as Campaign Tools

In 1960, both parties would be putting up first-time contenders for the presidency. Although the Republicans were sitting pretty in the White House with a now-healthy Eisenhower, whose popularity had never diminished, it was the Grand Old Party that had (out of anger over Roosevelt's four terms in office), in the late 1940s, pushed through the constitutional amendment limiting a president to two terms. They were the first fish caught in their own net.

Vice President Richard Nixon was the logical choice to top the Republican ticket. He had an excellent public service record; however, incidents like the "Checkers" speech made even a few members of his own party uncomfortable. Nonetheless, he seemed the best bet because of his familiarity to the public and his current political post. Republicans knew that Nixon's popularity was far below Eisenhower's, but they hoped that Ike's strength would help carry the party into another term. And though New York Governor Nelson Rockefeller expressed interest in the nomination early on, by the time the Republicans met in Chicago in late July, the nomination was Nixon's. Henry Cabot Lodge, former senator from Massachusetts, was nominated for vice president.

The Democrats met in Los Angeles, and there were four strong contenders, all senators: John Fitzgerald Kennedy (Massachusetts), Stuart Symington (Missouri), Lyndon Johnson (Texas) and Hubert Humphrey (Minnesota). Kennedy had shown good strength in the primaries and, even though no Catholic had ever been elected to the presidency, he achieved the nomination on the first ballot. He then asked Lyndon Baines Johnson to be his running mate.

Kennedy did not start campaigning until early September because of a late Congressional session, but Nixon began right after the convention, promising he would visit each of the 50 states, the first time a presidential candidate would have done so. (Candidates have always tended to invest most of their campaign time in the larger states with the greater number of electoral votes.)

From the campaign's start, both parties searched for the opposition's Achilles' heel. The Democrats labeled Nixon "Tricky Dick," called him unscrupulous and portrayed him as a man who shouldn't be entrusted with the power of the highest office in the land. The Republicans hammered at Kennedy's youth, lack of experience and his religion—many feared that Kennedy would take direct orders from the Pope! Kennedy tried to deflect the religious issue by tackling it head on. Kennedy spoke to a group of Protestant ministers meeting in Houston, Texas, and did a great deal to allay fears about his Catholicism. He stressed separation of church and state and insisted that the dictates of the Constitution were paramount, without taking into consideration issues of the church.

To his surprise, Nixon discovered himself up against an unexpected obstacle— Kennedy's personal magnetism. Though Kennedy spoke intelligently and well, people who came to campaign rallies were eager just to see him in person. He

*By bringing the election decision directly into the home via television, the Kennedy-Nixon debates ushered in the campaign style for today's election day where impressions gleaned through the media carry great weight with voters. The 1960 television audience for the series of four debates was huge, with the first debate witnessed by 70,000,000 people. (Only 69,000,000 people voted in the presidential election that year.) (Courtesy of CBS)*

seemed to carry with him the aura of a movie star. For Nixon, whose ambitious nature made him sometimes appear unlikable and insincere, it must have been like trying to fight machine gun fire with a slingshot.

But the television debates were the climax of the campaign. No longer did Americans have to leave their homes to participate in torchlight parades, attend rallies or go to the train station to hear a candidate speak. Now in the comfort of their own homes, they were going to see not one candidate, but both candidates side by side, and would be able to make a direct comparison of who seemed most fit to lead the nation.

In a series of four nighttime sessions (from September 26 to October 19) arranged by the three networks, Nixon, who had been sick early in the fall, appeared ill at ease, haggard and defensive, though well-prepared in his answers. His perspiration-dotted forehead seemed to gleam in the camera's glare. Kennedy projected a coolly confident image. He was articulate, witty and showed that he could be a natural leader. Though Nixon's aides did much to improve his image for subsequent debates, the harm had been done in the first one. The audience started off at 70,000,000 for the first debate, but tapered off somewhat for the subsequent ones.

As things continued to look bad for Nixon, the Republicans pulled out all the stops and asked Eisenhower to campaign for him. For eight days, the president traveled on Nixon's behalf, but it seemed to be too little, too late.

Although the press ultimately focused on Kennedy as the winner, early on election day the returns were inconclusive. It turned out to be one of the closest elections in American history and the votes were not decisive until noon on Wednesday when Nixon finally conceded defeat. (And Hawaii's three votes were not finally determined for Kennedy until the electoral college met.) Kennedy ended with 303 electoral votes to Nixon's 219, and the popular vote ended with Kennedy having only 119,450 votes more than Nixon out of a total of almost 69,000,000—a difference of .01% (34,226,731 to 34,108,157). Fraud was charged in the vote-counting in some states, and again, the electoral college system came under fire, but with no resulting change.

In 1960, Americans had elected a man who was to win their respect and capture their fantasies during the 1,000 days available to him.

## Blacks and the Vote

Almost 100 years after the Civil War, black Americans still were deprived of fundamental rights and subjected to ceaseless indignities. Black children in the South and in some parts of the North attended separate—and usually inferior—schools; state universities were closed to them; they sat at separate lunch counters, swam in segregated pools, could live only in black neighborhoods and received inferior work at inferior pay. Southerners sometimes thought little of solving a "Negro" problem with murder.

Yet there were signs of hope. Progress was being made by the Southern Christian Leadership Conference (SCLC), formed by Martin Luther King Jr., which had effectively organized a boycott against segregated bussing in Montgomery, Alabama; the Student Nonviolent Coordinating Committee (SNCC), which in 1960 fought for the right to equal service at lunch counters; and the Congress of Racial Equality (CORE) sent "Freedom Riders" of both races through the South in 1961 to test and break down segregation laws in interstate transportation.

In 1960, for the first time, large numbers of blacks voted in such southern cities as Memphis and Atlanta as well as throughout the North. This said less about equal justice and more about the fact that political parties were beginning to recognize the potential voting power of black Americans. It was a step forward all the same.

That year, black Americans launched an aggressive get-out-the-vote campaign. "Negro leaders are insisting that every available Negro voter must exercise his right to vote—and then call his friends to see to it that they vote, too," ran the text of an article in the *Chicago Defender*.[1]

Using the slogan, "Calls For Freedom," Dr. Martin Luther King, A. Philip Randolph and Roy Wilkins headed the Non-Partisan Crusade to Mobilize Negro Voters.

In a statement, the three leaders urged blacks to get out and vote, and then to go home and phone five friends and tell them to vote and then phone five more friends. "If you do this you can start a chain reaction that could easily result in thousands of Negroes voting, who otherwise would forget," the statement continued. "These are your CALLS FOR FREEDOM."[2]

In 1960, *The Chicago Defender* estimated that approximately 10.5 million blacks were eligible to vote and about 5,000,000 were registered.

In Alabama that year, the Federal Bureau of Investigation was locked in a court battle with the state in an effort to make photocopies of the voting records of Sumter County, Alabama, to obtain evidence to substantiate the charge that voting rights of scores of eligible black citizens had been willfully violated.

The Justice Department contended that of the 8,700 blacks of voting age living in Sumter County, only 178 were allowed to register. Since blacks outnumbered white residents of the county, the purpose in denying them the vote seemed clear. The Alabama attorney general tried to prevent the FBI from obtaining the copies, saying that it was a "high-handed attempt by Federal authorities to override the sovereignty of the state."[3]

In the summer of 1964—partly in reaction to the Civil Rights Act signed that year, a coalition of civil rights groups mounted a voter registration and education drive in Mississippi that sparked violence. Three civil rights workers were killed for their efforts to register blacks for the vote.

That November in Mississippi, the black-dominated Freedom Democratic Party decided to hold a four-day mock presidential election to give unregistered blacks the chance to express their political choices. Aided by 75 eastern and midwestern college students, the party put up ballot boxes for the "Freedom vote" in barbershops, cafes, cleaning establishments, churches and even in automobiles to reach the backwoods areas.

Said one of their leaders: "The freedom vote demonstrates how Negroes in Mississippi would vote if they were allowed to register. And it also shows that Negroes in Mississippi do want to vote and that the cause of the low Negro registration is intimidation rather than lethargy."[4]

Later, campaign workers for the Freedom Party were arrested for distributing handbills without a permit.

Under Lyndon Johnson, the Voting Rights Act of 1965 was passed, and it authorized federal intervention in areas where blacks were denied the vote. That legislation

*The UPI photograph above identifies this fellow as 68-year-old Tom Flowers, who registered to vote in June of 1966 after the "Mississippi Freedom March" stopped at the Panola County Courthouse in Batesville, Mississippi before moving on to Jackson. (Courtesy The Bettmann Archive)*

combined with the passage of the 24th Amendment, which outlaws poll taxes in federal elections, went a long way in guaranteeing black Americans the right to vote.

## 1964: "All the Way With LBJ"

On November 22, 1963, President John F. Kennedy had been assassinated in Dallas, Texas, leaving Vice President Lyndon Baines Johnson to push through the many liberal programs Kennedy had begun. Johnson had served his first months in office well and proved to be effective at getting through the legislation Kennedy began. When 1964 and the Democratic convention came around, the Party was ready to back him. The Democrats met in Atlantic City in August; it was a quiet convention with the only excitement provided by Johnson who flew in to personally announce his choice for running mate as Senator Hubert H. Humphrey.

The Republican convention in San Francisco in July was dominated by backers of Barry M. Goldwater, the ultraconservative senator from Arizona, who got the nomination. Goldwater chose another conservative, William Miller, a congressman from New York, for his running mate. After the "We Want Barry" convention cry, the Republicans replaced it with "In Your Heart You Know He's Right," a slogan that was parodied many times by the Democrats.

When Goldwater began his campaign, he tried to disassociate himself from all but the conservatives—he even distanced himself from Eisenhower, making it clear that he felt Ike was too liberal, too close in views to the opposition party. Goldwater promised to offer "A Choice, Not An Echo." But he almost immediately started alienating large constituencies. While in Florida, a state with many people receiving Social Security checks, he attacked the administration's Social Security program. In Tennessee, he noted that the Tennessee Valley Authority power system should be sold to private industry, and Tenneseeans responded with a slogan, "Sell the TVA? I'd rather sell Arizona!" When he indicated he was in favor of limited use of nuclear arms, the Democrats portrayed Goldwater as trigger-happy and unpredictable by creating a famous but controversial television commercial featuring the bucolic world of a little girl holding a daisy suddenly being destroyed by a mushroom-cloud nuclear explosion.

Johnson proved to be an able, albeit corny, campaigner, and because Goldwater was doing so well at keeping himself in trouble, Johnson generally gave campaign speeches in which he didn't bother to mention Goldwater at all.

Goldwater thought he saw a ray of hope when one of Johnson's closest aides was arrested for disorderly conduct only a short time before the election. But the aide quickly resigned, and world news (Khrushchev overthrown as Russia's premier, and Communist China exploding its first atomic bomb) soon pushed the aide's story out of the headlines.

On November 3, Johnson enjoyed one of the most decisive victories in history. Carrying 44 states with 486 electoral votes to Goldwater's six states with 52 electoral votes, Johnson had a popular plurality of almost 16,000,000. The popular total was 43,129,484 to 27,178,188.

This election, too, brought up a new issue that continues to plague modern elections—election forecasting based on results as they come in on election day. By 1964, the networks had developed advanced methods for gathering returns as they came in, and the news media were then able to make reasonably safe predictions as to trends and outcomes. Various forms of this exit-polling continue to be used, constantly raising a debate as to whether or not the reporting reflects or affects trends. Though certainly the cumulative effects of this kind of reporting on citizens of the western portion of the nation (who are more likely not to have gone to the polls by the time early returns from the East begin to be tabulated) have no precedent, it is not unlike what took place 175 years ago before there was a set date for election day. Since voting was held at a variety of times in many different places and reported on soon afterwards, many times a community would not yet have cast its ballots at the time that other results were known.

## Machine Politics Continue

When Richard Daley, the political boss of Chicago, died in 1976, it marked the end of an era and an end to the "old-style" political boss. Whether big-city machine politics is dead or merely languishing is debatable, but there is no doubt but what up through the '60s and '70s, Daley's machine was alive and well.

According to an article in the *New York Times* in 1964, teams of *Chicago Tribune* reporters touring the precincts observed instances of money changing hands before and after voters cast their ballots as well as other irregularities. One reporter said he saw a Democratic precinct captain ordering his aides to get drunks into a station wagon and off to the polls: "Get as many as you can, we need them," he's supposed to have said.[5]

One man supposedly voted four times, and a lady approached another voter asking, "Where's the lady who is supposed to pay me my $5 for voting like she promised?"[6]

Also in 1964 one precinct captain described to a reporter how he operated:

> I do maybe 150 favors a year. I have 15 notebooks at home with the list of favors I've done for my voters. Each time a voter calls me for a favor I get his phone number. I helped one woman get her citizenship after she had been trying for five years. I made seven trips downtown with her.
>
> Every night I look through the alleys on the way home. People call at midnight, 1 A.M., 3 A.M. Somebody might have gotten arrested and needs bond money. Sure, you go to the station. You got to go there. You stick by your word. You don't tell the people one thing and not do it."[7]

In return, the captain expected a payback on election day. Before the election he visited every household and followed up with a letter. A second letter reminding them to vote was sent to arrive the day before the election. Then on election day, seven people aided the captain. Several were "runners" who reminded people to get to the polls; others kept track of who had been at each polling place. A thank-you letter was always sent afterwards.

By 1968, there had been some cracking down on the political machine-controlled fraudulent voting. For many years, Skid Row drifters in Chicago did good business selling their votes for $1.00, but an investigation into fraudulent voting registration where derelicts and transients were paid to register by city employees put the Skid Row-ers out of business. They crowded the streets and polling places looking for buyers, but few were to be had. A new civil rights statute that made it a federal crime to pay or offer to pay someone to register or vote was also a deterrent. Needless to say, this development was not greeted with joy on Skid Row as one newspaper account describes:

> Many . . . were confused by the new voting provision which made no provision for the dollar payment or bottle of wine.
>
> Derelicts approached precinct captains and election officials and reporters they mistook for precinct workers and they asked:
> "Where's my breakfast money?"
> "I'm not gonna vote no more. You guys don't pay."
> "Where do I get my dollar?"[8]

Because little money changed hands, the number of voters dropped radically in some precincts. In the 31st, only 164 of 532 registered voters cast ballots; in 1960, a total of 422 voted.

Despite the crackdown, efforts at improper voting were still made. One man posed as a minister and attempted to convince election judges that certain individuals were staying at his mission and were eligible to vote. When a poll watcher went off to call the mission to ask about the man, the would-be minister fled by a back door.[9]

But the voting-fraud cleanup didn't wipe out the system. In 1970, another precinct captain told a reporter how he spent all of election day in one place: "Everyone knows where I am. They all come this way and stop by so I can give them advice on how to fill out their ballots."[10]

## 1968: Vietnam and the Vote

Vietnam and violence marked the 1968 election year. Until March when President Johnson announced that he would not seek reelection, "Hey, hey, LBJ, how many kids have you killed today?" well-summarized the acrimonious mood of the country. The ill will wrapped around Vietnam and stretched out to include violence over civil rights with racial violence very much a part of the day. The cause of racial reconciliation was set back by the assassination of Reverend Martin Luther King Jr. on April 4, 1968 in Memphis.

Prior to Johnson's announcement of noncandidacy, Eugene McCarthy had made a very strong showing in the New Hampshire primary with a peace message buttressed by the help of a very strong youth movement. The New Hampshire results also brought Robert F. Kennedy into the race, while the president's noncandidacy opened a door for Vice President Humphrey to make a run for the office.

In early June, California primaries showed a slight lead for Kennedy over McCarthy (Humphrey did not enter the primaries), but on the morning of June 5 Robert Kennedy became another victim of violence—he was assassinated in Los Angeles.

Among the Republicans, Richard Nixon, now 55 and the loser in several recent elections, appeared to be making a comeback, convincing party leaders that he alone could unite Goldwater conservatives and Rockefeller liberals to make a winning party. Though the Republican convention in Miami Beach that summer was surrounded by tension, the worst was yet to come. Miami took precautions that all would go well by building a six-foot chain-link fence around the convention hall, and stationing police everywhere. While there was racial violence on two nights of the convention, it was restricted to the Miami ghetto and delegates were hardly aware of it. With Nixon, Nelson Rockefeller and Ronald Reagan as leading contenders, the first ballot gave the nomination to Nixon. He selected Maryland Governor Spiro T. Agnew as his running mate.

The violence that was to shock the nation came in Mayor Richard Daley's town of Chicago where the Democrats met in August. Led by the National Mobilization Committee to End the War and the Youth International Party (the "Yippies"), thousands of protesters came to Chicago. Daley arranged for the International Amphitheater to be protected by seven feet of barbed wire, and an army of security guards as well as electronic credential scanners were placed at various checkpoints. Twelve thousand police worked 12-hour shifts, and the state National Guardsmen were called in as well. Throughout the week there were skirmishes, but it was on the night that Humphrey was to be nominated that the tension erupted into a major battle. Outraged when the protestors lowered an American flag, the police hurled tear gas into the crowd, and soon the police charged into the crowd attacking hippies, radicals, antiwar demonstrators, reporters, photographers and innocent bystanders. The event shocked the nation and killed the spirit of the convention.

Ultimately, of course, Humphrey won the nomination over the other contenders, choosing Edmund Muskie as his running mate, but the negative atmosphere of the August convention got them off to a poor start.

Amidst all this chaos, a third serious contender made an appearance on an American Independent Party ticket and worried both candidates, posing a particular threat to Nixon's ability to win the South. Though he had been a presence before in 1968, George Wallace, former governor of Alabama, made a particularly strong showing denouncing racial integration. General Curtis LeMay, a former Air Force chief of staff, eventually joined Wallace's ticket.

Humphrey started the campaign amidst chaos. Not only had the convention gone badly, but funds were low, and no one in his organization was doing well with planning and scheduling. As he began stumping, he was shocked to find that his connection with the Johnson administration made him the victim of all the antiwar sentiment that people were feeling. "Stop the War. Dump the Hump" became a cry he heard often from the hecklers. As the campaign continued, his organization strengthened, and it began to bring around his image, but it was slow going.

Wallace came out fighting with an anti–federal government, racist line of attack, and he had a certain appeal with some groups.

Nixon and his people remembered the campaign of 1960 where Nixon became overtired from his travel to all of the 50 states, so this campaign saw Nixon working at a more measured pace, appearing in person for major addresses and stumping only a little toward the end. Nixon was somewhat hurt by vice presidential candidate Agnew who became infamous for referring to the "Japs" and the "Polacks" and making remarks like "When you've seen one [ghetto], you've seen them all."[11]

Johnson remained removed from the campaign for the most part but finally endorsed Humphrey in mid-October and did even greater good on October 31 when he was able to announce an end to offensive bombing in Vietnam.

The student demonstrations of '68 were a part of that year's election day in various forms, though in Chicago little violence was reported. The radical Students for a Democratic Society (SDS) demonstrated throughout the day in Lincoln Park and the Loop to dramatize "the irrelevancy of the election." Despite the fact that Chicago had been the scene of such violence only a few months ago, turnout was down and what could have been a major event was relatively quiet. Members of the SDS did distribute leaflets at bus stops, train stations and polling places urging people not to vote. Their basic messages was:

> The reason we demonstrate is that we see that the elections offer no possibility of advance either for black people or for the white majority. By building our movement, we are trying to create this possibility.[12]

University of Chicago students marched behind a banner, "Not With My Head You Don't," in apparent reference to convention week disorders; students also sponsored a "death march" across the campus featuring students portraying Richard M. Nixon as the Ghost of Elections Past, Hubert H. Humphrey as the Ghost of Elections Present and George C. Wallace as the Ghost of Elections Future, but only a small crowd gathered. In Evanston, about 50 Northwestern University students marched to downtown Fountain Square where voter registration cards and absentee ballots were burned in an SDS-sponsored protest.[13]

Chicago police were watching high school polling places where militant black students had threatened to prevent voters from entering. Schools were closed at 2:00

P.M. on Monday, 75 minutes earlier than usual, so principals could see how many students were involved in the action. Since numbers were relatively small, administrators permitted "symbolic sit-ins"; however, at least 26 students were arrested as some sit-in attempts flared into violence. The night before, school administrators and policemen coaxed hundreds of student demonstrators from at least three high schools, destroying student plans for all-night sit-ins.[14]

Though it was not clear until Wednesday morning exactly what the final results were, Nixon walked away with 301 electoral votes to Humphrey's 191 and Wallace's 46. In the popular vote, Nixon had 43.4% (31,785,148) to Humphrey's 42.7% (31,274,503) and Wallace's 13.5% (9,901,151)—giving Wallace the largest vote ever cast for a third-party choice.

Again, the results were close enough that calls were made for change in the electoral system—once again the popular will could have been subverted if key states had gone differently.

At a time when much about election day seemed swathed in anger, it's heartening to see that there were still human interest stories reported about Election Day 1968: One woman insisted on casting her ballot on the way to the hospital to give birth; a gentleman in Detroit was arrested for spending more than an hour in an election booth—the Michigan limit sets two minutes as the time limit for voting. Jenkins Jones, 102, of Romance, West Virginia cast his ballot in his 20th consecutive presidential election. He proudly revealed that he had voted Democratic, just as he had done every time since he voted for Grover Cleveland in 1888; and in California police were busy rounding up the Democratic symbol—15 donkeys that had strayed onto a freeway at Riverside. In Los Angeles, the registrar of votes was late for work—he'd stopped off to cast his ballot.[15]

## Americans in Europe Celebrate Election Day

At a time when election parties were on the wane and when animosity at home created little thought of partying, it may have taken expatriates in Europe to celebrate election day in the manner of our forefathers. In 1968, the *Chicago Daily News* foreign service reported election interest throughout France and Britain, with expatriates numbering among the revelers:

> In Paris, there were noisy election parties on the Champs Elysees, at the United States information offices and at such pubs as Harry's New York Bar on the Rue Daunou.
>
> The crowd was so thick at Harry's that it extended down the street, reports William H. Stoneman, *Daily News* senior European correspondent. The turnout caused Andrew McElhone, Harry's son, to announce the bar would stay open

until the final returns were in. He added, however, that this wouldn't apply if the election had to be settled by the House of Representatives on Dec. 16.[16]

Special police squads directed auto and foot traffic as streams of night owls jammed the Hilton Hotel and the Pan American office, but the most elaborate election party was at the Hilton, where spare ribs were served amidst a wild west atmosphere spiced with dancing girls. A *papier mache* Statue of Liberty was erected outside the hotel.

At the U.S. embassy, a team of officers worked through the night answering telephone calls about individual races.

## 1972: Nixon and Creep

Despite intentions to end the war, Nixon did not do so. The years between elections were marred by continued opposition to involvement in Vietnam and a 1970 peace demonstration at Kent State in Ohio that resulted in four students being killed by National Guardsmen. The spring of '71 featured a march on Washington by more than 200,000 people to protest continued involvement in the war.

In '72, the Democrats ran Senator George McGovern of South Dakota, almost by default. One by one, the party had lost its better known candidates. Edward M. Kennedy had been ruled out because of the Chappaquiddick accident in which a young woman had drowned in his car, and George Wallace had been shot and paralyzed in an assassination attempt made in May of '72. Edmund Muskie had started out strong in the primaries but was unable to maintain his lead. (Muskie had become the subject of armchair psychoanalysis when, after his less-than-expected margin of victory in the New Hampshire primary, there had appeared an unflattering newspaper article about his wife. Muskie made a tearful defense of her that was carried on national television, and it left Americans wondering about his mental stability.)

As a result, when the convention met in Florida in July, McGovern, as the dark horse, appeared to be the best choice the delegates had. His choice for vice president was Thomas Eagleton of Missouri, but a revelation of Eagleton's treatment for depression forced McGovern to ask him to resign, with R. Sargent Shriver taking over the vice presidential spot on the ticket, but the incident hurt McGovern badly.

Nixon's popularity was at a low point according to a poll taken in the spring of '71. The president trailed Senator Edmund Muskie of Maine in a Harris survey that showed Muskie with 47% popularity to Nixon's 39%. But the White House took measures to stem the tide and areas such as foreign affairs began to take shape in Nixon's favor. A trip to Peking began establishing him as a foreign affairs expert, as he took the first few steps toward establishing relations between China and the United States. He also flew to Moscow, the first U.S. president to do so.

When the Republicans met in August, spirits were higher; Nixon and Agnew were renominated. In order to create a real landslide, a Committee to Re-Elect the President (CRP) was also created to help Nixon win by a large margin.

*The 26th Amendment was ratified in 1972 and enfranchised anyone over the age of 18 who was otherwise qualified to vote. Despite a 1972 candidate, George McGovern, who had been identified with young people throughout his campaign, less than half of the 18-to-20-year-olds bothered to vote in that first election for which they were eligible. (Courtesy, Richard Hutchings)*

When news was revealed of a break-in at Democratic Headquarters in the Watergate complex by burglars tied to Nixon's Committee, it was overshadowed by the Eagleton issue. At the time, Americans seemed to trust that political shenanigans were part of the process, the negative was being caught, and Nixon relied on his committee to campaign heavily for him until the end. The landslide Nixon hoped for was achieved and he carried 49 states with 521 electoral votes to McGovern's 17 (Massachusetts and the District of Columbia). In the popular vote, Nixon took 60.7% (47,170,179) to McGovern's 37.5% (29,171,791).

But that was the end of the good times for Nixon. Less than a year later, Agnew was charged with income-tax evasion and had to resign. Nixon replaced him with Congressman Gerald R. Ford of Michigan. Then word of the extent of CRP's activities began to leak out and soon there were hints of intimidation, forgery, sabotage, bribery and purjury that ran all the way up to the White House. Twenty members of Nixon's administration were convicted of various crimes related to what became known as "Watergate"; when impeachment proceedings were begun against Nixon, he finally resigned as president on August 8, 1974, making Gerald Ford the first president who had not been elected as president or vice president.

This was the first presidential election in which the lower voting age was put into effect. Under the new law, Americans 18 years of age and over who qualified in other respects were allowed to cast ballots.

## Primary System Becomes Dominant for Delegate Selection

1972 was a very significant year from a grass-roots standpoint because it represented a major change in the way delegates to the conventions were selected. In the 1820s, America moved from the congressional caucus system for selecting candidates to the national convention, and now in 1972, the primary system had come to dominate the delegate selection system. In 1968, there were only 17 primaries and 42% of the Democratic delegates came from primary states. By 1972, 23 states held primaries to select delegates and chose some 63% of them. This change affected the average voter because it lessened the power of the party by taking away the power to heavily influence convention proceedings. It also gave candidates greater influence on the selection process and handed much power to the media that reported on the primaries.[17]

## 1976: America Looks to an Outsider

"My name is Jimmy Carter, and I'm running for president," are the words that best convey the spirit of the election of 1976. The nation's bicentennial found a country ready to turn inward. The defeat in Vietnam had been a first for America, and there was disgruntlement about politics inspired by the continuing revelations about Watergate and the wrongdoings committed in the name of politics. It was this humble outsider with no pretensions—this Jimmy Carter—who best assessed what the nation wanted.

Starting two years prior to the election, Carter—peanut farmer, naval officer, one-term governor of Georgia, born-again Southern Baptist—felt that what the country wanted was someone untouched by mainline politics, so he traveled the country as a humble American. By the time of the Democratic convention in New York in July, Carter was popular enough to receive the nomination on the first ballot and then chose Senator Walter F. Mondale of Minnesota, an experienced insider, for vice president.

In the Republican race, incumbent Gerald Ford was in an awkward position. Since he had never run for a national office before, he had no national constituency. This opened the door for other candidates, and he had particularly tough competition from the popular two-term governor of California, Ronald Reagan. Ford won narrowly in early primaries, but Reagan took some important states, too, leaving the two neck-

and-neck when the Republicans were ready to meet in Kansas City in August. Reagan hoped to take the lead by announcing his selection of a running mate, but the announcement of Richard Schweiker of Pennsylvania alienated many and he lost support. The nomination went to Ford, by a narrow margin. Ford then asked Senator Robert Dole of Kansas to be his running mate.

By '76 candidates were using the power of television more and more, moving the selection of candidates even farther from party officials; they were turning to political consultants who could run a campaign based on image-building. Campaign decisions were made by media-oriented professional campaign managers who no longer rose up through party ranks and groomed potential candidates, but came into whatever campaign offered the best job. They had no lasting allegiance to the candidate and no deep commitment to the party. Television advertising, controlled media appearances, direct mail and polling and telephone banks were becoming the wave of the future for state-of-the-art campaigning.

Another change in campaigning was brought about by new election laws that limited the combined spending of the two candidates to $43.6 million— less than half of what both parties had spent in 1972. As a result, campaigns focused on putting their money into travel and television and had to dispense with many local headquarters as well as extras such as buttons, banners and bumper stickers.

Carter's Georgia advisors kept his campaign on track with a continuance of his image as moralistic and very traditional. His honesty, competency and trustworthiness were supported by his "I'll never tell a lie" campaign statement. Unfortunately, Carter was sometimes "fuzzy" on the issues (which the Republicans made the most of), and he made a serious error by granting an interview to a writer from *Playboy*. When the magazine appeared in the fall of 1976, Carter was quoted on a wide range of topics, but the most oft-repeated line was his comment about Jesus' views regarding adultery, and Carter's admission, "I've looked on a lot of women with lust. I've committed adultery in my heart many times." Carter was to regret this interview.

Since Ford had no automatic constituency, his campaign managers wanted to do all they could to help Ford "own" the White House. The Rose Garden campaign strategy was the result. Rather than having Ford campaign, the Republicans kept him in the White House doing presidential tasks and getting press coverage. They also used television advertising that portrayed Ford as a good, honest family man; another series portrayed Carter's "fuzziness" on the issues. However, his managers were unable to save Ford in the television debates.

In the second of three televised debates, Ford had to answer a question concerning the Soviet influence in eastern Europe, and Ford replied with a statement indicating that there was no Soviet domination of eastern Europe. He then went on to attempt to support that statement with additional misinformation on the eastern bloc countries. Newspapers ran long and hard with the story, and Ford's supporters were terribly frustrated. It was beginning to seem like a long campaign to both candidates.

While "earliest vote" honors in the 1950s were regularly taken by Asheville, in 1976, Dixville Notch, New Hampshire turned in the first votes for this election day with 26 votes. Ford edged out Carter 13 to 11 in the community, but an article noted that only in 1972—when the community favored Nixon over McGovern—was the town's vote predictive of victory.[18]

If somebody wanted to recreate an election day of old one could do no better than Plains, Georgia in 1976 when townspeople hoped to see one of their own become president of the United States. The community rallied by painting up the drab little town and dressing it with bunting. "Welcome President Carter" signs were tucked hopefully away at the railroad station. Tuesday morning the women were busy making sandwiches and cakes while the men were finishing a speaker's platform on Main Street. Everybody had a bad case of election day nerves.

Eighty-seven-year-old Alton Carter, Jimmy's uncle, might have been selling log cabin replicas as they did in 1840 when William Henry Harrison ran against John Tyler, but instead he was out selling Jimmy Carter T-shirts and Jimmy Carter posters and Jimmy Carter faces stamped on little gold peanuts to all the tourists (who must have voted absentee in order to come to Plains for election day).

What differed was the size and make-up of the crowd. The several thousand tourists and members of the press as well as security details that swarmed over the community were like nothing the people of 1840 had ever seen, but they were good for business. Candied peanuts, spiced peanuts, boiled peanuts, fried peanuts, cinnamon peanuts, gold peanuts and silver peanuts were all there for the buying, with all of Plains, Georgia—perhaps the entrepreneurs in particular—hoping for positive results and knowing that if they came in, this could go on forever—or at least for four more years.[19]

While Ford gained strength during the campaign, Carter lost some of his muscle. Had the election been held in September, Carter would have won by a landslide; by early November, his lead had ebbed away. Carter won the election, but he received only 50.1% (40,830,763) of the vote to Ford's 48% (39,147,793) and 297 electoral votes to 240 for Ford.


## 1980: Frustration Leads to Change

No one was much excited about the election of 1980. Inflation and unemployment were high, which meant no one was very happy, and while Carter had had his positive accomplishments like the Camp David accord between Israel and Egypt, the "outsider" president had worked poorly with Congress and was generally considered to be ineffective.

The hostage crisis in Iran occurred about a year before the election, and despite the fact that Carter's rescue attempt failed badly, he won the nomination on the first ballot and took Mondale for second place again.

When looking for a candidate, the Republicans turned quickly to Ronald Reagan who had made such a strong showing against Ford in '76. Meeting in Detroit in July, the Republicans chose Reagan on the first ballot with George Bush as running mate.

The 10-term Congressman from Illinois, John Anderson, put forth a serious effort as a third-party candidate, running as an independent on the National Unity ticket. With a progressive platform, he managed to get his name on ballots in all 50 states, and although it was felt that he could not achieve the presidency, he did have enough support to be considered a serious contender.

Carter's campaign did little to change his image of ineffectiveness. His attacks on Reagan, describing him as racist and eager for war, were often vicious enough to make Carter appear overly emotional.

John Anderson spoke out against both candidates, and when he was invited to participate with Carter and Reagan in the television debates sponsored by the League of Women Voters, Carter refused to appear, not wanting to add credibility to the third-party candidate for president. (Reagan was the lucky one—he gained extra television time, used his stage presence to good advantage and was the victor of the night.)

Carter appeared on October 28 in a televised debate with Reagan only, but he just couldn't do anything right. When he tried to add a human element to a serious topic by noting that his daughter Amy thought that nuclear arms control was very important, it served to trivialize the topic, and "Ask Amy" posters began to appear everywhere.

Reagan himself was smooth and comfortable and became known as the "Great Deflector" because of his ability to scoot away from issues he didn't want to talk about. He hadn't perfected his technique, though. When he indicated that trees, not cars, caused air pollution, environmentalists were up in arms; later he claimed that the United States' air pollution problem was solved, and the press made much of the fact that shortly thereafter Reagan was on a flight into Los Angeles that had to be rerouted because of smog. He also angered many, including China, when he indicated that he thought the U.S. ought to resume relations with Taiwan.

Nonetheless, as November neared, only a surprise breakthrough in the hostage negotiations would have prevented Reagan from achieving victory. It didn't happen, and though nearly half the eligible voters failed to go to the polls, Reagan won handily with 51% (43,899,248) of the popular vote to Carter's 41% (35,481,435) and Anderson's 7% (5,719,437). In the electoral college, Reagan took 489 votes to Carter's 49. Carter was the first incumbent Democrat to fail to gain reelection since Cleveland in 1888. Ironically, Iran freed the hostages the day of Reagan's inauguration.

## New Forms of Balloting Develop

Since 1964, different kinds of computer-based voting systems have gradually been installed in political districts large and small. In 1988, 55% of all votes were counted electronically.

Starting in the early 1960s, political jurisdictions began looking for alternatives to voting machines, which can be expensive to buy, store and maintain. In 1963, the Votomatic Ballot Tally System was developed by Joseph P. Harris, a political scientist at the University of California at Berkeley. This method was a punch-card system that has since been imitated by other companies. Generally, with the punch-card method, a voter places her ballot, actually a data-processing card, on a tray or in a specially-designed voting book. Then using a hand-held stylus, or sometimes a punching unit that slides along the tray, the voter punches a hole in the card to denote her choices. When the polls close, the cards are run through a computer to provide vote totals.

Some states feel computer cards bring with them all the possibilities for fraud that paper ballots entail and, therefore, have outlawed their use. Other states have welcomed a less expensive method for rapid ballot tallies. Voters have sometimes complained that the punch card balloting is a less private means of voting and can be slower—though once the method is mastered, it doesn't seem to cause major delays.[20]

Elsewhere, election officials are beginning to try optical-scanning methods. With these devices, the voter simply marks the ballot with a felt-tip pen or a No. 2 pencil, filling in boxes as one might on a standardized test. The ballots are then tabulated by computer. Thus far, this method is still costly. Another drawback is that sometimes the voter marks off more than one square for a candidate, thereby disqualifying the ballot.

Soon to be refined and brought into the voting system is almost assuredly a system where voters would ballot on a computer terminal, which can tabulate results quickly and also offer appropriate warnings, such as "Error. You may vote for only one candidate."

Of primary importance in the development of any new voting machinery will be the assurance that it is error-free and tamper-proof, and, with some of the new systems, that has yet to be proven.

## 1984: Reagan Rides High in the Saddle

Though from the beginning, Reagan looked like a strong contender for re-election, the Democrats got off to a running start in search of a candidate who could defeat the California "cowboy." As the Democratic primaries began selecting candidates, the choice narrowed down to three—Colorado Senator Gary Hart, Chicago civil-rights activist Jesse Jackson and former vice president Walter F. Mondale of Minnesota. When the Democrats met in San Francisco in July their choice was Mondale, who made history with his choice of a woman, New York Congresswoman Geraldine Ferraro, as his running mate.

The Republicans met in Dallas in August and quickly nominated Reagan and Bush.

In a touch of revisionist history, Harry Truman became the hero of the campaign. Mondale likened himself to Truman in that he expected to be the underdog who pulled ahead to achieve a well-earned victory. Reagan sometimes quoted Truman and then set about to copy Truman's 1948 Ohio whistle-stop campaign tour.

Both candidates had to address the budget deficit often; Mondale favored raising taxes while Reagan felt that reducing spending on social programs (while leaving the Pentagon untouched) would work. Abortion and prayer in the schools were two of the more emotional issues of the day, and the candidates often sidestepped them.

The most famous phrase of a recent campaign arose in 1984, but it came about during the Democratic primary while Gary Hart still appeared to be a strong contender for the Democratic nomination. He and Mondale were facing each other in a debate in Atlanta, and when Hart started talking again about his new ideas for economic growth, Mondale noted that whenever Hart talked of those "new ideas," Mondale was reminded of the television commercial where an elderly actress, representing a fast-food chain, examines a competing company's hamburger and querulously asks, "Where's the beef?" The phrase was used frequently throughout the campaign year.

Americans were better off in 1984 than in 1980, and among the few issues Reagan had to combat during the campaign was age. He would be almost 78 by the time he left office, and that was a concern. However, he carried it off with aplomb with his well-reported retort made during the second debate with Mondale: "I will not make age an issue . . . I'm not going to exploit for political purposes my opponent's youth and inexperience."

Just as Reagan was always up for a joke, so, too, have Americans always been ready for fun. While the dying out of the social aspects of election day have certainly reduced some of the day's levity, many people still enjoy the campaign to the fullest. Here are some instances from 1984 rounded up by *USA Today*:

- In San Francisco, voters at the Mansion Hotel and Restaurant—a polling place for three years—were treated to valet parking and chocolate truffles. "Why should citizens vote in smelly garages?" asked owner Bob Pritkin.

- In Emmetsburg, Iowa, a radio station took a "cess poll"—asking listeners to flush their toilets at a certain time to indicate support for their candidate. City officials measured the effect on the water level: Mondale won.

- A cookie poll in Evanston, Illinois, showed Reagan the winner. Since Friday, Maier's Bakery and Pastry Shoppe has been selling red-white-and-blue frosted cookies labeled "Reagan" or "Mondale."

- In Paris, Ronald Reagan won a straw poll, 367–234, taken by drinkers at the famous Harry's New York Bar. The poll of tourists, resident Americans and curious French has been wrong only once since 1924.[21]

On election day, Reagan took 525 electoral votes to 13 for Mondale; 59% (54,450,603) of the popular vote to Mondale's 41% (37,573,671). Reagan had enjoyed enormous popularity, times were good and the people felt comfortable with him.

## 1988: Dukakis Dampens Democratic Lead

In 1988 Reagan had served out his two terms in office, so it was time for a fresh face. For a moment, Americans thought they might get one in the form of idealistic Gary Hart, ever-interesting Robert Dole, strong contender Jesse Jackson or Michael

Dukakis, governor of Massachusetts. But all that soon faded in a campaign that just couldn't keep from slipping and sliding in and out of the mire.

Rumors that the Democratic convention in Atlanta might be "brokered" (settled in a backroom), soon died down as Gary Hart pulled out of the race because he couldn't escape rumors about his marital infidelity, and Jesse Jackson stood tall, but still lacked the votes to capture the nomination. Michael Dukakis, governor of Massachusetts, landed the nomination and selected Senator Lloyd Bentsen of Texas as his running mate.

Vice President George Bush took the lead in the Republican primaries, and when the party met in New Orleans, Bush had the nomination. For vice presidential running mate, he selected Senator Dan Quayle of Indiana. Quayle's lightweight background immediately became grist for the news mill, but Bush rejected suggestions that Quayle be dumped before the campaign even got under way.

*Today vote tallies and victory parties are sampled throughout election night by millions of Americans who follow the election events sporadically throughout the evening as they putter around home or chat at a local campaign celebration. Above, George Bush, as seen on the television screen, as he enjoys his 1988 presidential victory amidst a crowd of campaign workers, contributors and the press. (Courtesy CBS)*

Some called it the "dirtiest campaign" in history, but it was far from that. It just never focused on issues or got beyond the personal accusations of misdeeds, the parodying of Bush's "thousand points of light" speech, the funny hats the candidates always seemed to be donning or the media "sound bite."

In the 1988 campaign television became more important than ever. Campaign managers of both parties had learned by observing previous campaigns that it was the tearful (and televised) Muskie in 1972 whose image endured, and no matter what President Ford said, if he tripped on his way down from the podium, that was the picture that was sent round the world. There would be none of that in 1988. Everything done by both candidates was specifically arranged for the television cameras—no chance encounters were to be permitted.

In the early part of the campaign, Bush was stealing the nightly television news headlines as he appeared in various parts of America in picturesque settings, attacking his opponent in "sound bites" tailored for TV. When Dukakis's managers saw that his daily press conferences weren't being picked up by the electronic news media, Dukakis soon did everything from riding a tank to throwing a baseball to get coverage. Unfortunately, in playing almost totally to a medium whose broad and massive audience doesn't permit it to dwell long on any one serious problem, the issues, the candidates, the people, and the campaign were trivialized. Political pundits and editorial analysts say that 1992 will be different and that such controlled access to the candidates goes against American political tradition.

Though Dukakis had a solid lead in late summer, his lack of personality and his inability to maintain control of his campaign soon let that lead slip away. When Americans voted in November, Bush walked away with 426 electoral votes to Dukakis's 112, and 47,917,341 popular votes to 41,013,030 for the Massachusetts governor.

## The Latest in Getting out the Vote

Only 53.1% of the eligible voters turned out for the 1984 election, so 1988 saw different get-out-the-vote tactics. This time businesses participated. Though the Federal Election Commission requires that a qualified nonprofit, nonpartisan organization or appropriate government agency jointly sponsor any corporate voter registration campaign, there were still many businesses willing to help out.

Wal-Mart Stores, Inc. volunteered its more than 1,000 stores to operate as voter registration sites for a few days so that people could register as they shopped rather than making a special trip to town hall. (This was very successful in 1984 when the chain was responsible for 150,000 new registrants.) The Lord & Taylor chain offered a similar opportunity for voter registration. Other companies, including 7-Eleven stores and Southwest Airlines provided cards for registration by mail. At Hallmark Cards Inc., retired employees have sometimes been deputized by the county clerk to handle voter registration. These efforts are supported with fliers in the hallways and notices on the cafeteria tables to remind people to vote.

The League of Women Voters still operates on-site voter registration when asked.

## A Perennial Problem

A recurrent problem dating to the 19th century, when newspaper reports of "election results" often appeared before the close of polls in the West, seemed to be on the verge of a solution in 1989.

In an effort to respond to some of the western states' concerns about media reports of the early returns in the East (causing lower voter turnout), Congress has sought out possible solutions. A 24-hour voting day was discussed on Capitol Hill but was ultimately judged to be unwieldly. Holding elections on Sunday was considered but rejected for religious reasons. In 1989, as a partial solution, legislation was introduced in Congress for a "uniform poll closing" bill. This would mean that polls would close at the same hour across all time zones, for example, 10:00 P.M. in the East and 7:00 P.M. in the West. That way results from New York would not be available three hours before the polls close in California. The bill has passed in the House, but is stalled in the Senate. And, of course, this voting method would create new problems for voters because the time in the East might be more convenient than the time in the West. Currently, there is no obvious solution.

## At the Polls Today

An election inspector recently took the time to note down some of the items she found noteworthy at a recent election in Westchester, New York:

> More parents than ever before brought their young children to the polls. They brought them in order to take them into the voting booth and show them how to vote. Often there were six or even eight feet visible below the closed curtain . . . one pair of size 9s and a variety of much smaller ones. The children learned by example how democracy works in our town and our country.
>
> Young adults constituted another special group of voters. Many 18- year-olds came to vote for the first time. Some were hesitant, glancing back for reassurance before closing the curtain. Others strode in boldly. Without exception these new voters were visibly pleased to cast their first ballot. For many it was a family occasion. It was moving to witness the parents' pride as they stepped aside to allow their adult children into the voting booth on their own. . .
>
> The last two voters of the day arrived seconds before 9 o'clock, when we were looking for the equipment to close the polls. "We aren't too late, are we?" they panted. "We've raced against the clock to get here before 9!" They weren't

too late and while the woman waited for her husband to vote, she said, "That was awful. I haven't driven like that since I was a wild teen- ager." Then she paused thoughtfully and observed, "You know, I really can't complain. Most of the people in the world would give anything to vote like I just did."[22]

Certainly, torchlight parades and election day feasts are a thing of the past, but, for the most part, so are tissue ballots, election judges on the take, rigged voting and harassment at the polls. Today Americans can go to the polling place unmolested, vote a split ticket easily and cast their ballot in complete secrecy—things that American voters haven't always been able to do. Afterwards, most go back to work or to doing exactly what they please for the rest of the day, which after all, was part of the freedom the Founding Fathers had in mind when they came up with our system of government.

So though the celebratory aspects of election day have changed greatly, for the most part, our voting rights have gotten better and better. The new colonist who had to publicly announce his vote in front of his more powerful neighbors, the tenant-farmer who wasn't a property owner and therefore couldn't vote, the immigrant who had to vote as his precinct captain told him, the newly freed slave who risked being beaten, harassed or hanged for casting a vote, and women who didn't gain suffrage until the 20th century would likely be very envious and pleased with the way Americans who vote celebrate modern election day.

# Source Notes

## Chapter 1

1. Cortlandt F. Bishop, *The History of Elections in the American Colonies*, Burt Franklin, New York, 1893, 206.
2. *Ibid.*, p. 280
3. Nicholas Vargas, "Election Procedures and Practices in Colonial New York," *New York History*, 41:3, July 1960, 265–266.
4. M. E. Powel, "The Story of Election Day," *Bulletin of the Newport Historical Society*, Number 15, January 1915, 1–16.
5. A. W. Plumstead, *The Wall and the Garden*, University of Minnesota Press, Minneapolis, 1968, 6.
6. Samuel Sewall, *The Diary of Samuel Sewall*, edited by Richard C. Robey, Arno Press, New York, 1972, 386.
7. Plumstead, *The Wall and the Garden*, 17.
8. Rhys Isaac, *The Transformation of Virginia 1740–90*, University of North Carolina Press, Chapel Hill, 1982, 56.
9. Bishop, *The History of Elections in the American Colonies*, 113.
10. Albert E. McKinley, *The Suffrage Franchise in the English Colonies*, Burt Franklin, 1905; reprinted 1969, 277.
11. Daniel J. Boorstin, *The Americans: The Colonial Experience*, Vintage Books, New York, 1958, 115.
12. Charles S. Sydnor and Noble E. Cunningham Jr., "Voting in Early America," *American Heritage*, 4:1, Fall 1952, 6.
13. David Paul Peltier, "Border State Democracy, A History of Voting in Delaware 1682–1897," (unpublished thesis, 1967), 17.
14. Bishop, *The History of Elections in the American Colonies*, 141.
15. *Ibid.*, 173.
16. *Ibid.*, 129.
17. *Ibid.*
18. *Ibid.*, 135–136.
19. Marchette Chute, *The First Liberty, A History of the Right to Vote in America, 1619–1850*, E P. Dutton and Co., New York, 1969, 17.
20. *Ibid.*, 18.
21. Richard P. McCormick, *The History of Voting in New Jersey, A Study of the Development of Election Machinery 1664–1911*, Rutgers University Press, New Brunswick, N.J., 1958, 36.

22. McKinley, *The Suffrage Franchise in the English Colonies*, 480.
23. *Ibid.*, 487–488.
24. Bishop, *The History of Elections in the American Colonies*, 44.
25. Vargas, *New York History*, 266.
26. McCormick, *The History of Voting in New Jersey*, 59–60.
27. *Ibid.*, 48.
28. *Ibid.*, 48.
29. *Ibid.*, 79.

## Chapter 2

1. Samuel Eliot Morison, *The Oxford History of the American People*, Oxford University Press, New York, 1965, 305.
2. Quoted in Chute, *The First Liberty*, 253.
3. *Ibid.*, 254.
4. Quoted in Lucius Wilmerding Jr., *The Electoral College*, Rutgers University Press, New Brunswick, N.J., 1958, 3.
5. *Ibid.*, 5.
6. Quoted in Chute, *The First Liberty*, 256.
7. Catherine Drinker Bowen, *Miracle at Philadelphia, The Story of the Constitutional Convention*, Little, Brown and Company, Boston, 1966, 272.
8. Quoted in Daniel P. Jordan, *Political Leadership in Jefferson's Virginia*, University Press at Virginia, Charlottesville, 219–220.
9. Quoted in Bowen, *Miracle at Philadelphia*, 286.
10. *Ibid.*, 287.
11. *Ibid.*, 290.

## Chapter 3

1. Kenneth Russell Bowling, "Politics in the First Congress, 1789–1791," (unpublished Ph.D. thesis, University of Wisconsin, 1968), 32.
2. Kirk Harold Porter, *A History of Suffrage in the United States*, AMS Press, New York, 1971, 23.
3. Quoted in Bowling, "Politics in the First Congress," 18.
4. *Ibid.*, 20.
5. *Ibid.*, 42.
6. Edward Stanwood, *A History of the Presidency From 1788 to 1897*, Houghton Mifflin Co., Boston, 1905, 21–22.
7. Richard P. McCormick, *The Presidential Game*, Oxford University Press, New York, 1982, 28.
8. Stanwood, *A History of the Presidency*, 28.

9. McCormick, *The Presidential Game*, 33.
10. Stanwood, *A History of the Presidency*, 29.
11. David Jacobs, "John Adams," *American Heritage Book of the Presidents and Famous Americans*, vol. 1, Dell Publishing Co., New York, 1967, 67.

## Chapter 4

1. George Tucker, *Valley of Shenandoah*, C. Wiley, New York, 1824, 217.
2. McCormick, *The Presidential Game*, 243.
3. Wilson Sullivan, "George Washington," *American Heritage Book of the Presidents and Famous Americans*, vol. 1, Dell Publishing Co., New York, 1967, 9.
4. McCormick, *The Presidential Game*, 50.
5. *Ibid.*, 51.
6. Stanwood, *A History of the Presidency*, 51.
7. Page Smith, "The Election of 1796," *History of American Presidential Elections 1789–1968*, McGraw-Hill Book Co., New York, 1971, 89.
8. Jordan, *Political Leadership in Jefferson's Virginia*, 96.
9. *Ibid.*, 119.
10. *Ibid.*, 103.
11. Peltier, "Border State Democracy" 102.
12. See note 11 above.
13. McCormick, *A History of Voting in New Jersey*, 98.
14. Lynn Warren Turner, *The Ninth State*, The University of North Carolina Press, Chapel Hill, 1983, 61.
15. *Delaware: A History of the First State*, vol. 1, edited by H. Clay Reed, Lewis Historical Publishing Co., New York, 1947, 233–235.

## Chapter 5

1. *A History of the Presidency*, 59.
2. Wallace S. Sayre and Judith H. Parris, *Voting for President, The Electoral College and the American Political System*, The Brookings Institution, Washington, D.C. 1970, 46–47.
3. McCormick, *The History of Voting in New Jersey*, 106.
4. Alfred Connable and Edward Silberfarb, *Tigers of Tammany*, Holt, Rinehart & Winston, New York, 1967, 51–52.
5. Norman K. Risjord, *Chesapeake Politics 1781–1800*, Columbia University Press, New York, 1978, 235–236.
6. Wilson Sullivan's, "Thomas Jefferson," *American Heritage Book of the Presidents and Famous Americans*, vol. 2, Dell Publishing Co., New York, 1967, 103–104.

7. Quoted in Paul F. Boller's *Presidential Campaigns*, Oxford University Press, New York, 1985, 13.
8. Jordan, *Political Leadership in Jefferson's Virginia*, 134–135.
9. Stanwood, *A History of the Presidency*, 69.
10. Noble E. Cunningham, "Election of 1800," *History of American Presidential Elections 1789–1968*, edited by Arthur M. Schlesinger Jr., McGraw-Hill Book Co., New York, 1971, 133.
11. Quoted in Sullivan's, "Thomas Jefferson," 104–105.
12. John Dos Passos, *The Shackles of Power: Three Jeffersonian Decades*, Doubleday & Company, New York, 1966, 15–16.
13. McCormick, *The History of Voting in New Jersey*, 113.
14. Edward Raymond Turner, "Women's Suffrage in New Jersey: 1790–1807," *Smith College Studies in History*, 1:4, 1916, 172.
15. *Ibid.*, 181–182.
16. *Ibid.*, 182.

## Chapter 6

1. Peltier, "Border State Democracy" 178–179.
2. *Ibid.*, 132.
3. Adam W. Leonard, "Personal Politics in Indiana 1816 to 1840," *Indiana Magazine of History*, 19:1, March 1923, 7.
4. See note 3 above.
5. Leonard, "Personal Politics in Indiana," 8.
6. Logan Esarey, "Pioneer Politics in Indiana," *Indiana History Magazine*, 18:2, June 1917, 120.
7. *Ibid.*, 121.
8. *Missouri Gazette*, St. Louis, August 9, 1817.
9. Walter B. Stevens, *Centennial History of Missouri (The Center State) One Hundred Years in the Union, 1820–1921* vol. 2, S. J. Clarke Publishing Co., St. Louis and Chicago, 1921, 128.
10. Jerome O. Steffen, "William Clark: A New Perspective of Missouri Territorial Politics 1813–1820," *Missouri Historical Review*, 67:2, January 1973, 189.
11. Quoted in *A History of Suffrage in the United States*, 57.
12. *Ibid.*, 59.
13. *Ibid.*, 15.
14. *Ibid.*, 62–65.
15. William Plumer, "Excerpt from William Plumer Papers," *History of Presidential Elections 1789–1968*, edited by Arthur M. Schlesinger Jr., McGraw-Hill Book Co., New York, 1971, 342–343.
16. *Ibid.*, 343.
17. See note 16 above.

18. Robert P. Hay, "The American Revolution Twice Recalled: Lafayette's Visit and the Election of 1824," *Indiana Quarterly Magazine of History*, vol. 2, 1906, 46.
19. *Ibid.*, 53.
20. Leonard, "Personal Politics in Indiana," 2.

## Chapter 7

1. *Missouri Republican*, St. Louis, November 29, 1827.
2. *Missouri Intelligencer*, Fayette, July 25, 1828.
3. See note 2 above.
4. Paul F. Boller Jr., *Presidential Campaigns*, Oxford University Press, New York, 1985, 44.
5. *The Alabama Journal*, Montgomery, August 5, 1840.
6. See note 5 above.
7. Jim Kelly, Museum Collection Notes, Tennessee State Museum.
8. Robert V. Remini, *The Election of Andrew Jackson*, Greenwood, Westport, Conn., 1980, 200–201.
9. Margaret Bayard Smith quoted in Clement Eaton, ed., *The Leaven of Democracy: The Growth of the Democratic Spirit in the Time of Jackson*, Braziller, New York, 1963, 41.
10. *Ibid.*, 41.
11. Porter, *A History of Suffrage in the United States*, 76.
12. Patrick T. Conley, *Democracy in Decline: Rhode Island's Constitutional Development 1776–1841*, Rhode Island Historical Society, Providence, 1977, 221.
13. *A History of Suffrage in the United States*, 106.
14. *Ibid.*, 90.
15. *Ibid.*, 83.
16. See note 14. above.
17. Noah J. Major, *Pioneers of Morgan County*, 374 seq., quoted in "Pioneer Politics in Indiana," by Logan Esarey, *Indiana History Magazine*, 13:2, June 1917, 121.
18. J. Mills Thornton III, *Politics and Power in a Slave Society, Alabama, 1800–1860*, Louisiana State University Press, Baton Rouge and London, 1978, 146.
19. *Ibid.*, 147–149.
20. David L. Cohn, *The Fabulous Democrats*, G. P. Putnam's Sons, New York, 1956, 43.
21. See note 20 above.
22. Union Inn Register, 1836, in the collection of the Indiana Historical Society.
23. Derke Hackett, "The Days of This Republic Will Be Numbered: Abolition, Slavery, and the Presidential Election of 1836," *Louisiana Studies*, 15:2, Summer, 1976, 143.

24. *The Republican*, St. Louis, November 7, 1836.
25. *Ibid.*, November 8, 1836.
26. *Ibid.*, November 9, 1836.
27. *Ibid.*, November 10, 1836.
28. *Ibid.*, November 12, 1836.
29. *History of Voting in New Jersey*, 116–117.
30. *Ibid.*, 117.
31. See note 30 above.

## Chapter 8

1. Fon W. Boardman Jr., *America and the Jacksonian Era 1825–50*, Henry Z. Walck, Inc., New York, 1975, 34.
2. David Jacobs, "Log Cabin Campaign," *American Heritage Book of the Presidents and Famous Americans*, vol. 4, Dell Publishing Co., New York, 1967, 283.
3. Boller, *Presidential Campaigns*, 66.
4. Esarey, "Pioneer Politics in Indiana," 126–127.
5. Kelly, Museum Collection Notes, 29–30.
6. Nashville *Whig*, June 1, 1840.
7. See note 6 above.
8. John L. Ferguson, *Historic Arkansas*, Arkansas History Commission, Little Rock, 1966, 65–66.
9. Peltier, "Border State Democracy," 230.
10. *Daily Missouri Republican*, November 2, 1840.
11. *Ibid.*, November 3, 1840.
12. Peltier, "Border State Democracy," 231.
13. David Jacobs, "William Henry Harrison," *American Heritage Book of the Presidents and Famous Americans*, vol. 4, Dell Publishing Co., New York, 1967, 275.
14. Kelly, Museum Collection Notes, quoting Mary French Caldwell, *Tennessee, the Dangerous Example*, Nashville, 1974, 305.
15. Joseph D. Masterson, to Miss Elizabeth Simpson, October 19, 1840, Elizabeth Simpson Collection, Indiana Historical Society.
16. Esarey, "Pioneer Politics," 128.
17. *Ibid.*, 128.
18. Ferguson, *Historic Arkansas*, 67.
19. Quoted in McCormick, *The History of Voting in New Jersey*, 135.
20. *Daily Missouri Republican*, October 29, 1840.
21. Peltier, "Border State Democracy," 235.
22. See note 10 above.
23. Peltier, "*Border State Democracy*," 235.

24. Cyprian Clamorgan, *The Colored Aristocracy of St. Louis*, St. Louis, 1858, reprinted in *Missouri Historical Society Bulletin*, 3:1, October 1974.
25. *Daily Missouri Republican*, November 5, 1840.
26. *Ibid.*, November 2, 1840.
27. Denis Tilden Lynch, *"Boss" Tweed: The Story of a Grim Generation*, Blue Ribbon Books, New York, 1931, 49.
28. Quoted in Lynch, *"Boss" Tweed*, 160.
29. *Ibid.*, 161.
30. Quoted in McCormick, *The History of Voting in New Jersey*, 125.
31. "Election Day in Newport," *Bulletin of the Newport Historical Society*, July 1913, 2.
32. *Ibid.*, 10–11.
33. *Ibid.*, 11.
34. *Ibid.*, 11–12.
35. Boller, *Presidential Campaigns*, 80.
36. C. Louis Barzee, *Oregon in the Making '60's to Gay '90's*, Statesman Publishing Co., Salem, Oregon, circa 1936, 47.
37. *Ibid.*, 49.
38. See note 37 above.
39. Robert W. Johannsen, *Frontier Politics and the Sectional Conflict*, University of Washington Press, Seattle, 1955, 146.
40. Ammon Underwood, "Journal of Ammon Underwood," edited by James K. Greer, *Southwestern Historical Quarterly*, 32:2, October 1928, 147.
41. Adolphus Sterne, "Diary of Adolphus Sterne," edited by Harriet Smither, *Southwestern Historical Quarterly*, 34: 1, July 1930, 70.
42. Diene Harris, "The Reminiscences of Mrs. Diene Harris, Part II," *Quarterly of the Texas State Historical Association*, 4:3, June 1901, 155.
43. Matthew P. Blue papers, Alabama Dept. of Archives and History, Montgomery.
44. *Ibid.*
45. Emerson Wilson, "Delaware's Whigs had a Ball in 1844," *Wilmington News Journal*, January 5, 1974.
46. James K. Polk, *Polk, The Diary of a President, 1845–49*, edited by Allan Nevins, Longmans, Green and Co., London, New York, Toronto, 1929, 351.
47. James Schouler, *History of the United States*, Kraus, New York, 1908, 13, vol. 4, 202.
48. McCormick, *The History of Voting in New Jersey*, 142–143.
49. Porter, *A History of Suffrage in the United States*, 120–121.
50. "The First Congressional Election in Colorado (1858)," *Colorado Magazine*, 6:2, March 1929, State Historical Society of Colorado, 46.
51. *Ibid.*, 47.
52. *Ibid.*, 47.
53. J. E. Wharton, *History of the City of Denver*, Byers and Dailey, Printers News Office, 1866, 85.

54. Quoted in Ned North, "Let's Vote for President Anyway!," *Paradise of the Pacific*, 54:4, April 1940, 27.
55. *Ibid.*, 28.

## Chapter 9

1. Ingomar, St. Louis, November 1, 1856.
2. Wilson Sullivan, "Abraham Lincoln," *The American Heritage Book of the Presidents and Famous Americans*, vol. 5, Dell Publishing Co., New York, 1967, 409.
3. Julius G. Rathbun, "The 'Wide Awakes'," *The Connecticut Quarterly*, 1:4, 327–333.
4. *Daily Missouri Democrat*, November 6, 1860.
5. John Edward Young, "An Illinois Farmer During the Civil War: Extracts from the Journal of John Edward Young, 1859–66," *Journal of the Illinois State Historical Society*, 24: 1–2, April–July 1933, 84.
6. *Ibid.*, 84–85.
7. Boller, *Presidential Campaigns*, 110.
8. *Daily Missouri Democrat*, November 7, 1860.
9. See note 8 above.
10. Young, "An Illinois Farmer," 87–88.
11. *Daily Missouri Democrat*, November 7, 1860.
12. Robert W. Johannsen, *Frontier Politics and the Sectional Conflict*, University of Washington Press, Seattle, 1955, 146.
13. *Ibid.*, 148.
14. Sullivan, "Abraham Lincoln," 427.
15. Ellis Merton Coulter, *The Confederate States of America*, Louisiana State University Press, Baton Rouge, 1950, 22–26.
16. Quoted in Cohn, *The Fabulous Democrats*, 77.
17. Norman B. Wilkinson, "The Brandywine Home Front During the Civil War, Part III: 1863," *Delaware History*, 11:2, 137.
18. Wilkinson, "The Brandywine Home Front During the Civil War, Part IV: 1864–65," *Delaware History*, 11:4, 317.
19. *The War of the Rebellion: A Compilation of the Official Records of the Union and Confederate Armies*, Series I, volume 42, part 2, chapter 54, "Correspondence, etc.," Government Printing Office, Washington, D.C. 1893, 1045–1046.
20. George Frederick Miller, *Absentee Voters and Suffrage Laws*, Washington, D.C., 1948, 30–31.
21. *The War of the Rebellion*, 435–436; 570.
22. *John Ransom's Diary*, Paul S. Eriksson Inc., New York 1963, 166.
23. *Daily Missouri Democrat*, November 5, 1860.
24. *The Virginia Daily Union*, Virginia, Nevada, November 9, 1864.

25. *The Evening News*, Gold Hill, Nevada, November 12, 1864.

## Chapter 10

1. Allen W. Trelease, *White Terror: The Ku Klux Klan Conspiracy and Southern Reconstruction*, Harper & Row, New York, 1971, xl.
2. Leon Litwack, *Been in the Storm So Long*, Vintage Books, New York, 1979, 554.
3. Walter L. Fleming, *Documentary History of Reconstruction*, Arthur H. Clark Company, Cleveland, 1907, 87.
4. *Ibid.*, 88.
5. *Ibid.*, 90.
6. Myrta Lockett Avary, *Dixie After the War*, Doubleday, Page & Company, New York, 1906, 286.
7. Litwack, *Been in the Storm So Long*, 555.
8. Eric Foner, *Reconstruction: America's Unfinished Revolution 1863–77*, Harper & Row, New York, 1988, 341.
9. Litwack, *Been in the Storm So Long*, 555.
10. Fleming, *Documentary History of Reconstruction*, 84–85.
11. *Ibid.*, 88.
12. Avary, *Dixie After the War*, 291.
13. Litwack, *Been in the Storm So Long*, 546.
14. *Ibid.*, 547.
15. Avary, *Dixie After the War*, 283.
16. Litwack, *Been in the Storm So Long*, 555–556.
17. John William De Forest, *A Union Officer in the Reconstruction*, Yale University Press, New Haven, 1948, 126–127.
18. Fleming, *Documentary History of Reconstruction*, 82–83.
19. *Ibid.*, 85–86.
20. Avary, *Dixie After the War*, 287.
21. Quoted in Avary, *Dixie After the War*, 288.
22. *Ibid.*, 289–290.
23. *Ibid.,* 115–116.
24. Foner, *Reconstruction*, 342.
25. *Ibid.*, 551.
26. Quoted in Fleming, *Documentary History of Reconstruction*, 370.
27. Melinda Meek Hennessey, "Race and Violence in Reconstruction New Orleans: The 1868 Riot," *Louisiana History*, Louisiana Historical Association, Winter 1979, 77–88.
28. *The Daily Picayune*, New Orleans, November 4, 1868.
29. *KKK Report*, South Carolina testimony, Negro's statement, 1871, 371–373.
30. Ibid., 373.
31. Trelease, *White Terror*, 177.

32. Luther E. Smith, April 13, 1871, Mobile Alabama, Archives of Missouri Historical Society, St. Louis.
33. James M. Wells, *The Chisolm Massacre: A Picture of "Home Rule" in Mississippi*, Chisolm Monument Association, Washington, D.C., 190.
34. *Missouri Republican*, November 4, 1868.
35. David L. Cohn, *The Fabulous Democrats*, quoting Hofstadter, *The American Political Tradition, 2nd Ed.*, Alfred A. Knopf, New York, 1973, 85.
36. *The Missouri Republican*, November 6, 1872.
37. Eleanor Flexner, *Century of Struggle*, Atheneum, New York, 1972, 164–165.
38. Porter, *A History of Suffrage in the United States* citing *U.S.* v. *Anthony*, Fed. Cases 14459, 194.
39. *Ibid.*, citing *Minor* v. *Happersett*, 194.
40. Boller, *Presidential Campaigns*, 134.
41. Eugene J. Roseboom and Alfred E. Eckes Jr. *A History of Presidential Elections*, 4th ed., Macmillan Publishing Company, New York, 1979, 92.
42. Letter of H. W. Leffing Well, the U.S. Marshall in the Eastern District of Missouri, 1876, the Honorable Albert Todd, Albert Todd papers, Missouri Historical Society.
43. W. Emerson Wilson, "Political Dirty Tricks 100 Years Ago," *Wilmington News Journal*, October 30, 1976.
44. Lamont Johnson, *Ballot for Americans: A Pictorial History of American Elections and Electioneering with the Top Political Personalities 1789–1956*, E. P. Dutton and Company, New York, 1976, 59.
45. *St. Helena Star*, November 3, 1876.
46. Robert Murken Miglian, "California's Reaction to the Disputed Presidential Election of 1876," *Journal of the West*, 15:1, January 1976, 21–23.

# Chapter 11

1. Richard Kotter, "An Examination of Mormon and Non-Mormon Influences in Odgen City Politics, 1847–69," (unpublished Master's thesis, Utah State University, 1967), 28.
2. Ronald Collett Jack, "Utah Territorial Politics 1847–1876" (unpublished Ph.D. thesis, University of Utah, 1970), 77.
3. *Ibid.*, 93, quoting Shaffer to Fish, July 22, 1870. (National Archives, State Department MSS, Utah, II, No. 706).
4. *Salt Lake Herald*, Salt Lake City, August 2, 1870.
5. *Salt Lake Daily Tribune*, Salt Lake City, August 16, 1871, quoted in Jack, "Utah Territorial Politics," 244.
6. *Salt Lake Daily Tribune*, August 12, 1871, quoted in Jack, "Utah Territorial Politics," 245.

7. T. A. Larson, "Petticoats at the Polls," *Pacific Northwest Quarterly*, 44:2, April 1953, 75.
8. Maude B. Ingham, "Women's First Ballot Here Was Like 'Shot Heard 'Round World,'" unpublished, undated paper of Wyoming Historical Society, Laramie, 2.
9. Quoted in Larson, "Petticoats," 77.
10. Quoted in *The History of Woman Suffrage*, edited by Elizabeth Cady Stanton, Susan Anthony, and Mathilda Joslyn, New York, Rochester, 1886, 739.
11. Quoted in Jay J. Wagoner, *Arizona Territory 1863–1912: A Political History*, University of Arizona Press, Tucson, 1970, 83.
12. *The Pueblo Chieftain*, November 9, 1904.
13. *Journal of the General Assembly of the State of Colorado in Joint Session*, 15th session, 1905, 122.
14. Marjorie Hornbein, "Three Governors in a Day," *The Colorado Magazine*, 45:3, 1968, 244.
15. *Ibid.*, 245.
16. Michael R. Green, reference archivist, Texas State Archives to Kate Kelly, December 17, 1987.
17. Cited in Eric Burns, "Elections of Yesteryear: The Debate Got So Hot, One Candidate Bit the Other on the Thumb," *TV Guide*, March 19, 1988, 30–31.
18. *The Texas Pioneer*, Fairfield, June–July 1931.
19. *Ibid.*

## Chapter 12

1. Michael Arthur, "Chester Alan Arthur," *American Heritage Book of the Presidents and Famous Americans*, vol. 7, Dell Publishing Co., New York, 1967, 567.
2. Boller, *Presidential Campaigns*, 143.
3. Leonard Dinnerstein, "Election of 1880," *A History of American Presidential Elections*, edited by Arthur M. Schlesinger Jr., 4 vols., New York, 1971, vol 2, 1509–1510.
4. Porter, *A History of Suffrage in the United States*, 208–210.
5. *Ibid.*, 211.
6. Cohn, *The Fabulous Democrats*, 91.
7. Roseboom and Eckes, *A History of Presidential Elections*, 4th ed., 106.
8. *Ibid.*, 158.
9. David Jacobs, "The Election Expenses," *American Heritage Book of the Presidents and Famous Americans*, vol. 7, Dell Publishing Co., New York, 1967, 621.
10. Boller, *Presidential Campaigns*, 158.
11. Roseboom and Eckes, *A History of Presidential Elections*, 110.

12. Quoted in Charles L. Mee Jr., "Grover Cleveland," *American Heritage Book of the Presidents and Famous Americans*, vol. 7, Dell Publishing, Co., New York, 1967,

13. Samuel P. Orth, *The Boss and the Machine*, Yale University Press, New Haven, 1919, 150.

14. L. E. Fredman, *The Australian Ballot: The Story of an American Reform*, Michigan State University Press, East Lansing, 1968, 30–31.

15. *Ibid.*, 46.

16. *Daily Enterprise*, Virginia, Nevada, November 6, 1892.

17. Roseboom and Eckes, *A History of Presidential Elections*, 119.

18. *Ibid.*, 119.

19. Donald Young, "William McKinley," *American Heritage Book of the Presidents and Famous Americans*, vol. 8, Dell Publishing Co., New York, 1967, 638.

20. Boller, *Presidential Campaigns*, 177.

21. Roseboom and Eckes, *A History of Presidential Elections*, 120.

22. Cohn, *Fabulous Democrats*, 106.

23. Edward V. P. Schneiderhahn, Journals and Diaries, Archives of Missouri Historical Society, St. Louis, vol. 3, 28–33.

24. Elizabeth Johnson Wright, "Return Day in Sussex County," *Delaware: A History of the First State*, vol. I, Lewis Historical Publishing Co., New York, 1947, 233.

25. *Sunday Star*, November 12, 1882.

26. Wright, "Return Day," 235.

27. *Rocky Mountain News*, Denver, Colorado, September 23, 1880.

28. *Ibid.*, September 22, 1880.

29. Lamont Buchanan, *Ballot for Americans: A Pictorial History of American Elections and Electioneering with the Top Political Personalities 1789–1956*, E. P. Dutton & Company, New York, 1976, 73.

30. *Haverhill Weekly Bulletin*, Haverhill, Massachusetts, November 17, 1888.

31. Louis F. Post and Fred C. Leubuscher, *Henry George's 1886 Campaign*, Hyperion Press, Inc. Westport, Connecticut, 1961, 154.

32. Colonel Adna G. Clarke, "First American Election in Hawaii," *Paradise of the Pacific*, 53:4, April 1939, 27.

33. *Ibid.*, 28.

34. Quoted in Boller, *Presidential Campaigns*, 180.

## *Chapter 13*

1. Carl Abbott, Stephen J. Leonard, and David McComb, *Colorado: A History of the Centennial State*, revised edition, Colorado Associated University Press, Boulder, 1982, 201.

2. *Chicago Daily Tribune*, July 8, 1908.

3. *The Denver Republican*, July 7, 1908.

 4. *The History of Voting in New Jersey*, 200–201.
 5. *Ibid.*, 206.
 6. Miller, *Absentee Voters and Suffrage Laws*, 25.
 7. *Ibid.*, 45.
 8. Michael Harwood, "William Howard Taft," *The American Heritage Book of the Presidents and Famous Americans*, vol. 8, Dell Publishing Co., New York, 1967, 718.
 9. Stephen C. Shadegg, *Arizona Politics: The Struggle to End One-Party Rule*, Arizona State University Press, Tempe, 1986, 12.
10. *Coconino Sun*, Flagstaff, Arizona, November 18, 1912.
11. *Arizona Gazette*, Phoenix, November 6, 1916, November 7, 1916, 1:3.
12. *Arizona Republican*, Phoenix, November 7, 1916.
13. Letter from Merideth Nicholson of Indianapolis to Mr. F. G. Darlington of Hyannisport, Massachusetts, July 6, 1907, Frank G. Darlington Papers, Indiana Historical Society, SC 482.
14. *Pueblo Star Journal and Chieftain*, Pueblo, Colorado, July 17, 1960.
15. *The Cheyenne Leader*, November 6, 1900.
16. Journals and Diaries, Archives of Missouri Historical Society, St. Louis, vol. 5, 48–49, vol. 6, 58–59.
17. Annie H. Wood, "Election Eve in 1906," *Paradise of the Pacific*, 58:11, November 1944, 24–25.
18. *From Parlor to Prison: Five American Suffragists Talk About Their Lives*, edited by Sherna Gluck, Vintage Books, New York, 1976, 17.
19. *St. Louis Post-Dispatch*, July 20, 1984, sec. E, p. 3.
20. Collins Thompson, to David R. Francis, ambassador to Russia, Petrograd, November 14, 1916, Francis Collection, Archives of the Missouri Historical Society, St. Louis.

## Chapter 14

 1. *St. Louis Times*, November 2, 1920.
 2. *Ibid.*, November 3, 1920.
 3. *St. Louis Post-Dispatch*, November 1, 1920.
 4. *St. Louis Post-Dispatch*, November 2, 1920.
 5. See note 4 above.
 6. *St. Louis Times*, November 3, 1920.
 7. See note 6 above.
 8. *St. Louis Times*, November 1, 1920.
 9. See note 8 above.
10. See note 6 above.
11. See note 6 above.
12. *St. Louis Times*, November 4, 1920.

13. Harold F. Gosnell, *Getting Out the Vote: An Experiment in the Stimulation of Voting*, University of Chicago Press, Chicago, 1927, 38–39.
14. Mrs. Harry Carlson, "The First Decade of the St. Louis League of Women Voters," *Bulletin*, 26:1, October 1969, 49.
15. *St. Louis Post-Dispatch*, November 4, 1924.
16. *St. Louis Post-Dispatch*, November 5, 1924.
17. See note 16 above.
18. See note 12 above.
19. Wesley, Charles H., dean of the Graduate School, Howard University, in foreword to *The Attitude of the Southern White Press Toward Negro Suffrage 1932–40*, edited by Rayford W. Logan, The Foundation Publishers, Washington, D.C., 1940, v.
20. *Ibid.*, v.
21. *Ibid.*, vi.
22. Roseboom and Eckes, *A History of Presidential Elections*, 158.
23. *Globe Democrat*, October 27, 1928.

## Chapter 15

1. *The Nation*, 135:3506, August 31, 1932, 224.
2. Thomas Griffith, "Newswatch," *Time*, 131:16 April 18, 1988, 46–47.
3. Stefan Lorant, *The Presidency: A Pictorial History of Presidential Elections from Washington to Truman*, Macmillan, New York, 1953, 586.
4. *St. Louis Post-Dispatch*, November 8, 1932.
5. *Pittsburgh Courier*, September 10, 1932.
6. *St. Louis Globe-Democrat*, November 9, 1932.
7. *Chicago Defender*, November 12, 1932.
8. *St. Louis Post-Dispatch*, November 8, 1932.
9. *News-Week*, 8:19, November 7, 1936, 9.
10. *Ibid.*, 7.
11. See note 9 above.
12. Wilson Sullivan, "Franklin Delano Roosevelt," *American Heritage Book of the Presidents and Famous Americans*, vol. 10, Dell Publishing Co., New York, 1967, 857.
13. *New York Times Magazine*, July 26, 1987, 21.
14. *Pittsburgh Courier*, November 23, 1940.
15. *Ibid.*, November 2, 1940.
16. *The Pittsburgh Courier*, November 2, 1940.
17. *New York Times*, November 6, 1944.
18. Cohn, *The Fabulous Democrats*, 162.
19. *New York Times*, November 8, 1944.
20. *New York Times*, November 7, 1944.

21. *St. Louis Post-Dispatch*, November 7, 1944.
22. See note 20 above.
23. *Delaware; A History of the First State*, 233.
24. See note 20 above.
25. *Time*, 44:20, November 13, 1944, 20.
26. See note 21 above.
27. *Chicago Defender*, November 4, 1944.
28. See note 27 above.
29. See note 27 above.
30. *New York Times*, November 8, 1944.
31. See note 30 above.
32. See note 30 above.
33. *St. Louis Post-Dispatch*, November 7, 1944.
34. *The New York Times*, November 8, 1944.
35. See note 34 above.
36. See note 34 above.
37. See note 34 above.
38. *New York Times*, November 8, 1944.
39. *Ibid.*
40. See note 20 above.
41. See note 20 above.
42. See note 20 above.
43. Cohn, *The Fabulous Democrats*, 166.

## Chapter 16

1. Cohn, *The Fabulous Democrats*, 179.
2. Charles L. Mee Jr., "Dwight David Eisenhower," *American Heritage Book of the Presidents and Famous Americans*, vol. 11, Dell Publishing Co., New York, 1967, 953.
3. *Time*, 60:7 August 18, 1952, 11.
4. *Time*, 60:9 September 1, 1952, 14.
5. See note 4 above.
6. *Chicago Defender*, October 4, 1952.
7. *Newsweek*, 40:17, October 27, 1952, 4.
8. *Time*, 60:19 November 10, 1952, 22.
9. See note 8 above.
10. See note 8 above.
11. *New York Times*, November 3, 1952.
12. *Ibid.*
13. *New York Times*, November 5, 1952.
14. See note 13 above.

15. See note 13 above.
16. See note 13 above.
17. *Time*, 68:20, November 12, 1956, 18.
18. *Chicago Defender*, November 6, 1948.
19. See note 18 above.
20. *Chicago Defender*, November 8, 1952.
21. See note 20 above.
22. *Chicago Defender*, November 15, 1952.
23. See note 22 above.
24. See note 22 above.
25. *Chicago Defender*, November 1, 1952.
26. *New York Times*, November 3, 1952.
27. See note 13 above.
28. See note 13 above.
29. See note 13 above.
30. See note 13 above.

## Chapter 17

1. *Chicago Defender*, October 29, 1960.
2. See note 1 above.
3. *Chicago Defender*, November 5, 1960.
4. *New York Times*, November 1, 1964.
5. *New York Times*, November 4, 1964.
6. See note 5 above.
7. *Chicago Daily News*, April 22, 1964.
8. *Chicago Daily News*, November 6, 1968.
9. See note 8 above.
10. Milton L. Rakove, *Don't Make No Waves Don't Back No Losers*, Indiana University Press, Bloomington, 1975, 125.
11. Roseboom and Eckes, *A History of Presidential Elections*, 290.
12. *Chicago Daily News*, November 5, 1968.
13. See note 12 above.
14. See note 12 above.
15. *Chicago Daily News*, November 6, 1968.
16. See note 15 above.
17. Roseboom and Eckes, *A History of Presidential Elections*, 300.
18. *Chicago Daily News*, November 2, 1976.
19. See note 18 above.
20. See note 18 above.
21. *USA Today*, November 7, 1984.
22. Jane Adcock, "An Election Inspector Files Report From the Front Lines," *New York Times*, November 1, 1987.

# Index

273